IGNORED HISTORIES

IGNORED HISTORIES

The Politics of History Education
and Indigenous-Settler Relations
in Australia and Kanaky/New Caledonia

Angélique Stastny

UNIVERSITY OF HAWAI'I PRESS

HONOLULU

Library of Congress Cataloging-in-Publication Data

Names: Stastny, Angélique, author.
Title: Ignored histories : the politics of history education and
    indigenous-settler relations in Australia and Kanaky/New Caledonia /
    Angélique Stastny.
Description: Honolulu : University of Hawai'i Press, 2022. | Includes
    bibliographical references and index.
Identifiers: LCCN 2021050539 | ISBN 9780824889975 (cloth) | ISBN
    9780824890353 (pdf) | ISBN 9780824890360 (epub) | ISBN
    9780824891664
    (kindle edition)
Subjects: LCSH: Settler colonialism—Study and teaching—Australia. |
    Settler colonialism—Study and teaching—New Caledonia. |
    Australia—History—Study and teaching—Evaluation. | New
    Caledonia—History—Study and teaching—Evaluation.
Classification: LCC DU109.5 .S73 2022 | DDC 994.007202—dc23/
    eng/20220125
LC record available at https://lccn.loc.gov/2021050539

ISBN 9780824890377 (paperback)

Cover art: *Top,* artwork by Ignace Wéma honoring pro-independence
freedom fighter Eloi Machoro on a bus shelter in Kanaky/New Caledonia,
2016. Photo by author. *Bottom,* banners at the Invasion Day protest,
Parliament Gardens, Naarm (Melbourne), 2015. Photo by Snehargho Ghosh.

À toi, Papa, qui m'a encouragée à prendre cette longue route
et m'a toujours soutenue et, sans qui, ce livre n'aurait jamais vu le jour.
Pour toujours dans mon cœur et à mes côtés dans le Rêve et l'Invisible.

To not hide anything, to follow one's soul, to be afraid of nothing but one's cowardice, to head straight and welcome all sides...

Gonzague Phélip,
Kanaky Kanaky Kanaky (2001, 21)

Contents

ACKNOWLEDGMENTS

I have lived for seven years on the land of the Wurundjeri and Boonwurrung peoples of the Kulin Nation in Narrm (Melbourne). This research project was born and brought to completion while I was living on these lands. Living on Wurundjeri and Boonwurrung Countries has taught me a great deal over the years, and I pay my respects to the Elders of these lands, past, present and emerging. I am also very grateful for the generosity of spirit that those I have met here, and in other First Nations, have extended to me, despite continuing attacks to their sovereignty, freedom, and dignity as human beings. In acknowledging this Country, I also accept what I see as being my responsibility to listen, to learn, to confront colonialism, to challenge white supremacy, and push for justice, reciprocity, and relationships of shared responsibility through which our humanity can flourish. This book is one humble attempt in such a direction.

This book is a personal endeavor, but even more so, a node of relationships where my paths and the paths of others have crossed. Many people have supported me during the research, writing, and publication of this book; their contributions have given shape to this project and been fundamental to its completion.

I am very grateful to the history teachers in both Australia and Kanaky/New Caledonia who have participated in this research project. I thank them all for their time, their interest, and their thought-provoking accounts of their teaching experience. I also wish to thank those who referred history teachers to me.

The subject matter of this book originates from my doctoral research. I wholeheartedly thank Mélanie Torrent and Raymond Orr for supporting my endeavour at the outset. My deepest gratitude and appreciation go to my supervisors at the time at the University of Melbourne for their inestimable support: Sarah Maddison, whose enthusiastic, conscientious guidance and expertise helped bring this research to completion. She showed unwavering support in the most crucial times. Raymond Orr supported me right from the start. This journey wouldn't have been as worthwhile without his insightful comments, encouragements, calm demeanor, sense of humor, and friendship. Grace Moore provided valuable support, guidance, kindness, and careful readings of my writing.

This research was also made possible thanks to the crucial financial support I received in the form of scholarships and travel grants from the Australian Government, the Arts Faculty and the School of Social and Political Sciences at the University of Melbourne, the ARC Centre of Excellence for the History of Emotions, and from donors Colin Nettelbeck and the late Colin Duckworth via the University of Melbourne French Trust Fund.

Thanks to the archivists in Australia, Kanaky/New Caledonia and France for their help. My thanks also go to all those who helped organize and advertise the public conferences I gave in Kanaky/New Caledonia.

I thank those who offered me hospitality in Kanaky/New Caledonia, to those beautiful souls who gave me a ride when I was hitchhiking in the Loyalty Islands and those who gave me company and shared insightful conversations when I gave them a ride on the Grande Terre. These moments remain precious in my heart. To Macki Wéa and his family in Gossanah for welcoming me at the yearly commemorative exhibition and ceremonies of the 1988 Ouvéa massacre. To the Weneki and Wadrilla chiefdoms for their hospitality during the thirty-year commemoration of the massacre and during the sharing and recording of testimonies organized by the Comité du 5 mai. Listening to these stories in Gossanah, Weneki, and Wadrilla was a critical learning experience. I salute their courage and dedication to talk about local history and share these memories.

Thank you to this book's editor, Emma Ching, at the University of Hawai'i Press, who supported this book to publication, as well as to the three anonymous reviewers for their suggestions and endorsement of the book.

I thank Alissa, Caroline, Craig, Emmanuel, Jemimah, Marianne, Matthew, Paul, Rowan, Sabine, and Snehargho for their support during the research and writing. A very big thank you to James Bourne (and the reliable Choofm!) for his wonderful support and networking magic in Broken Hill and Paakantyi Country more widely. I am also extremely grateful to him for providing editorial suggestions on an early version of the work.

My deepest and heartfelt thanks to my family, Papa, Maman, and Gilles, for their unfailing support, love, and understanding.

Finally, for all the beautiful encounters and relationships I have made on this path and that I keep in my heart, thank you for planting the seeds of possibility.

Author's Note

Australia is home to several hundred First Nations peoples, generally recognized as two groups: Aboriginal peoples and Torres Strait Islander peoples. In Kanaky/New Caledonia, one distinct group is recognized: the Kanak people. Wherever possible in this book, Indigenous Nation or language affiliation names are used, such as "Wurundjeri" or "Warlpiri," but, because this book is an analysis across two societies, Australia and Kanaky/New Caledonia, I predominantly use the term "Indigenous people(s)" when referring to the comparative context.

The terms "Indigenous" and "settlers" are political identities constructed by colonial discourses. These terms convey some of the specificity of power relations within settler colonial societies. I use the generic term "Indigenous" to refer to those whose ancestors lived on those lands before colonization and who have faced the invasion of their territories, specifically, Aboriginal people and Torres Strait Islanders in Australia and Kanak people in Kanaky/New Caledonia. Bringing indigeneity into the frame exposes the questions of Indigenous sovereignty and challenges settler nativism.[1] I use the term "settler" both for any person who has come to Australia or Kanaky/New Caledonia at any time from the early days of colonization to the present and for their descendants.

The implied binary between "Indigenous" and "settler" has certain flaws and limitations. In fact, by engaging with a state apparatus—the school system—that has helped give this colonial binary form and content, I seek to unpack the strategies behind it, the problems with it, and the possibilities beyond it. Using the colonial signifiers "Indigenous" and "settlers" challenges any apparent neutrality and enables a discussion of the articulations of settler colonial structures. It may also enable a better understanding of the positions that have been left out of or do not fit neatly into such a binary. The usage of these terms in this book aims at unpacking the processes of how such identity markers came to be, rather than accepting them as constituted identities.

I have chosen not to use the citizenship denominations "Australian" or "New Caledonian" for either Indigenous or settler people unless the topic specifically attends to a question related to citizenship. This is for two main reasons. First, the citizenship denomination continues to be an assimilatory framework. It is a denomination with which many Indigenous people in these two societies do not primarily identify, if at all. Second, the Indigenous-settler relations that are at stake in this book and the issue of responsibility that is attached to them go beyond citizenship status, rights, and responsibilities within the nation-state framework, and reach the ontological level. Although citizenship certainly comes with additional responsibilities and possibilities to engage within Indigenous-settler relations, the core element of these relations remains the physical presence of Indigenous people and settlers within one space, regardless of their citizenship.

Wherever possible, and available, I use Indigenous place names. The correspondent English/French place names have been indicated in parentheses () on the first occurrence of the term only.

The name "New Caledonia" was given by James Cook on sighting the main island in 1774. The English term has been gallicized, and Nouvelle-Calédonie is the only name currently recognized by the French Republic. Kanaky, although a more recent coinage (officially adopted in 1984), goes back to a much older and deeper affiliation to place. It reflects the affirmation in the name of a unified Kanak people of unceded Kanak sovereignties. It is constituted by the Kanak people. According to the late Kanak politician Jean-Marie Tjibaou and many Kanak people today, it includes the non-Kanak communities peopling the country as well (Mokaddem 2009, 17). New Caledonia is a colonial appropriation through naming; Kanaky is an Indigenous reappropriation and resurgence through renaming. In that sense, "Kanaky" is a decolonial form of identification. It is a process of disidentification and reidentification, of delinking from the colonial identification of "New Caledonia."[2] The dual appellation "Kanaky/New Caledonia" is used in this book to reflect the sociopolitical realities of the territory and to problematize the ongoing political antagonism within it. It is also used to render the identification and affiliation with Kanaky, which is usually ignored or silenced, more visible in the current political context. In this sense, the name seeks to reflect and respect the freedom and right of Indigenous people to define themselves in their own terms. The ordering of the terms in this double appellation reflects the primacy of Kanak sovereignty.

Power, the School System, and Ignorance

TEACHING INDIGENOUS-SETTLER HISTORY in schools is highly contested across many settler colonized societies. Indigenous-settler histories are often marginalized or excluded outright from history curricula in favor of a nationalistic settler-centered historical narrative and of the histories of foreign countries. In these societies, learning about the history of one's country at school is certainly not a given. Its inclusion in the history curricula, when it is included, has often necessitated a sustained Indigenous, activist, and academic push for curriculum reforms and lengthy political debates. The issue remains topical and very polemic.

In Aotearoa (New Zealand), Prime Minister Jacinda Arden announced in September 2019 that New Zealand history would be made compulsory across schools and *kura* (Māori-language immersion schools) by 2022. This was the result of years of grassroots efforts, protests, and petitions. In 2014, a group of students from Ōtorohanga College (in the Waikato region in the North Island) began a campaign calling for a commemorative day to nationally recognize the New Zealand wars of the nineteenth century and for their inclusion in the national curriculum. Led by Waimarama Anderson and Leah Bell, the students gathered thirteen thousand signatures on a petition, which was presented to the Māori Affairs Select Committee at Parliament in 2016. In 2018, Taitimu Maipi defaced the colonial statue of Captain John Hamilton with red paint and a hammer in Hamilton. Concomitantly, a grassroots campaign—Time to Tell Our Story—spearheaded by the media organization Stuff got under way. In turn, in early 2019, the New

1

Zealand History Teachers' Association launched a petition to the government titled "Give me my history" that called for "raising our own veil of ignorance." The planned inclusion of Māori-Pākehā relations in the curriculum was hard won because the Ministry of Education had been opposed to compulsion.

The question of whether the history of one's country should be optional or compulsory has also stirred up debate in Canada. In 2018, Ontario cut planned curriculum revisions and reversed the previous government commitment to make Indigenous content compulsory; meanwhile, Quebec declared that it had no plans to change the history curriculum. These decisions were made despite criticism from Indigenous communities that the provinces should work more closely with them and that the Truth and Reconciliation Commission recommendations should be implemented. In the United States, the 2019 "Becoming Visible" report by the National Congress of American Indians found that 87 percent of state history standards do not include any mention of Native American history after 1900, and that twenty-seven states do not mention Native Americans in their K–12 curriculum.

In South Africa, apartheid has not been a mandatory component of the school history curriculum. In March 2015, Chumani Maxwele, a student at the University of Cape Town in South Africa, threw a bucket of feces against a bronze statue of Cecil John Rhodes located on the university's campus. This started the #RhodesMustFall student movement, which called for the decolonization of education and reform of the university curriculum. This movement highlighted the more critical need for South Africa to conduct education reform at all levels. In September 2019, a ministerial task team started writing a revised curriculum that included greater focus on South African history up to grade twelve. Minister of Basic Education Angie Motshekga also announced that a new compulsory history curriculum would be introduced following public consultations. Such a move remains politically controversial, however.

In Australia, the country's history is often squeezed out of the school curricula and students are left ignorant of Indigenous-settler history, and even more so of colonial wars and massacres. Bringing Indigenous perspectives in the classroom is not compulsory. It is up to the schools and state governments to include them. In November 2019, the federal minister for Indigenous Australians, Ken Wyatt, called for more truth-telling in classrooms on these issues. Meanwhile, in the nearby Pacific archipelago of Kanaky/New Caledonia—a French-speaking settler colonial society—recent education reforms have removed some aspects of colonial history from the history curriculum and, with the exception of isolated initiatives by individual teachers, the 1984–1988 war for the independence of the territory remains untaught.

The inclusion of Indigenous-settler history in school curricula has been met with skepticism and reluctance. An anxiety in these societies is that discussing the hostilities and conflicts that have taken place in the past will stir up bad feelings and animosity. However, ignoring settler colonial history and remaining silent about the past have not resolved these issues or resulted in just and long-lasting peace between Indigenous people and settlers. This book delves into the international debate about the teaching of colonial, Indigenous-settler history in schools and investigates how it plays out in two settler colonial societies of the South Pacific: Australia and Kanaky/New Caledonia.

The South Pacific region includes six of the seventeen UN-listed Non-Self-Governing Territories and three settler colonial societies—Australia, Kanaky/New Caledonia, and Aotearoa New Zealand. The question of decolonization is unfinished business and remains critical. Decolonization has therefore been a growing education concern in the region as well. The development of courses on Indigenous and Pacific histories and knowledges, colonialism, and critical race and whiteness studies, as well as the growing contribution and impact of Indigenous and Pasifika activists, researchers, and practitioners reflect such a decolonizing education agenda.[1] Although the idea of decolonizing education seems to have received greater attention and gained more ground in higher education, the imperative to decolonize history teaching has also manifested itself at the school level. This book provides a unique contribution to comparative and international education discussions in the South Pacific region.

Viewing Australia and Kanaky/New Caledonia together is useful for several reasons. These two neighboring societies have experienced strikingly similar colonial patterns: penal colonization, settler and exploitation colonialism, attempted genocide of Indigenous people, Christianization, extensive mining, forced and indentured labor, segregation, reservation systems, desegregation, assimilation, and current closing-the-gap and reconciliation policies without the preliminary processes of truth-telling and justice. Bringing these two settler colonial societies of the Pacific—the products of two colonial empires—into one analysis thus enables us to improve and sharpen our understanding of the mechanisms, polymorphism, and imperviousness of settler colonialism beyond the specificities of nationalisms and the cultural legacies of colonial empires. It also enables us to better scope the possibilities to contest and destabilize settler colonialism, to provoke change, and—ultimately—to decolonize Indigenous-settler relations. In these fraught settler colonial contexts, the question of how colonial histories are passed down from one generation to the next is pivotal to this decolonizing agenda.

I became aware of the pivotal yet precarious place of the teaching of colonial, Indigenous-settler history in these societies when I moved to the region from France more than nine years ago. "Why are you interested in Australian history?" I was first asked this question, shortly after arriving in Australia as a postgraduate student, by an Australian peer during the first week of classes. She paused, looked at me with a hint of curiosity, and continued, "I mean, you know, you come from a country with such a long history. Here, with our just over two hundred years, you'll probably find there's not much to look at unless you take into account Indigenous Australia before that." As I experienced similar sentiments over the following weeks, months, and years, I became aware of a pattern. This pattern seems to almost reflect an Australian "normality," of not feeling an interest or a need to understand Australian history, of not knowing the land on which you stand. Yet when my research on Australian colonial history and politics comes up in conversations, at times it seems to hit a nerve and at other times to spark an interest. It can lead to long conversations or else cut them short. It may bring up painful stories or be received with a blunt racist comment. It is an issue that seems to leave no one unmoved.

A different country, a different scene, but a similar pattern. It's a balmy night; the sun has long since set. As we drive from Tontouta Airport to Nouméa in the darkness of the night, the warm air of that late tropical night, the sounds and scents from the surrounding landscape all feel so unlike France, save for the road signs that flash by and the language we speak in the car. Yet, two thousand kilometers from the Australian east coast and seventeen thousand kilometers from metropolitan France, Kanaky/New Caledonia remains French territory. It is my first time here, and the airport shuttle driver asks why I am here. I tell him about my research on New Caledonian history and politics. He snaps back, "Don't you want to get married and have kids instead?" A few weeks later, as I exchange a few words with a historian before departing, he tells me, "It's good that people like you, from the outside, are taking up research on these issues because once you live and work here, it becomes difficult to say what you want." In Kanaky/New Caledonia as well, local history and politics are issues that seem to leave no one unmoved. It is a politically contentious place between a desire to not know and a struggle to know.

These two anecdotes seem to reveal the same problematic place that history occupies in these two societies. The recent histories of Australia and Kanaky/New Caledonia have been scarred by settler colonialism. In the former case, the colonialism was led by the British against Aboriginal and Torres Strait Island peoples, in the latter by the French against the Kanak peoples. Whether that colonial history is belittled and ignored or sought out and held up for accountability, it runs deep in the social fabric. In fact, colonial history continues to be a source of fierce, emotionally charged social and political conflicts in both societies. This suggests that the historical knowledge that is created and disseminated is fundamental to how settler colonial power is constituted, sustained, and challenged.

This book analyzes the ways that settler colonial power constitutes historical knowledge and how it affects Indigenous-settler power relations. It attends to the ways that historical knowledge is constituted in the school system. To undertake this analysis, I looked at both school history curricula and history textbooks and conducted interviews with school history teachers in Australia and Kanaky/New Caledonia. Based on the findings, I argue that settler colonial power rests on "settler regimes of ignorance" that sustain the political status quo. In other words, if knowledge is power, so is ignorance. Ignorance is the result of invested efforts and of a political struggle between different groups within settler colonial societies. The central contribution of this book is that the failure to comprehend the realities of colonialism is the social achievement of settler colonial power. The need to produce knowledge to fight settler ignorance is an attitude commonly adopted in settler colonial studies and studies on decolonization. However, multiplying media through which knowledge can be accessed does not necessarily reduce ignorance or, for that matter, shift power relations.[2] Such a conclusion remains a conundrum for educators and researchers. I demonstrate in this book that the mere production of knowledge is not a solution. Instead, I suggest that attitudes to the ignorance is both where the problem is and where the solution lies.

Public Schools: A Key Institutional Site of Settler Colonial Power

Settler colonial power constitutes and disseminates historical knowledge through a variety of media. These include the press, the radio, the television, arts, public commemorations, monuments, museums, and the public school system. Schools are a compelling site because they are a compulsory form of education and therefore a major source of learning in the formative years of human life, having an impact—on a daily basis and over an extended period—on the development and worldview of the children involved. Schools are a key institutional site in which discourses are presented as historical truth. Schools are institutions for the dissemination of knowledge but at the same time also sites of power. They inculcate students into specific ideological and emotional norms and social relations. That is, they disseminate government-sanctioned ways of understanding and engaging in Indigenous-settler relations. Schooling as a form of power has particular salience in settler colonial societies such as Australia and Kanaky/New Caledonia. In these societies, schools have been a crucial tool for the assimilation and oppression of Indigenous people. Yet against the background of decolonization and social movements internationally, Indigenous contestations have continued. In Australia, these culminated in the 1988 bicentenary protests and history syllabus boycotts; in Kanaky/New Caledonia, a state of war from 1984 to 1988 led to the creation of dissident Kanak schools.[3] In the face of continued Indigenous resistance, schools have attempted more recently to reform historical knowledge and redefine Indigenous-settler relations.

These attempts to reform historical knowledge and transform Indigenous-settler relations have been carried out in conflict-filled and tense political contexts characterized by polarized political positions: conservative and progressive in Australia, for and against independence in Kanaky/New Caledonia. In the latter, the names used in the vicinity of the school to refer to the territory reflect this schism all the more: Kanaky, New Caledonia. In Australia, Aboriginal and Torres Strait Island people have not coined another name for the continent. They have, however, created an Aboriginal flag (1971) and a Torres Strait Island flag (1992) as symbols of their affiliation to place and their unified sovereignties. More recently, some have challenged the colonial naming (English explorer Matthew Flinders suggested the name Australia in 1804) and speak instead of so-called Australia.

History teaching in schools in both Australia and Kanaky/New Caledonia has therefore been inscribed by often antagonistic political positions. As a result, attempts by the school system to reform historical knowledge and transform Indigenous-settler relations have received mixed political and emotional responses. Historical knowledge has been in the clutches of conflicting people and groups claiming control over both the past and present. Thus reforms of historical knowledge and resistance to it are key terrain for political struggles in both Australia and Kanaky/New Caledonia. As a result, teaching Indigenous-settler history remains a controversial issue, swaying between a desire to not know (ignorance) and a struggle to know (knowledge).

Settler Regimes of Ignorance

The focus has been on the relationship between power and knowledge. Far less attention has been given to the relationship between power and ignorance.[4] Yet an analysis of the historical knowledge produced by settler colonial power also requires an analysis of the how and why of ignorance about specific aspects of that history.

Ignorance is not understood here as the mere absence of knowledge but instead as the active desire to not know. It is a deliberate ignorance, a willful ignorance, when people do not care about knowing or refuse to know. To ignore is an act, not a passive state, an act of turning away from specific, unwanted, and unsettling knowledge. Knowing and ignoring are mutually constitutive and happen simultaneously. More than the episodic forgetting of aspects of history, not knowing is a strategic ignorance that consists of "the constant policing of boundaries between the known and the unknown" (McGoey 2007, 13). In 1882, the renowned French historian Ernest Renan declared that forgetting, even historical error, is an essential and brutal factor in the creation of a nation. For distinct peoples to unite and become nations, they "must have forgotten many things about their own origins." Although Renan uses the misleading word "forgetting," he does evoke its active nature, its political purpose and the key role of the instrumentalization of history in the creation of modern nations. Likewise, the English historian Eric Hobsbawm observes that national histories comprise "anachronism, omission, decontextualisation and, in extreme cases, lies" (1997, 357). Oppression often works through ignorance. Thus ignorance can be considered germane to colonial contexts. France's active disassociation with colonialism is characteristic of the dominant French historical narrative (Stoler 2011, 125). Likewise, in Kanaky/New Caledonia, Louis-José Barbançon observes that in Kanak societies "memory was life" (2006, 208), whereas for European settlers it has been exactly the opposite: "for a long time, the right to forget prevailed over the duty to remember. Heretical and sacrilegious was the one who dared to break the unsaid [*le non-dit*]." Building on these observations, and in view of the findings from this research, I argue that ignorance is foundational and fundamental to the two settler colonial societies of Australia and Kanaky/New Caledonia.

I coined the expression "settler regimes of ignorance" to reflect and raise the issue of the foundational place of ignorance within settler colonial societies. The notion of a regime of ignorance has only begun to emerge in the academic literature (Dilley and Kirsch 2015). However, further reflection as to its relevance to settler colonial contexts is lacking. In these contexts, a regime underpins the notions of domination—of settler colonial domination and norms—in all spheres of life. This domination is emotionally invested and socially and politically reproduced. This political regime consists of discourses and power relations that generate gaps in knowledge to buttress colonial military might and sustain settlers' political domination.

This type of political regime coincides with an epistemic and emotional regime of ignorance. An emotional regime is created by an emotional community that dominates the social and cultural norms, language, and media of a large part of society.[5] In Australia and Kanaky/New Caledonia, these regimes thus consist of settler regimes: settlers dominating the political, epistemic, and emotional spheres of these settler colonial societies. Settler colonial regimes and regimes of ignorance therefore intersect. In fact, ignorance is constitutive of settler privilege and power. Settler ignorance is "the profound investment in maintaining the failure to comprehend the realities of colonialism by those people who might most benefit from these conditions" (Vimalassery et al. 2016). This failure to comprehend the realities of colonialism is the social achievement of settler colonial power. The act of ignoring has been observed in several settler colonial societies and is one characteristic of colonialism, and even more so of settler colonialism. The

Bermudan political scientist Charles Mills speaks of a racial contract that relies on an epistemology of ignorance, consisting of "white misunderstanding, misrepresentation, evasion and self-deception on matters related to race," and producing "the ironic outcome that whites will in general be unable to understand the world they themselves have made." This racial contract requires a structured blindness to maintain the white polity (Mills 1997, 18–19). The racial contract is an ignorance contract. Writing about South Africa under apartheid, Melissa Steyn argues that the ignorance contract may be regarded as "a subclause of the racial contract" (2012, 21)—that is, ignorance buttresses racial discrimination and domination. Likewise, in North America and the Caribbean, Manu Vimalassery, Juliana Pegues, and Alyosha Goldstein observe that the lack of acknowledgment or engagement with colonial histories and legacies is "not simply a matter of collective amnesia or omission," a passive relation to colonialism that might suspend culpability (2016). They suggest instead that "this ignorance—this act of ignoring—is aggressively made and reproduced, affectively invested and effectively distributed in ways that conform the social relations and economies of the here and now." Any production of knowledge is also production of ignorance. This is due to the perspicacity, the epistemological choices, and the political agenda of the transmitter of knowledge. Knowing and not knowing are subject to political, personal, and historiographical dispositions and have political consequences. Therefore, what the school system tries to ignore matters as much as or probably more than what it tries to teach.

Discussion about how people have been, and are, taught about Australia's colonial history at school has been considerable. In 1968, the anthropologist William Stanner made a partial survey of early twentieth-century Australian history books and denounced the absence, in several books, of the history of contacts and conflicts between Indigenous people and settlers, an absence he named "the great Australian silence" (1991, 25). This notion has since then been widely mobilized in historiographical and political debates in Australia. However, no scholar has undertaken a long-term analysis of Australian school textbooks to answer the question of how Indigenous-settler history has been taught and thus to test Stanner's claim that previous generations were silent on the presence of widespread colonial violence and wars. This is one significant contribution of this book. Not only does it provide the first long-term analysis of Australian school history textbooks, but the findings from the research also challenge the great Australian silence theory. Colonial violence and wars are mentioned throughout the period and in almost all textbooks of the sample. The ignorance that has been generated in the school system is different from mere absence of knowledge. Such contribution is significant for two reasons. First, it calls for a closer examination of one of the fundamental tenets of Australian historiography; second, it provides a more precise understanding of settler colonial power at work in the production of historical knowledge, and therefore in the production of ignorance. My interest in the long-term corpus of history textbooks is in the present because "it selects out of the past" (Wolfe 1999, 3). My concern is with the role of textbooks as teachers' historiographical inheritance, that is, as a corpus of text, a historiography, that shapes the political work of knowledge production in the present. This inheritance amounts to an inherited settler regime of ignorance that influences the processes of knowledge and ignorance production in the present.

This book engages in a comparative analysis of the ways that Indigenous-settler history is taught in public schools in Australia and Kanaky/New Caledonia. Based on an analysis of history curricula, school textbooks, and interviews with history teachers across Australia and Kanaky/New Caledonia, it addresses the following questions: What shape does this memorial and intrinsically political work take in the history class? What are the conditions and practices in and through which knowledge is acquired and ignorance cultivated? To what extent can, or does, the teacher—as the ultimate institutional actor, the inheritor of a historiography, and a political and emotional agent—affect what is taught and what is ignored in schools and therefore shape the power relations between Indigenous people and settlers? This book explores the ways that teachers deal with settler regimes of ignorance and their capacity or lack of capacity to challenge them.

I do not argue that settler regimes of ignorance should be replaced with regimes of knowledge. As outlined, knowledge and ignorance are not opposites but mutually constitutive. Asking whether ignorance varies by degree thus seems a futile exercise. As the French philosopher Jacques Rancière points out, ignorance is resistant both to mastery and to monopolization and "there is no hierarchy in ignorance" (1991, 32). Instead, I am interested in the individual and institutional attitudes toward that ignorance. The desire to not know and the struggle to know both emanate from ignorance. The crucial difference is one's attitude to and use of that ignorance. What is problematic is not ignorance per se but that it is constituted as a regime, that is, as a tool for and a product of political rule and domination. Settler regimes of ignorance seem inescapable. Yet they are at times challenged by an individual's willingness to address such ignorance. That is, surprisingly, ignorance can act as a lever for change. This dynamic deserves more attention. This book analyzes the dynamism between knowledge and ignorance and the different uses of ignorance that help maintain or disrupt settler colonial power.

Before engaging in an analysis of the processes of knowledge production and ignorance cultivation, mapping the establishment of colonial systems and hierarchy of knowledge from which such processes take root and placing them in the larger historical and political contexts of Australia and Kanaky/New Caledonia is each necessary.

The Establishment of Colonial Systems and Hierarchy of Knowledge

Australia consists of Aboriginal and Torres Strait Island lands and seas. Kanaky/New Caledonia consists of Kanak lands and seas. At present, many settlers whose ancestral roots are elsewhere also live on these lands and off these seas. Settlers have come to make up 97 percent of Australia's population on a land area more than four hundred times larger than Kanaky/New Caledonia. In the latter, settlers are a significantly lower proportion, about 60 percent of the population. These demographic and geographical differences are significant factors in understanding how Indigenous-settler political relations have unfolded in these two neighboring societies.

The Preliminary: Securing Domination through Military Might

The British-led colonization of Australia started in 1788 in Eora Nation, one of several hundred Indigenous Nations existing at the time.[6] The French-led colonization of Kanaky/New Caledonia began in 1853 in the Hoot ma Waap customary area, which became one of the two settler colonies of the French empire (the other being Algeria). Invasion spread from the southeast of Australia across the continent, and throughout the main island (Grande Terre) in Kanaky/New Caledonia.[7] These invasions were met with resistance. Indigenous-settler relations were often marked by brutal physical violence. In Australia, Indigenous people were massacred by government officials, settlers, and Native Police, starved, poisoned, and saw their agriculture destroyed. Until the 1860s, guerrilla wars and massacres occurred regularly; after that, until the early twentieth century, they were more sporadic. The last known massacre of Indigenous people in Australian history is the 1928 Coniston Massacre in Central Australia. In Kanaky/New Caledonia, mobile columns composed of colonial troops, European settlers, and Kanak auxiliaries were sent to crush the resistance. Settlers used a scorched-earth military strategy, destroying villages, plantations, and irrigation systems to starve Kanak people on the main island. From the 1850s to the 1870s, Kanaky/New Caledonia saw frequent uprisings, wars, and constant military expeditions. Armed conflicts and wars went on for many decades and continued sporadically in the twentieth century, notably in 1878 and 1917 and from 1984 to 1988. The last massacre of Kanak people in New Caledonian history occurred in 1988 in Iaai (Ouvéa). Kanak resistance has been dealt with by imprisonment, massacre, capital punishment, displacement, and exile.[8]

These colonial wars were undeclared but nevertheless total wars, both involving and directed at civilians. Such practices were later supported by racialist Social Darwinist theories and the legal theory of *terra nullius*, according to which land could be legitimately seized. Australia's Indigenous peoples and Kanak peoples were degraded and considered to be primitive people doomed to imminent and inevitable extinction. Deploying these theories for colonial ends, French, British, and Australian governments confiscated Indigenous land and seas and attempted to exterminate Indigenous people. Colonization led to genocide, land dispossession, and loss of languages and cultures. The pace, intensity, and geography of spatial appropriation (and expropriation) varied from place to place and in the course of time.[9] Yet throughout colonization damaged Indigenous societal structures, displaced entire peoples, disempowered existing political organization, and ignored Indigenous voices. Conflicts and wars between Indigenous peoples and settlers in both Australia and Kanaky/New Caledonia have indeed been asymmetric conflicts.

As a result, the extent and the ways settler colonial powers attempted to exterminate Indigenous people are significant. Currently accepted estimates evaluate the Indigenous population in Australia at the time of invasion to be more than one million (Butlin 1983; Williams 2013). By 1901, it was reduced to twenty thousand, which amounts to a 98 percent decrease. Even if the most conservative figure of three hundred thousand at the time of invasion is taken, the decrease would still amount to 93 percent. In Kanaky/New Caledonia, from the beginning of colonization to the 1930s, the Kanak population declined markedly. Kanak population at the time of colonization has been estimated to be between one hundred thousand (Roberts 1929, 523; Hickman 2016, 45) and two hundred thousand (Ounei 1985, 3). Since colonization, it reached its lowest level in 1921 of 18,600 on the main island (Saussol 1988, 49). This amounts to a decrease of approximately 81 to 91 percent. Many factors account for these declines: massacres, executions, poisoned food, and waterholes (in Australia); widespread use of the scorched-earth military tactic (in Kanaky/New Caledonia); and starvation, malnutrition, and diseases such as smallpox and sexually transmitted diseases (many of which spread as a result of the widespread rape of Indigenous women by settlers).

In colonial contexts, invasion and domination involving brutal physical violence and military might only have necessitated limited knowledge from the colonial powers (mapping, resources, basic knowledge of Indigenous peoples and their military capability), enough to break Indigenous resistance and administer Indigenous territories. Following colonial wars, and under a colonial administration, colonial powers needed to craft a discourse in which European military superiority was matched with a perceived intellectual superiority. Discourses of superior knowledge on one side and primitivity on the other fed policies of segregation. The receptiveness of such discourses rested on the settlers' willful ignorance of Indigenous people and knowledge.

Colonial Systems: Segregation, Public Schools, and Debased Curricula

From the second half of the nineteenth century, and following periods of brutal colonial conflicts and wars, governments moved to create Indigenous reserves to subdue Indigenous people by confining and controlling them and to facilitate land dispossession. Such procedures were called policies of protection in Australia and policies of cantonment in Kanaky/New Caledonia. These policies expropriated the Indigenous land and workforce.[10] Indigenous people in Australia and Kanaky/New Caledonia were heavily controlled and had to pay in kind or in cash (through taxes) for their own subjugation. In Australia, all British colonies and states (after 1901) passed legislation to heavily control Indigenous people in their movement, work, and association. Likewise, the Indigenous Code—a set of laws establishing an inferior status for Indigenous people—applied across Kanaky/New Caledonia from 1887 to 1946 had a similar function. In parallel with Indigenous free labor, colonialism in Australia and Kanaky/New Caledonia also relied on an intercolonial human trafficking of contracted or forced labor. Pacific Island people were sent to plantations in Queensland (Australia) for instance, and settler colonial power in Kanaky/New Caledonia contracted Southeast Asian people to work in the mines and plantations.

Relationships and reciprocity between Indigenous people and settlers of all origins were discouraged or outlawed. Love between Indigenous people and settlers became "illicit love" (McGrath 2015). Children of combined Indigenous and settler ancestry were at risk of forced assimilation into the white settler society. In Australia, these children were systematically removed from their parents by governments and missions, eventually becoming known as the Stolen Generation. In Kanaky/New Caledonia, such children could lose their customary inheritance under the Indigenous Code. Such policies enforced a biological apartheid, under which people were categorized according to their blood quantum. Although European or white "blood" could "stand admixture" and remain "pure," Indigenous blood could not and "Indigeneity" was compromised (Wolfe 1994, 116; Ellinghaus 2003, 203). Physical and biological apartheid led to a mental apartheid. These policies and practices restricted interaction and communication between Indigenous people and settlers, helped feed colonial myths about the believed inferiority of Indigenous people and knowledge, and contributed to a continuing lack of intercultural communication. The reserve system, missions, and accompanying racialist policies of separation segregated Indigenous people from settlers in all social spheres, including education.[11]

In the last quarter of the nineteenth century, between 1872 and 1894, the British colonies in Australia introduced free, secular, and compulsory primary education. The compulsory schooling age was usually between six and thirteen, with slight variations from colony to colony. Educational institution-building was led by the colonies and supported by colony-specific curricula. At the time of federation in 1901, education was not included as a commonwealth power in the constitution and remained under the jurisdiction of the states, which had the power to define the curriculum and enact regulatory measures. State education was run by a centralized administration that ensured uniform teaching across the state. Australia therefore did not have a uniform, nationwide educational provision. To date, states and territories remain responsible for the delivery of education in schools. The Australian government contributes to the funding of public schools, and national education policy is decided by all state and territory governments working through the Council of Australian Governments system.

The states' school systems continued to expand and were the main provider (ahead of denominational schools) of education in Australia (ABS 2001a). Public, free, and compulsory secondary schooling emerged later. Public secondary systems of education were initially developed in each state between 1905 and 1915, but those had fees and were specifically for children after school-leaving age. It is only after World War II, the economic and demographic boom, and the steep rise in enrolment that tuition fees were abolished in public secondary education and the school-leaving age extended. Enrollment in public schools rose from about six hundred thousand in 1900 to two million in 1969 and accounted for 78 percent of the student population (Burke and Spauli 2001; Australian Bureau of Statistics 2001).[12] However, schooling often remained out of reach of the most isolated communities, and the laws did not apply to Indigenous people.

Indigenous people were segregated from settlers in education, both by removal policies for Indigenous children and by pressure from settler families, which led to the exclusion of Indigenous students from school. The removal and education of Indigenous people was carried out mostly under coercion by governmental authorities, missions, families, and police forces. Indigenous people were moved to homes and missions to be controlled, assimilated, and made beneficial, through their labor, to the settler colonial society. Until World War II, most Australian states removed children to institutions and placed them in foster or adoptive families.

Although Aboriginal children were briefly, in the early years of the school system, allowed to attend school, regulations in the 1880s enabled their removal from schools under the racist "clad and courteous" and "exclusion on demand" policies. Exclusion of Aboriginal children was implemented at the discretion of the school principal or as a result of complaints by parents. In the Protection era, children on reserves had to attend Aboriginal-only schools and others were placed in segregated classes within government schools. Unlike in public school systems, education directed at Indigenous people did not take place in a secular school system. Indigenous children were also taught a debased curriculum, mostly focused on manual and domestic labor, which prepared them to work for settlers (Burridge and Chodkiewicz 2012, 12, 14). It took long decades of struggles by Indigenous parents and communities before Indigenous children could have full access to unsegregated government education.

In Kanaky/New Caledonia, from 1881 to 1886, member of the French government Jules Ferry designed laws to introduce free, compulsory, and secular primary schooling for children aged six to thirteen. From 1885, a segregated, public, secular school system was set up in Kanaky/New Caledonia.[13] Primary school teaching was linked to the structure of the French school system and took in most school age settler children. At first, the French government did not make the promotion of education in the colonies a priority. It was therefore the responsibility of French authorities in the colonies to make schooling a government concern. Primary school was made compulsory for European children only later, in 1902, and every town (*commune*) was required to have a school. In practice, however, schools developed earlier in urban than in remote areas (Laurens and Vareille 1984, 113–114).

In parallel, in 1885, noncompulsory secular Indigenous schools (*écoles indigènes*) were opened and existed until the dismantling of the Indigenous Code in 1946 (Salaün 2005). Indigenous schools in Kanaky/New Caledonia aimed at controlling Kanak people by creating conciliatory elites and useful masses for the colony, through their labor. Georges Hardy, director of the Colonial School (1926–1933) and one of the most fervent promoters of a racialist differentiated teaching in the French colonies, considered that the sole purpose of Indigenous schools was to train "the elites that the authorities need to make the inner workings of colonisation work, by disseminating a minimal teaching to the masses" (Surun 2012, 349). This transmission and reproduction of the colonial order was also carried out through the inferiorization and ban of Kanak languages in 1921. Thereafter, the "French monolingual ideology was implanted in a territory traditionally favouring plurilinguilism" (Colombel and Fillol 2009, 2).

Thus schools in Australia and Kanaky/New Caledonia were "miseducating" Indigenous people and preparing them for basic manual labor for settlers (Angulo 2016). The aim of colonization was an incomplete assimilation, which educated and trained people enough to function within the system but not enough to question its foundation. As the sociologist Aníbal Quijano explains in another context, "at first, they placed these patterns far out of reach of the dominated. Later, they taught them in a partial and selective way, in order to co-opt some of the dominated into their own power institutions" (2007, 169). Through policies of seg-regation, Indigenous people were largely excluded from colonial systems of learning and considered to be on a lower rung of humanity. Ignorance helped create a colonial social hierarchy. Indigenous people were rel-egated to a position of ignorance within the settler knowledge system, and settler colonial power controlled access to this restrictive knowledge.

The Colonial Systems and Hierarchy of Knowledge Contested

Indigenous parents and communities in Australia fought against segre-gation practices in various ways: moving their children to more accept-ing schools, holding rallies, and writing petitions to state governments and the English monarch. In 1940, the government adopted a policy of assimilation for children with both Aboriginal and settler ances-tries. Indigenous struggles against segregation continued unabated. In 1956, Aboriginal teaching graduates began teaching in New South Wales. In 1963, the first Aboriginal Education Consultative Committee in New South Wales was formed to lobby regarding education issues for Aboriginal people. The 1960s and 1970s began to witness a shift in Commonwealth intervention in the state and territory public school systems. After the 1967 referendum, the federal government had the power to legislate on education and provide support for Indigenous peo-ple through grants and the establishment of an Aboriginal Education Consultative Group in each state. In 1972, almost a century after the first exclusionary practices, the law allowing principals to exclude Indigenous children from schools was abolished.

Around that time, the assimilationist educational provision by the states was facing growing criticism from various sections of the popu-lation—among both Indigenous and non-Anglo-Celtic settler popu-lations. The former pushed for recognition of their sovereignty, the latter for recognition of their cultural diversity and specific needs. The Indigenous populations in both countries had begun to rise again from the 1920s to 1930s, and Indigenous resistance rebuilt momentum. Indigenous voices pushed for the opening of a political debate and for their voices to be heard. Aboriginal and Torres Strait Island activism from the 1930s and the Black Power–inspired Indigenous movements of the 1960s and 1970s in both Australia and Kanaky/New Caledonia, saw Indigenous people using what power they had to fight for their rights, freedom, self-determination, and independence.[14]

Indigenous people appropriated and adapted imported tools of political struggle and knowledge production to fight against their continuing marginalization within the settler colonial socio-political system. In Australia, the Australian Aboriginal Progressive Association was created in 1924 by Fred Maynard and lobbied for Indigenous people in meetings, marches, newspaper articles, and petitions. A number of Indigenous actions, including the 1946 Aboriginal Stockmen's Strike, the 1963 Yirrkala bark petitions, and the 1966 Wave Hill Walk-Off pushed for a political debate on the recognition of Indigenous people's rights to land. The decades that followed continued to be marked by strikes and protests, which intensified and changed forms from the late 1960s. Inspired by the Black Power movement in the United States, Indigenous people used stronger and faster methods to make their voices heard. They condemned institutional racism, called for human rights (not just civil rights), continued to fight against mining and for land rights, and asserted their sovereignty and self-determination through community-based programs, the creation of the Aboriginal Tent Embassy (in 1972), and diplomatic relations with Indigenous peoples overseas. They published books on history, politics, and law and continued developing their own media and arts.

This Indigenous resurgence was opposed to the political context of assimilation but often met with state repression or fell on deaf ears. Although the 1967 referendum created the prospect of the commonwealth government overriding discriminatory state laws toward Indigenous people and therefore creating prospects for a better future, in reality positive changes were limited. Indigenous land claims continued to be rejected. Indigenous self-determination was co-opted through the institutionalization of community-run programs in the 1980s.[15] Finally, the triumphalist 1988 bicentennial celebrated the colonial invasion.[16] All these testified to the continued ignorance and indifference of the majority of the population of Australia's treatment of Indigenous people. The growing protests against the bicentenary, however, challenged the narrative by bringing colonial history and Indigenous-settler social conflicts to the fore. These protests pushed state governments to reform curricula and devolve authority to schools.

In Kanaky/New Caledonia, a large majority of European settler children were enrolled in public schools and, as in Australia, the post–World War II years witnessed a sharp increase in school enrolments. Unlike settler children, until the 1950s, most Kanak children were enrolled in denominational schools and only about one-quarter attended Indigenous schools. In 1946, the Indigenous code was abolished. Indigenous schools were progressively closed, and Indigenous students were relocated to government schools. In 1951, an estimated 50 percent of school-age Kanak children attended a government school (Grangier 1950; Bruy-Hebert 2010).

From then on, school and university certifications were made available to Kanak students as well as Europeans. Until the 1960s, however, secondary teaching was often reserved for the elite, and exclusion based on race and class was common. Since the 1970s, the place of public education has expanded at the expense of the private sector. The public sector represented 54 percent of education in 1970, 71 percent in 2000, and 73 percent in 2014 (Cour des Comptes 2016, 286). However, the integration of Kanak people as citizens within the French Republic and into previously exclusively "white" schools marginalized Kanak languages (Colombel and Fillol 2009, 2). New Caledonian government schools followed programs of the French mainland, recruited their teachers mostly in mainland France, and used French textbooks. Such staffing and curricular patterns received increasing criticism and fed the growing Kanak nationalist movement.

Many Kanak people—several of whom studied in France in the 1960s and went through the 1968 uprising—and some settler supporters organized themselves politically. They demanded more political, cultural, economic and land rights, and, later, independence. Several activist groups were created, such as the Red Scarves (Les Foulards Rouge) and the 1878 Group, and organized political meetings and demonstrations. At the end of the 1970s, the movement for independence placed the government school system at the center of their political struggle. The "colonial school" was perceived as a source of alienation and acculturation for Kanak people. During the 1984–1988 war, the independence movement's politics of refusal targeted both the electoral and schooling systems.[17] An active boycott of the school system by Kanak people was put in place across Kanaky/New Caledonia, and Kanak Popular Schools were created as an alternative. These ran for several years, some even for a couple of decades, but the French government's decision to apply sanctions to families who had withdrawn their children from government schools and the eroding support from Kanak people undermined the movement. Nonetheless, the school boycott and the ongoing conflict precipitated changes in the public school system.

Thus, by 1988, in both Australia and Kanaky/New Caledonia, the school system and the colonial hierarchy of knowledge it was made to sustain had come under considerable challenge. In Australia, the ever-growing Indigenous-led protests surrounding the 1988 bicentennial celebrations against the Australian government's treatment of Indigenous people as well as the 1991 Royal Commission on Aboriginal Deaths in Custody, which revealed institutionalized racism and violations of human rights, led the Australian government to pursue a policy of reconciliation to silence Indigenous demands for land rights and treaty. In Kanaky/New Caledonia, the 1984–1988 war ended with an amnesty, which was followed by a subsequent reconciliation process focused on the notion of "common destiny" (*destin commun*). Educational institutions recognized the importance of adapting the school system to local social realities. The political urgency of the war and the lingering resentment in its aftermath accelerated the process. Jurisdiction for primary schooling was transferred from mainland France to New Caledonian provinces in 2000. The transfer of jurisdiction over secondary schooling partially followed in 2012. In both countries, the school system therefore became a vector of government-led reconciliation processes. Yet reconciliation has not necessarily amounted to a fundamental shift in Indigenous-settler power relations in either Australia or Kanaky/New Caledonia. The public education systems in these two societies still bear the marks of colonialism in that they sustain settler colonial political institutions and the hegemony of Western knowledge systems, lack relevance to local sociolinguistic and economic realities, marginalize Indigenous power and epistemologies, and perpetuate discrimination along Indigenous-settler lines (Mokaddem 1999; Fillol 2009; Salaün 2013). These signs of ongoing settler colonialism become all the more apparent when looking at the institutions concerned with Indigenous-settler relations that maintain the political status quo. At the core are issues of land, political representation, and Indigenous sovereignties.

Indigenous-Settler Relations: The Political Contexts

In response to Indigenous struggle and protest, Indigenous people have achieved piecemeal efforts toward land restitution over the decades. A process of returning land to Indigenous people has been under way in both Australia and Kanaky/New Caledonia. The 1992

Mabo legal case and subsequent 1993 Native Title Act created a national framework under which Indigenous peoples' native title could be recognized.[18] However, this recognition was later weakened by the 1998 Native Title Amendment Act and, as many deplore, native title remains constrained within a settler colonial political framework and does not consist of either land rights or justice.[19] In 2016, Indigenous lands and reserves made up 13 percent of Australian territory. If the native title exclusive possession were also included, Indigenous people would hold 23 percent of Australia's land area (see map 1).

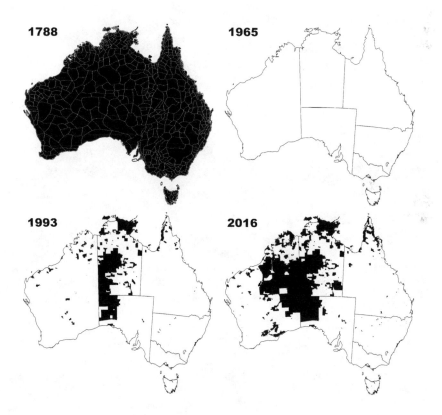

Map depicting the evolution of Indigenous-held land in Australia. From Jon Altman, and Francis Markham, "Burgeoning Indigenous Land Ownership: Diverse Values and Strategic Potentialities," in *Native Title from Mabo to Akiba: A Vehicle for Change and Empowerment?* edited by Sean Brennan, Megan Davis, Brendan Edgeworth, and Leon Terrill (Annandale, NSW: Federation Press, 2015).

In Kanaky/New Caledonia, after unabated Kanak demands for
the restitution of their lands, the government launched land reform
in the 1970s. This measure was furthered when Jean-Marie Tjibaou, at
the head of the Governing Council of New Caledonia between 1982
and 1984, established two institutions that promoted Kanak cultures
and political rights: the Kanak Technical and Scientific Cultural Office
(Office culturel scientifique et technique kanak) and the Land Office
(Office foncier).[20] As of 1999, Kanak customary lands are inalienable,
unseizable, incommutable, and nontransferable. They make up 27 percent of the territory's land area today (see map 2).

Political Representation

Progress has been made in terms of the political representation of
Indigenous people in Australia and Kanaky/New Caledonia, but settler

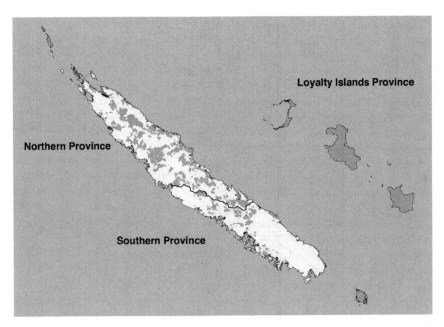

Map of Kanak customary lands in Kanaky/New Caledonia as of December 1, 2020. The land
marked in grey represents the location of the Kanak customary lands, totaling 27 percent
of the land in Kanaky/New Caledonia. Northern Province: 251,030 hectares (50 percent of
customary lands); Loyalty Islands Province: 189,390 hectares (38 percent of customary lands);
Southern Province: 62,870 hectares (12 percent of customary lands). Courtesy of ADRAF.

colonial power continues to exclude Indigenous sovereignties and allow only a consultative role to Indigenous political bodies. In Australia, the first national body elected by Aboriginal people was the National Aboriginal Consultative Committee (1972–1977). An Indigenous representative body, the Aboriginal and Torres Strait Islander Commission was created in 1990, though abolished in 2004 under the Howard government. The subsequent National Indigenous Council (2004–2008), made up of fourteen members (politicians, economists, artists, and sportspeople), had a purely consultative role. In 2010, the National Congress of Australia's First Peoples—a national representative body independent of government, and the largest Aboriginal and Torres Strait Islander organization in the country—was established. Today, within the institutional framework, the Indigenous Advisory Council is appointed by the prime minister and the minister for Indigenous Affairs and has only a consultative role.[21] Egalitarian parliamentarism and racism has also maintained the political marginalization of Indigenous people since Federation. Since the establishment of the federal parliament in 1901, only eight Indigenous people have been members, six in the Senate and two in the House of Representatives. Two Indigenous senators (Pat Dodson and Malarndirri McCarthy) and two members of the House of Representatives (Ken Wyatt and Linda Burney) at the federal level are currently in office. Indigenous people have achieved greater representation in state and territorial institutions, especially in the Northern Territory. At the time of writing, twenty-two Indigenous people have been members of parliament in the Northern Territory, five in Western Australia, four in Queensland, and one in the Australian Capital Territory, New South Wales, Victoria, and Tasmania.

In Kanaky/New Caledonia, considering the stronger demographic weight of Kanak people and of the pro-independence voices, political representation has been greater. Since the Nouméa Agreement, Kanaky/New Caledonia has been composed of five institutions specific to this territory: the Congress (the deliberative assembly), the Government (the executive), the Customary Senate, and the Environmental, Social and Economic Boards.[22] Political powers are shared between the three provinces and the territory but not with the customary institutions (the Customary Senate). The Customary Senate is constituted on the basis of the eight Kanak customary areas and composed of male members exclusively.[23] It is consulted for matters relating only to Kanak identity and does not have any decision-making or legislative power. In the lead-up to the 2018 referendum for independence, a transfer of political powers was initiated from institutions in mainland France to New Caledonian institutions to support the emancipation of the territory. These transferred powers do not, however, include sovereign powers (defense, foreign affairs, justice, law and order, and currency). The Congress has witnessed a tug-of-war between loyalist and pro-independence parties, which currently hold twenty-eight seats and twenty-six seats, respectively. The current government, like the previous one, is composed of eleven members: six loyalist members and five pro-independence members, which reflects a strong antagonism within New Caledonian society.

Indigenous Sovereignties

Reconciliatory processes have remained fraught processes in both Australia and Kanaky/New Caledonia. Many condemn the ineffectiveness or hypocrisy of such policies.[24] Meanwhile, demands for self-determination for Indigenous people and the question of Indigenous sovereignties have been ignored. As a result, the political struggle continues both within and beyond existing institutional frameworks. First, Indigenous people continue to run several campaigns: for instance, the campaigns in Australia for an Indigenous representative body and the political campaigns in Kanaky/New Caledonia for the conduct of the 2018–2022 referenda for independence and the constitution of a special, restricted electorate. Second, it takes the shape of a refusal to confront settler power on its own terms, what Andrew Mack identifies as "the first condition for avoiding defeat" in asymmetric conflicts (1975, 176). The growing refusal of constitutional recognition by many Aboriginal and Torres Strait Island people in Australia, and their push instead for nation-to-nation treaties, is one such example. Although some Aboriginal and Torres Strait Island people seek constitutional recognition and better political representation, an ever-growing majority call for Australia-wide, statewide, and nation-to-nation treaties. Australian citizenship has also been contested by several Aboriginal and Torres Strait Island people in the form of refusal of the compulsory voting system, acquisition of an Aboriginal passport, and declaration of independence. The Aboriginal passport was first created in the late 1980s and has, since the early 1990s, been delivered by the Aboriginal Provisional Government, which has fought for Aboriginal sovereignty, self-determination, and self-government. In recent years, several Indigenous Nations have declared their independence, such as the Murrawarri Republic (2013), the Euahlayi Peoples Republic (2013), the Republic of Mbarbaram (2013), the Wiradjuri Central West Republic (2014), the Yidindji Government (2014), the Yuggera Ugarapul Tribal Peoples (2016), and the Mirrabooka Sovereign United Nations (2017). Indigenous sovereignty, whether in the form of a treaty or treaties (Australia) or independence (Kanaky/New Caledonia) continues to be fought for on several fronts. Reconciliatory policies have translated into a reinforcement of settler power whereby, in crisis situations, the state managed to maintain access to Indigenous lands and resources by proposing some sorts of recognition and reconciliation. In Kanaky/New Caledonia for instance, power-sharing has emerged as an instrument of peacemaking. The 1984–1988 war led to the Matignon-Oudinot Agreements, which set up the political and economic "rebalancing" of the territory. This process was furthered with the 1998 Nouméa Agreement, which set in motion the gradual transfer of political powers (except for sovereign powers) to territorial institutions. Political scientists Denis Tull and Andreas Mehler warn, however, that "the short-term quelling of conflicts in the guise of power-sharing is not to be confounded with peace" (2005, 395). Likewise, the Nouméa-based philosopher Hamid Mokaddem observes that "the Nouméa Agreement is the political name of an actual instability behind an apparent peace" (2007, 119).

Indigenous people often face a double challenge: both from the metropole (which maintains economic interests in the region) and from a large majority of the local settler population (whose political and economic interests are a powerful impediment to a potential shift of power). When Indigenous power seems close to overturning settler colonial power, Mack observes that, typically, settlers will bitterly resist any attempt to hand over control to Indigenous people; and "if pressures in the metropolis are such that withdrawal from the colonies appears likely . . . there may well be moves by the settlers to attempt a type of 'go-it-alone.'" In such case, "the settlers will in many ways prove to be a more formidable enemy than was the vastly more powerful metropolitan power, because the constraints over the use of force will be almost completely absent in their case" (Mack 1975, 190–191). It is instructive that several Indigenous struggles that have challenged Australian governments' unresponsiveness, from William Cooper in the 1930s to Clinton's Walk for Justice in 2016–2017, have addressed the English monarch directly.[25] It is also indicative that, in 2012, former French Minister for Overseas Territories Victorin Lurel's using the word Kanaky in addition to New Caledonia, "to respect all parties" because "we say New Caledonia but it has a connotation" led to political contestations from local loyalist politicians. They condemned it as a provocation and warned the government in mainland France that they would "fight against any unilateral proposition that would go against the maintaining of New Caledonia within France" (Agence France Presse 2012). According to the historian Bouda Etemad, emancipation in settler colonial societies was carried out "under the guidance of the European settler polity, without destruction of colonial structures" so that in countries of North America (United States and Canada) and South America (Argentina, Uruguay, Chile) or the Pacific (Australia, New Zealand), "the Europeans maintained themselves at the top of the social and political hierarchy." Thus, he concludes, "in all those cases, 'decolonisation' marks the triumph of European colonisation" (2012, 198). The Federation of Australia in 1901 reflected the maintenance of colonial structures. Depending on the aftermath of the 2018–2022 referenda, Kanaky/New Caledonia might continue on that path, should institutional continuity and the nonrecognition and implementation of Kanak sovereignty prevail.

These two societies indeed face the challenge that settlers have become "too comfortable and complacent about living on stolen Indigenous homelands" (Corntassel 2011) as Indigenous people and a segment of the settler population call for historical truth and justice and continue to affirm Indigenous sovereignty. That in both Australia and Kanaky/New Caledonia these reconciliatory policies happened without preliminary truth-telling and justice remains problematic. One recurring problem is the incapacity to conceive a common vision of the future.

As in other settler colonial societies, the current struggle between Indigenous people and settler colonial power in Australia and Kanaky/New Caledonia rests on two competing visions of the future. One consists of juridical homogeneity and the enforcement by the state of "one standard of values, behavior, and vision," and the other is based on "coexistence, a social balance between independence and interdependence of peoples, and a political relationship founded on an ethic of pluralism in a framework of respect" (Alfred 2004, 92). As Customary Senator Gilbert Téin explains, "what is striking is that instead of just asking their place on the existing fabric, the *natte* [mat] as we say back home on which we sit, they [settlers] want to weave another new *natte*. That's what's a bit annoying" (2011). This situation bears many contradictions in both Australia and Kanaky/New Caledonia. Indigenous people are both affirmed (in their civil rights) and denied (in their sovereignty), appreciated (for their artistic, cultural and sporting achievements), and vilified (for their political dissidence).

Such divisions between settler colonial power and Indigenous power have been reflected in the school systems in Australia and Kanaky/New Caledonia. Beyond its intellectual function, the public school system has been a privileged state apparatus and a political tool for social and political engineering. The politics of history curriculum has played a key role. The ways that history is taught and what Indigenous and settler people learn about their past and the present continue to shape Indigenous-settler relations significantly. Yet the fundamental political aspect of the school system is often overlooked by scholars interested in education in favor of pedagogical or statistical questions. This book attempts to fill that gap and to unpack the political purpose and impact of history curricula, and history teaching more broadly, on Indigenous-settler relations in the present.

This book therefore also provides a useful contribution to current scholarship on decolonization. After the wave of decolonization beginning in the mid-1940s, decolonization is back on academic and political agendas worldwide. Although the United Nations records only seventeen nongoverning territories, among which is Kanaky/New Caledonia, the question of decolonization continues to stir political debates internationally. Unabated Indigenous movements for sovereignty worldwide, widespread cultural identity crises (in the form of culturally bereft nationalisms, xenophobia, and religious fundamentalism), and evidence of the exhaustion of current democratic political models, given their origins in colonialism and modernity, all point to the relevance of decolonizing processes. The necessity of decolonizing processes in societies that claim to have already been or to be in the process of being decolonized—through the transfer of political authority from the metropole to the majoritarian colonial polity in the colony—can be more difficult to advocate for or implement, and therefore is all the more crucial. This is the case of settler colonial societies such as Australia and Kanaky/New Caledonia. As I suggest toward the end of this book, decolonization is all the more desirable in that it has the potential to lead to a situation whereby political relations can be reshaped, human plurality can express itself, and true politics be achieved.

Outline of the Book

This book is organized into three parts: policy and directives, texts, and pedagogy. As prelude, chapter 1 scopes the societal debate that takes place in Australia and Kanaky/New Caledonia around the contested concepts of settler colonialism and decolonization and interrogates common understandings and usage. The usage is further assessed against the academic research on the topic in the field of settler colonial studies and decolonization (decolonization intersecting two standpoints: decolonial thinking and Indigenous resurgence). The chapter then introduces the methods and materials for this research and their usefulness to our understanding of settler colonialism and potential ways to undermine settler colonial power.

Part 1 focuses on government education policies. It looks at the initial stage of history teaching: curriculum development, staffing and teacher training, that is, the official directives and skills provided to history teachers. Chapter 2 opens the analysis with a review of the recent evolution of history curricula. I analyze the place and importance of history curricula in the political battlefield as well as the content of the history curricula and the variables behind these curricular choices. I demonstrate that the production of history curricula is in both Australia and Kanaky/New Caledonia a highly politically divisive issue, in the throes of political antagonism, and that it continues to at worst exclude outright, at best marginalize, Indigenous people from the curriculum development process. Chapter 3 looks into teacher training on Indigenous-settler history. Together with chapter 2's focus on curricular reforms, it provides a comprehensive basis for understanding the educational policies and directives of the settler colonial powers.

Part 2 examines government-sanctioned interpretations of its content. Exploring the historiography that shapes teachers' historical knowledge and teaching work, it delves into the production and content of textbooks, that is, history teachers' historiographical inheritance and inherited settler regime of ignorance. Chapter 4 explores the evolution of textbook publishing, in particular, the trends and variations in the authorial power of textbooks. It considers logics of inclusion and exclusion in the processes of generating official knowledge. In chapter

5, I undertake a systematic analysis of the content of these school history textbooks—their stereotypical enunciations of Indigenous-settler history and the kinds of identities and power relations they create to sustain ignorance.

Part 3 looks at the adaptation of such historiographical inheritance by teachers in their pedagogical choices. It moves on to the implementation, by teachers, of educational policies and directives. Chapter 6 pays attention to teachers' responses to these institutional directives and institution-sanctioned materials. It discusses teachers' approaches to teaching and the strategies they report adopting to teach Indigenous-settler history; that is, what their educational objectives are and the ways they believe such goals may be achieved. It considers the ways that teachers reinforce, circumvent, or contest these settler regimes of ignorance, the possibilities they offer, and the continuing obstacles they face in doing so. Whereas chapter 6 explores possibilities and achievements, the last chapter engages with the ongoing obstacles to teaching Indigenous-settler history. I suggest that although even for the most willing teachers, settler regimes of ignorance often prove inescapable, attitudes to ignorance also reveal its potential in shifting Indigenous-settler power relations. In an effort to find out whether this potential can be tapped at a larger-than-individual level—in other words, the likelihood of its being implemented at the institutional level—the conclusion provides the key answers to the research questions and closes with a reflection on the role of schools, in their current iteration, to effectively teach Indigenous-settler history and their potential to decolonize—or at least start shifting—power relations between Indigenous people and settlers.

CHAPTER 1

Settler Colonialism and Decolonization

*The Societal Debates, the Academic Field,
and the Research*

COLONIALISM AND DECOLONIZATION remain contested concepts and processes in Australia and Kanaky/New Caledonia. The French anthropologist Alban Bensa, renowned for his work on Kanak cultures and New Caledonian society, observes that "in a colonized country, words are parcel bombs that each one handles with caution. Words are not free there, they are scared of themselves and of others because the ones who use them don't have the same references" (1997, 11). Indeed, in these two societies, historians, political actors and commentators, and teachers use divergent frames of reference to define what colonialism and decolonization mean and consist of, which in turn affects the teaching of Indigenous-settler history in the public school system.

Debunking Myths about Colonialism and Decolonization

Some see decolonization as an obsolete notion. For instance, Philippe Boyer, former history teacher, textbook author, and former director of the Territorial Centre for Research and Pedagogical Documentation (1995–1996) in Kanaky/New Caledonia and president of the academic association CORAIL (Coordination for Oceania in Research on the Arts, Ideas and Literatures), argued in 1996 that "the era is no longer one of decolonization" given that the "Territory has come out of the colonial era" (Wénéhoua 1996, 62).[1] Such comments define colonization as a strictly institutional status now abolished. Common historical demarcation is often made in the historiographies of Australia and Kanaky/New Caledonia between a "colonial period" and a contemporary, "modern," "postcolonial" society. In Australia, the line of demarcation is 1901, the date of the federation of Australia, when British colonies became Australian States and Territories. In Kanaky/New Caledonia, it is 1946, when its status changed from colony to Overseas Territory (Territoire d'Outre-mer) and the Indigenous code was abolished. Such demarcation defines colonization and therefore decolonization as a purely legal status and as a historical period (1788–1901 in Australia and 1853–1946 in Kanaky/New Caledonia). To understand colonialism as legal status defined by a historical period omits the social, psychological, economic, political, cultural, and ontological articulations and implications of colonialism and is therefore inadequate and insufficient for achieving decolonization in education.

Colonialism has also been presented in a morally ambivalent way, as having both negative and positive effects, or "lights" and "shadows" as the 1998 Nouméa Agreement states. For instance, New Caledonian politician Philippe Gomès argues that despite being "barbarous," colonization "enabled peoples who were excluded from development to progress" (Massau 2017). Such formulation is typical of a discursive strategy of colonial expansion and domination, which constructs "a hierarchy of superior and inferior knowledge and, thus, of superior and inferior people around the world." According to this hierarchy, as the decolonial thinker Ramón Grosfoguel observes, the colonial representations of colonised peoples moved from "people without writing," "people without history," "people without development," to "people without democracy" (2007, 214). Likewise, one of the most prolific New Caledonian historians, Frédéric Angleviel, contends that, after weighing the pros and the cons,

> the balance is towards the French side, for despite regrettable facts, the French colonial period remains largely positive *if one avoids anachronisms,* and *if one puts it back in the global context of the time:* The life of European workers was hard, the fate of Aboriginal people dramatic, Africa, Asia and even the United States until the War of Secession had slavery. (Wénéhoua 1996, 28–29, emphasis added)

A decade later again, Angleviel condemned the critiques of colonisation that he sees as its "diabolisation . . . according to our current criteria," in short as both an "intellectual and factual anachronism" (2004, 87). Such arguments have been contested by scholars using historical sources. First, it is inconsistent with some historical accounts, even from the most fervent actors of colonization. Albert Sarraut, former minister of the Colonies and later prime minister of France, admitted in the 1930s that the aim of colonization has never been to be "positive" toward the colonized populations: "colonisation . . . has been an act of force, a self-interested force. . . . colonisation is but a self-interested, unilateral, selfish enterprise, achieved by the stronger over the weaker. Such is the reality of history" (1931, 107–108). Second, self-righteous comparison is a dangerous tool that downplays colonial violence and evades moral responsibility and anxiety (Welch 2003, 247, 252). Duncan Bell observes that it is widespread in British and French debates to relativize and downplay the brutality of conquest by arguing that the subjugated populations are better off governed by them than by another colonial power (2016, 100). Third, regarding supposed anachronisms, a common misleading assumption is that all Europeans were once bereft of morality, human dignity, and awareness to manifest attitudes and discourses critical of colonialism. Although such assumptions have the advantage of providing a moral distancing from a supposedly more racist past, they seem historically flawed. Such observation is indeed based on the erroneous assumption that critiques of colonization are only contemporary to our times. In fact, several such critiques have been offered since the onset of colonization.[2] Today's criticism of past colonial practices therefore does not necessarily cast an anachronistic look but is inscribed in a long, albeit marginal, critique of it.

These frames of reference, as articulated by historians, educators, and political actors, have a considerable impact on the historical narrative disseminated in schools. The teaching of Indigenous-settler history is guided by curricula, institutional directives, teaching materials, and practices that engage with, if not emanate from, such frames of reference to serve a specific political purpose. Thus it seems necessary to problematize these frames of reference and make our understanding of colonialism more complex than that of a bygone, morally ambivalent historical period.

Colonialism is a mechanism of domination and "systematic repression" (Quijano 2007, 169). That is, it is acted. It is not just a situation of "communities privileged by history" (Angleviel quoted in Wénéhoua 1996, 14) passively inherited from the mere "tide of history" (Gerard Brennan in High Court of Australia 1992). Colonialism is not fate. It must be continuously, critically analyzed as a phenomenon, in constant reformulation, of destruction of the reciprocity and love between peoples. Detractors of the critiques of colonialism speak of the guilt and "self-flagellation" necessarily imposed on settlers in such endeavors. Yet engaging in a critique of colonialism is not about self-hatred, bearing grudges, or being vengeful, but instead about educating ourselves and taking responsibility. Being critical of colonialism is not about Us v. Them or Indigenous v. Settler. Yet it is also not about fence-sitting opinions to please everyone.

In politics, critiques of colonialism, especially ongoing colonialism, remain largely marginal and ignored. "A struggle over who controls this past, who can influence the interpretation of this past, and who can determine the historical truth about the nature of colonialism" has been ongoing (Attwood 2005, 1–2). The instrumentalization of the past has been key in the formation of nation-states and in the maintenance of settler colonial power. Such understandings of colonialism have affected the meanings given to decolonization and thereby the decolonization process itself. In Australia, the government has established no official decolonization policy. Official discourses focus instead on social justice. The question of decolonization is limited to activist and academic circles in regard to Indigenous sovereignties and debates about treaties. Kanaky/New Caledonia has been on the UN list of Non-Self-Governing Territories since 1986. An official process of transfer of political powers from mainland France to Kanaky/New Caledonia is virtual. Yet, as Tracey Banivanua Mar points out, the United Nations and decolonizing administrations have "reconfigured decolonisation as a procedural event through which non-self-governing territories—rather than peoples—would be gifted nationhood, but not necessarily of their own making." So that, after 1960, "sovereignty of territory would always be privileged above and against the sovereignty of peoples" (Muckle et al. 2016, 461). The sovereignty of territories is different from the sovereignty of peoples, and procedural decolonization falls short of addressing Indigenous demands for self-governance and enabling the actual decolonization of Indigenous-settler relations. The current political framework of the 1998 Nouméa Agreement thus runs the risk of co-opting Kanak sovereignty into a "new sovereignty, shared in a common destiny," which will continue to marginalize Kanak people. The absence of a basic common ground about what colonialism means and what decolonization entails continues to entrench the political impasse in both Australia and Kanaky/New Caledonia on Indigenous-settler relations.

Decolonial Thinking and Indigenous Resurgence

In the face of this impasse, scholars and activists have continued to reflect on the ongoing issue of colonialism. Settler colonial studies and the theories and practices of decolonization developed by decolonial thinking and Indigenous resurgence are particularly useful and efficient in understanding and contesting settler colonialism. Decolonial thinking, though interrelated with Indigenous resurgence in the struggle for decolonization, does not necessarily emerge from Indigenous standpoints or epistemologies, but focuses instead on modern colonial discourses in order to critique them. Yet decolonial thinking and Indigenous resurgence have several commonalities: they understand colonialism as an ongoing phenomenon; they problematize the relation between colonialism and capitalism; they place race, gender, and white privilege at the center of the reflection; they critique Western epistemology and call to transcend current epistemological and political systems; and they articulate the need to disrupt "colonialism, heteropatriarchy and capitalism" for the "disruption of settler colonialism" (Snelgrove, Dhamoon, and Corntassel 2014, 2). As a white settler scholar, I approach decolonial thinking as an intellectual destabilizer of settler colonialism and an intellectual enabler for Indigenous resurgence, as a permissive space and an epistemic leveler. This initial leveling stage and this permissive space enables engaging with Indigenous resurgence and can facilitate the restoration of, and primacy of Indigenous ontologies, epistemologies, and governances. Although settler colonial studies are useful for laying out the issue, decolonization supplies the framework for contemplating the possibilities beyond it.

Settler Colonialism Is Structural and Total

Settler colonialism is a distinct form of colonialism. In settler colonialism, unlike other forms, "settler-colonisers come to stay" (Wolfe 2006, 388) and "carry their sovereignty and lifestyles with them" (Veracini 2011b, 206). The historian Patrick Wolfe stresses that settler colonialism is "a structure not an event" (1999, 3). Settler colonialism has its own structures, articulations, and effects. Forms of domination in settler colonial societies have more in common with one another than with their respective (former) colonial metropoles. Forms of domination in settler colonial societies are also distinct from other (formerly) colonized contexts. Settler colonialism and exploitation colonialism for instance aim at two different things, Lorenzo Veracini explains: "the exploitation coloniser say 'you, work for me' while the settler coloniser say 'you, work for me while we wait for you to disappear' or 'you, move on so you can work for us'" (2011a, 1–2). Yet settler colonialism is not a mere descriptive typology but instead specific processes, relations, and sets of conditions that take place to maintain settler colonial power and domination. Settler colonialism rests on the binary Indigenous or settler, on the hegemony of the latter over the former, and, among settlers, on the hegemony of European settlers over non-European settler workers. Non-European settler subjugation and Indigenous elimination take place simultaneously (Tuck, McKenzie, and McCoy 2014, 7). Settler colonialism is grounded in a logic of elimination of Indigenous people through either genocide or assimilation (Wolfe 2006). Yet ultimately settler colonial societies work on their "refusal to recognize themselves as such, requiring a continuing disavowal of history . . . and how settler colonialism is indeed ongoing" (Tuck, McKenzie, and McCoy 2014, 7).

The political scientist Taiaiake Alfred observes that "our common understanding of what that term means is lacking." This lack evidences itself in the fact that colonialism is understood "mainly in material terms" (political injustices, domination, dispossession of lands, or economic oppression), and also in psychological or spiritual terms (dysfunctional or self-destructive behaviors). Alfred argues, however, that "the true meaning of 'colonialism' emerges from a consideration of how we as Indigenous peoples have lost the freedom to exist as Indigenous peoples in almost every single sphere of our existence" (2004, 89–90). The issue of colonialism goes beyond the economic, the political, or the psychological and touches on the ontological level. He adds, "It is the fundamental denial of our freedom to be Indigenous in a meaningful way, and the unjust occupation of the physical, social, and political spaces we need in order to survive as Indigenous peoples" (89–90). It is indicative that the English word "free" comes from the Indo-European root "$prī$," meaning "to love"; and its French equivalent "$libre$" from the Indo-European "h_1leud^h," meaning "people, which belongs to the people." Thus, and following Alfred, colonialism can be understood as the denial of reciprocity (love) and the separation of the self from the other, of the individual from its people. It is the alteration of a fundamental human condition by political methods: the denial of reciprocity through policies of domination, segregation, sterilization, assimilation, and genocide; and the separation of the individual from their people through displacement, containment, abduction, cultural prohibition, and assimilation. Colonialism is therefore not a historical era, an institutional context, or merely a political and economic relationship; it is "a total existence" that "has separated all of us as human beings from other beings and the earth" and that has "created a culture of fear among both the subdued and dominant peoples" (89–90).

Colonialism indeed affects both the colonized and the colonizer. Bringing this reflection further, Jeff Corntassel suggests that "if colonization is about disconnecting peoples from their lands and territories and depriving them of their cultural practices, then acts of decolonization—including decolonizing knowledge—are, in part, about reconnection and community resurgence" (2011). According to Winona Wheeler, decolonization entails developing a "critical consciousness about the cause(s) of our oppression, the distortion of history, our own collaboration, and the degrees to which we have internalised colonialist ideas and practices" (Stevenson 2000, 212). It requires auto-criticism, self-reflection, and a rejection of victimage.

The Colonial Binary and the Logics of Race

The experiences of Indigenous people under colonialism are varied. Likewise, settlers do not all have the same position within settler colonial societies. Nor do they all benefit equally from settler colonialism. Many people have been brought to settler states as convicts, indentured servants, or economic and political refugees; others have been government officials and migrants moving for greater professional and educational gains or for the mere lure of profit. Some have come from a position of domination and privilege in their home country; others have themselves been colonized or marginalized in their homeland. Ethnic background, skin color, gender, and class have also influenced which settlers benefit the most from stolen Indigenous lands and waters. The settler category intersects with whiteness. As Andrea Smith puts it, analyses of the Indigenous-settler binary are insufficient and replicate the logic of settler colonialism if they do not engage the analytics of race and logics of white supremacy (2012, 77–78). Colonial contexts are racialized contexts.

An important manifestation of settler colonialism is indeed white privilege. White privilege is, for instance, feeling safe and not targeted when surrounded by police force. It is not being refused a taxi based on one's indigeneity or not be subjected, disproportionately, to police routine check and police violence. White privilege is being able to ignore that white privilege exists. White privilege, however, does not necessarily depend on biological notions; it is also shaped by our history and by our actions. Taiaiake Alfred contends that today "the 'white man' has been deracialised and reformed as a mentality within colonizers of all colors" (2004, 96). Indeed, White privilege also morphs into settler privilege, that is, the privilege of occupying Indigenous lands and benefiting from such dispossession. Thus, although settlers benefit from colonization to varying degrees depending on skin color, class, and gender, the colonial system is "a political, economic, cultural and social system that grants numerous privileges to settlers, regardless of their social status" (Bancel, Blanchard, and Vergès 2007, 5). Thus "while colonialism's effects can be seen externally, the landscape of colonialism lies within us. . . . Unless we confront and dominate the colonialism inside, confronting it outside will be a futile exercise. That is the struggle in which to be engaged" (Alfred 2011). Likewise, Harry Brod warns that "there is no such thing as giving up one's privilege to be 'outside' the system" because one is always in the system and privilege is something that society gives us (1989, 280). Thus the "only question is whether one is part of the system in a way that challenges or strengthens the status quo." Brod argues that unless one changes the institutions that give it to us, they will continue to give it, and one will continue to have it, regardless of how noble and equalitarian our intentions are. As Emmanuel Lévinas points out, "we are thus responsible beyond our intentions" (1996, 4).

In undertaking a critical analysis of settler colonialism so that I might challenge it, I do not claim to speak from a decolonized position or with a decolonized mindset. Decolonization requires a life-long vigilance and diligent efforts of unlearning and relearning. In that respect, this book is such work in practice, and with it, equipped with a growing literature on settler colonialism and decolonization, I hope to contribute to our understanding of settler colonialism and possibilities for decolonization. Although an examination of settler colonialism allows a better understanding of the historical-political context specific to settler colonial societies, decolonial thinking and Indigenous scholarship provide, at the moment, the most thought-through and effective tools to understand and challenge settler colonialism.

Settler Decolonization

Settler colonialism is also differentiated from other forms of colonialism by the challenges it brings to the question of settler decolonization. Patrick Wolfe has remarked that "settler colonialism is relatively impervious to regime change" (2006, 402). Likewise, Lorenzo Veracini observes that "settler colonial forms have existed in a variety of sites of European colonial expansion . . . and contrary to other colonial forms, settler colonialism has been remarkably resistant to decolonisation" (2007). He identifies three often overlapping "general experiences of settler decolonisation": settler evacuation (such as in Algeria, Libya), promotion of various processes of Indigenous reconciliation, and denial (associated with a rejection of proposals to reform the settler body politic) (2011b, 210). He argues, however, that all these experiences have failed to effectively decolonize territories because even settler evacuation—"the decolonisation of territory"—is "not matched, even symbolically, by an attempt to build decolonised relationships)" (2011b, 210). The second (processes of reconciliation) and third (denial) experiences of settler decolonization in fact work to sustain a settler colonial polity and therefore sustain settler colonialism.

Yet, as Smith writes, when we do not presume that settler colonial states will always continue to exist, "we create the space to reflect on what might be more just forms of governance, not only for Native peoples, but for the rest of the world" (2008, 311–312). Indigenous people and nations hold centuries-long histories of indigenous self-governance, in all their variety, that are indispensable to foster this reflection, to challenge liberal politics and capitalism, and to put decolonization in practice.

Colonialism Is Constitutive of Modernity and Capitalism

Modernity and colonialism emerged concomitantly and are interdependent. Colonialism and modernity are mutually constitutive and not derivative (Vásquez 2012, 242). Grosfoguel argues that "one of the most powerful myths of the twentieth century was the notion that the elimination of colonial administrations amounted to the decolonisation of the world," when in fact, "we continue to live under the same 'colonial power matrix'" (2007, 219). This colonial power matrix is commonly referred to as "the coloniality of power."[3] Coloniality is "the continuity of colonial forms of domination after the end of colonial administrations, produced by colonial cultures and structures in the modern/colonial capitalist/patriarchal world-system" (219). Likewise, according to Aníbal Quijano, race (as a social organization) and capitalism (as a mode of operational control) are the two pillars of the coloniality of power (2000). They are the foundations of the social, epistemic, and political orders that keep shaping societies.

As a result, Indigenous resurgence advocates for a form of decolonization that focuses on Indigenous people and Indigenous forms of governance and ways of being. Indigenous resurgence theorists stress the need to dismantle and rethink power structures for Indigenous liberation. The works of scholars such as Taiaiake Alfred (2005, 2013), Leanne Simpson (2008, 2011, 2016), and Glen Coulthard (2014) are foundational to this field. For Simpson, Indigenous resurgence is "nation building, not nation-state building" (2016, 22). In contrast to nation-state building, she explains, this resurgence generates nations as "networks of complex, layered, multidimensional, intimate relationships with human and nonhuman beings" (2016, 22–23). Indigenous resurgence results from collective processes that are "fundamentally nonhierarchical, nonexploitative, nonextractivist, and nonauthoritarian" and attempts to disrupt both capitalism and the colonial gender systems put in place by settler colonial power (Simpson 2011, 87). Likewise, Glen Coulthard declares that "for Indigenous nations to live, capitalism must die" and calls for a resistance to settler colonialism that moves beyond state politics (2013). In this context, decolonization becomes a stateless site of independence and Indigenous sovereignty that contests mere procedural decolonization.

Political Research on Contested Grounds

Studies of settler colonialism and decolonization commonly differentiate between European colonialisms. That is, British, French, Spanish, or Dutch forms are generally studied separately. Within the literature in English, comparative research mostly adopts Australia, New Zealand, South Africa, Canada, or the United States as its focus. The two settler societies of the French Empire—Kanaky/New Caledonia and Algeria—are usually studied independently. No research in English or French engaging with settler colonialism across European colonialisms in a comparative perspective could be traced.[4] The only published books that address the decolonizing of the curriculum, or the navigation of rival and conflicting narratives of a nation's past, tend to be edited collections examining a wide range of national contexts.[5] Although a noticeable focus of these works is on settler colonial societies, they are studied independently, not comparatively. This book calls for opening up such space and integrating British/Australian and French settler colonialisms, specifically Australia and Kanaky/New Caledonia, into a comparative analysis and thus offers a unique comparison of two settler colonial societies in the Pacific region.

Australian and New Zealand historians have historically engaged more readily with the Pacific or Oceania as a field of research than scholars from France and the Francophone Pacific have.[6] Meanwhile, French and New Caledonian historiographies continued to largely overlook the logic of colonial invasions and relations in Oceania. It was only with the Indigenous political movements of the 1960s and 1970s that scholars began to focus on New Caledonia's colonial history.

> One must wait until France's politics in the Pacific is given a rough ride, even contested by part of the populations of these territories and by their South Pacific neighbours, for historians to pay more attention to these islands. The history of the French archipelagos of the Pacific set itself as a recent specialisation that developed in a tensed context. (Mohamed-Gaillard 2009, 162)

Sarah Mohamed-Gaillard notes that "the comparative framework . . . between the thoughts and practices put into place in Oceania remains a little-explored avenue of research" (2009, 166). Likewise, Seu'ula Johansson-Fua observes that "despite over 100 years of comparative and international education discourse, there remains little contribution from the Pacific region to this field" (2016, 30). This book attempts to reveal some of the workings of settler colonial power and explain the education mechanisms and strategies that maintain domination and hierarchies within the Australia and Kanaky/New Caledonia contexts.

The question of knowledge is central to settler colonization and decolonization. It is the control of knowledge that holds the different areas of the settler colonial structure together. In this book, power is defined as control. Knowledge gives power and power gives control. Therefore, one must ask who is to benefit from the historical knowledge disseminated in public schools. As power is control, Susan Fiske explains, people pay attention to those who have power, to "those who control their outcomes" (1993, 621). Attention is therefore "directed up the hierarchy" and follows control. Conversely, those with more power "need not attend very much to those with less power" or "may not want to attend," because they have less "at stake" (621). Settler power necessitates this lack of attention, this ignorance, to sustain itself. One key way of exercising settler control and domination is through ignorance, or at least by regulating what knowledge is transmitted. How then to identify and raise the issue of colonialism, or settler control, in the school system?

In their analysis of colonization and schooling in Oceania, Murray Thomas and Neville Postlethwaite suggest that "if colonialism is defined as the control of people's affairs by outsiders, then one way to judge the degree of colonialism in a school system is to identify who carries power and responsibility at different levels of the educational hierarchy" (1984, 23). These levels are financing, the administrative structure of the school system, the education personnel and the content of curriculum, and the instructional materials and instruction. This book takes into account all these factors but takes the last two as entry points because they engage teachers' sphere of influence. How does settler colonial power control and manage the production and enunciation of historical knowledge within that institution? If modernity is "the age that has expelled the 'other' out of History," "the age of amnesia, the age without history," as Rolando Vásquez suggests, what then is in the teaching of history (2012, 248)? What is "expelled," ignored, in what specific contexts, and for what particular purpose? This book seeks to highlight how settler colonial power constitutes historical knowledge, and how this knowledge is in turn shaped by, and affects, power relations between Indigenous people and settlers. To do so, I have used and developed three key resources: history curricula, history textbooks, and interviews with history teachers.

Curricula

Curriculum exists within a recent institution, the school system, and is then "an invention of modernity" that "involves forms of knowledge whose functions are to regulate and discipline the individual" (Popkewitz 1997a, 140). This regulation is twofold: it "defines the boundaries of what is to be known" and inculcates "politically-sanctioned ways" for individuals to "organize, and understand their world and "self" (144). Curriculum is therefore the outcome of power and abides by the underlying settler political agenda.

Relevant existing curriculum research in Australia often focuses on the evolution of curricula as a whole and their implementation (Cranston et al. 2010; Yates and Collins 2010). In that respect, the place of Indigenous knowledges in Australian curricula and education systems has gained increasing attention among education scholars in the last two decades (Nakata 2002, 2011; Lowe and Yunkaporta 2013). These works make a significant contribution to education theory as well as to Indigenous and critical pedagogy. However, the evolution of history curricula in Australia has, in comparison, been little researched. Among the exceptions are Robert Parkes (2007, 2009) and Anna Clark (2006), who focused on the impact of the History Wars on history curriculum reforms in Australia. The place of Indigenous people in history curricula is often marginal, if not lacking in such analyses in favor of a multicultural or broadly national angle. The education scholar Heather Sharp (2010, 2012) provides valuable longer-term analyses of representations of Indigenous people and settlers of British descent in Queenland history curriculum at three specific times: around World War 1, during the Australian Black Power Movement (1960s–1970s), and during the 1988 bicentennial (2010, 2012). An analysis of the more recent evolution of Indigenous-settler history in national history curricula, which engages with both the ideological debate and the content of the history curricula, is wanting. Likewise, in Kanaky/New Caledonia, with the exception of a scientific work in the late 2000s on the recent evolution of history curricula (Hardouin 2008), no research on history curricula or history teaching in Kanaky/New Caledonia more widely could be traced. This book builds on these works and contributes to filling this gap. It focuses on the implementation of a national curricular framework in Australia in 2012 and the curricular debates both preceding and surrounding it and on the latest curricular reforms, from around the year 2010s, in Kanaky/New Caledonia. The curriculum policy texts in both countries are studied and tested against the viewpoints of the teachers I interviewed and of key education and political commentators in order to capture the points of contention in the debate and to contest and politicize the curriculum reforms.

Textbook Analysis

Although this book deals with the ways that Indigenous-settler history is taught today, a long-term analysis of school history textbooks is crucial to the analysis. The historiography of Indigenous-settler relations—in its quality, inadequacy, or even the lack of it—incontestably shape teachers' work. In the school system, this historiography is tailored into a pedagogical product: the history textbook. The textbook is therefore a key element of teachers' work, regardless of how they use it. As a historiographical inheritance, it has three core political qualities: first, it is a communication tool that assembles scientific knowledge and official educational policies and programs into an accessible and usable format; second, it is a structuring tool that guides teachers as to how to steer their knowledge and teaching in line with official educational policies and programs; and, third, it is an ideological tool that disseminates specific values and ideas. Bryan Smith and his colleagues argue that "the hegemony of this particular form of textual documents creates conditions in which the textbook becomes the arbiter of truth. . . . the text comes to constitute acceptable forms of knowledge and engagement with historical ideas" (2011, 55). Textbooks produce social meanings and constitute a resource that individuals use to learn their place in history and in society. Besides, textbooks are highly responsive to the changing policies of the state, given its institutional role. In that sense, they are shaped by, and reflect, much broader political and emotional motives and shifts. Textbooks do not mirror the knowledge of the time. Instead, they produce the knowledge and ideologies that adults consider children should know and value (Bradford 2001, 5). As Damien Riggs suggests,

> history may be understood not as an "objective truth" arrived at by those who correctly study "the facts" but, rather, as a meaning-making practice that privileges certain groups of people over others, and which thus legitimates the worldview of particular groups to the exclusion and oppression of others. (2004, 37)

The role of textbooks in privileging certain historical knowledge and ideologies and therefore consolidating certain political groups has drawn growing scholarly interest. A literature on the representation of marginalized groups in textbooks, located at the junction of Indigenous, ethnic, and gender studies, has emerged in settler colonial societies. These studies have focused, for instance, on the representation of Native Americans and Black Americans in North America, racial stereotyping in South Africa, and of Māori people in Aotearoa New Zealand.[7] In the Francophone colonial context, a substantial literature has analyzed the role of historiography in colonial domination, the representation of colonization in textbooks, and the role of schools in the colonial process. Existing literature, however, largely focuses on France, Africa, and Asia, focusing on Algeria and Vietnam (see Leon 1991; Chenntouf 2006; Lantheaume 2007; Boyer, Clerc, and Zancarini-Fournel 2013; Falaize 2014; de Suremain 2009; and Hutchins 2016).

Australia and Kanaky/New Caledonia have received comparatively less attention. The few existing textbook analyses in Australia focus on school values (Firth 1970), multiculturalism (Cope 1987), and Indigenous content (Fien 1985; Sauvage 2010; Bradford 2001; Sharp 2013). Stewart Firth looks at school values in school texts from the 1880 to 1914 (1970). Bill Cope explores the changing historical narrative in textbooks from 1945 to 1985 (1987). A more systematic analysis of the representation of Indigenous people in social sciences school textbooks is John Fien's survey of sixty-four lower secondary school geography textbooks published between the 1970s and 1985, among which only eight, he observes, mention Indigenous people (1985). His analysis exposes textbooks' omission or misinformation of Aboriginal content, which he terms "structural silence." More recent is Alexandra Sauvage's analysis of representations of the Frontier in 1990s school textbooks (2010). Clare Bradford looks at Australian school texts from 1900 to 1960 from a postcolonial perspective (2001). Heather Sharp studies the representations of Indigenous people in Queensland social studies textbooks from the 1960s to the 1980s (2013). Robyn Moore analyzes discourses of whiteness and Aboriginality in textbooks from 1950 to 2010 (2020).

In the case of Kanaky/New Caledonia, only one scholar seems to have engaged in an analysis of history textbooks, Jacqueline Dahlem, who in her thesis and again in a book analyzes the political project and identity positions around the production of the 1992 history textbook (1997, 2002). In short, scholarship on Australian textbooks usually focuses on a specific period, and the works by Dahlem attend only to the 1992 New Caledonian textbook. This book therefore offers what I would argue is the first scholarly work to engage in a long-term, systematic analysis of the historical knowledge disseminated in school textbooks in Australia and Kanaky/New Caledonia.

Textbooks have been selected according to three criteria: they post-date the institution of the free and compulsory public school systems in Australia and Kanaky/New Caledonia, respectively; they have been produced in Australia and Kanaky/New Caledonia for use in the public schools of these two societies, and are adapted to the official curricula; and they cover the respective history of these societies as a whole rather than a specific period or locality. I then randomly selected one text-book per decade. The earliest one for use in public schools that could be found in the archives dates to 1877. Two have been retained for the 2010s decade in the Australian sample because postcolonization history of Australia is no longer covered within one textbook but over two years under the Australian Curriculum. The selected set consists of sixteen textbooks in the Australian case, from the 1870s to the 2010s, and three textbooks in the New Caledonian, from the 1990s to the 2010s. The time frame for the New Caledonian textbooks is significantly shorter because the territory started publishing its own history textbooks only in the 1990s (see appendix 1).

Judging textbooks by their covers and content, early Australian text-books (pocket-size, mostly single-authored, black and white, with long, chronologically or geographically ordered narratives) differ greatly from recent ones (larger formats, multi-authored, colorful, richly illustrated, and thematically organized). Yet a common definition and function unite them all: they are standardized texts, designed for the instruction of pupils in the classroom that include their author's his-torical enunciation, pedagogical guidelines and drills, and inculcate specific historical notions to a specific year level. They are not a mere collection of documents but instead a crafted, oriented set of texts with a pedagogical aim.

The sample includes both primary and secondary school textbooks. This decision seems judicious for at least two reasons. First, compulsory schooling was for a long time limited to the primary years, and therefore the majority of the population would not have accessed school materi-als for the secondary years, when they existed. This explains why several Australian textbooks until the mid-twentieth century are primary school textbooks. Second, despite the fact that the early textbooks in the sam-ple are mostly for primary school and the latest for secondary school, the level of literacy and historical thinking is fairly consistent. In fact,

current Australian primary school textbooks (thin, including numerous illustrations and drawing exercises) can hardly be compared with
primary school textbooks of the late nineteenth and early twentieth
century (often more than two hundred pages of text with few if any illustrations). The current range of primary school textbooks in Australia
is very limited and none of the primary school teachers I interviewed
reported using any textbook. Given the small size of the sample from
Kanaky/New Caledonia, both primary and secondary textbooks have
been included. As in early Australian primary school textbooks, the
high level of literacy of New Caledonian primary school textbooks
makes them adequate for the analysis.

Ultimately, my interest is less in the content of each textbook per
se than in what the content reveals about longer trends in settler colonial knowledge production. In other words, what can the corpus tell
us about power and authority in the public school system and about
today's teachers' historiographical inheritance? Does this archival corpus, largely overlooked so far, bring new clues as to the ways that history
has been written and disseminated and how settler regimes of ignorance
play out in these societies?

Interviews with History Teachers

The history class is a politically charged place, empowering certain peo-
ple and marginalizing others. In her reflection on teaching Australian
Society at a tertiary Australian institution as a non-Indigenous person,
Alice Healy-Ingram observes that

> the very classroom space is underscored with normalised struc-
> tures of power, that language is affected with connotations that
> privilege and exclude, that educational institutions both open up
> and close possibilities for challenging the persistence of colonial
> governance (2011, 77).

As much as the classroom is not a neutral teaching or learning space,
neither is the teacher a neutral transmitter of historical knowledge.
Pablo Toro Blanco argues, in his research on education and emotion,
that teachers "cannot be perceived just as simple transmission devices
of official curriculum" (2015, 596). Instead, the complex situation
of teachers in the transmission of knowledge equates to a black box

situation. History teachers therefore sit in the complex juncture of the political instrumentalization of history (curriculum), their own socially constructed historical knowledge (historiographical inheritance and lived experience), and that of the students. The teachers are not, however, in a powerless situation. The classroom is their sphere of influence and, as the ultimate institutional agent, they have some capacity to affect the power dynamic in their classrooms. Interviewing history teachers about their philosophy and practices enabled reading that black box.

In Kanaky/New Caledonia, nineteen teachers participated in the project, an 86 percent participation rate. In Australia, of all contacted teachers, fourteen eventually participated, a 38 percent rate (see appendix 2). Two key issues have emerged that may explain the lower rate and do indicate general attitudes toward Indigenous-settler history in this country. First, whereas Indigenous-settler relations in Kanaky/New Caledonia have been treated as a pressing political question (considering the demographic and electoral tug-of-war), the subject is more marginalized in Australian politics. This may have translated to a general disinterest and ignorance of Indigenous-settler history even from within the teaching profession. Indeed, three responses from teachers who declined to participate reveal that Indigenous-settler history is viewed as relevant and of interest to Indigenous students only. Although the research project explicitly targeted teachers of mainstream Australian history and the teachers were informed of this focus, one history teacher advised me to turn instead to teachers who taught Aboriginal studies to mainly Aboriginal students because they might be in a better position to relate and participate. Another teacher replied that they did not think they could contribute meaningfully to the research because it had been a long time since they worked with a cohort of Aboriginal students. Second, the curricular priorities set by the government in mostly Indigenous schools—which focus on literacy, numeracy, and attendance—mean that history and other social sciences subjects are often not taught at all in these schools. A few teachers from the Northern Territory replied by expressing their incapacity to participate for these very reasons despite their interest in the project. One intermediary replied, for instance, that they couldn't "think of one teacher . . . who teaches either of these things in the regions [they] work in" because "one of the issues . . . in remote schools is that the political focus on Closing the Gap means that all of the policy attention and funding is directed to things like truancy and NAPLAN and the Humanities and Social Sciences are entirely left out of the curriculum."[8]

Interviews with history teachers aimed at investigating experiences of teaching Indigenous-settler history in Australian and New Caledonian schools. In Australia, at the time of this writing, twelve of the fourteen interviewees are current teachers at varying stages of their careers, and two are former or retired school teachers. Although I aimed for an equal distribution in background, three are Indigenous teachers and eleven are settlers.[9] Although teachers were contacted across all states and territories, the teachers I interviewed work or worked only in two states—Victoria and New South Wales—and the Northern Territory, and in six Indigenous Countries: Wurundjeri (Melbourne), Eora (Sydney), Yorta Yorta (Shepparton), Paakantyi (Broken Hill and Menindee), Warlpiri (Lajamanu), and Warumungu (Tennant Creek).[10] Among the six teachers who work in predominantly Indigenous Country areas, commonly referred to as "remote" in the colonial geography of Australia, two are Indigenous and four are settlers. Two of the settler teachers have spent a considerable amount of time in the same area (more than a decade) and are speakers of the local Aboriginal language. The two others are part of the Teach for Australia program.[11] Of the two Indigenous teachers, one is working on her Country and the other is Gamilaraay and working off-country in New South Wales.

In Kanaky/New Caledonia, of the nineteen teachers interviewed, fifteen are history teachers, two are teacher educators, and two are former or retired teachers. Likewise, equal distribution regarding background was attempted but not attained: five are Kanak teachers and fourteen are settlers.[12] Teachers are located in each of the three provinces and in five of the eight Kanak customary areas, including Drubea-Kapumë, Xârâcùù, Paicî-Cèmuhî, and Drehu.[13] Of the ten teachers interviewed who work in predominantly Kanak schools in Kanaky/New Caledonia, four are Kanak and six are settlers. Three of the settler teachers have spent more than two years working in the same school, but none reported speaking the local Kanak language. For the three others, it is their first teaching position and they have worked in the school for less than two years.

The time, the pace, the intensity, and the geography of colonization vary considerably from place to place and over the course of time across the locations where these teachers work. Colonization happened at very different times in Australia depending on the location. The Dharug were the first to experience invasion, in 1788 in Paakantyi Country. In Menindee, the beginning of colonial contact was with explorer Thomas Mitchell in 1835. For the Warlpiri people, the first colonial contact is for a few within living memory. In Kanaky/New Caledonia, considering the far smaller size of the territory, colonization was not as spaced out in time, but the experience of colonization has been diverse nonetheless. Some are located in urban areas (Nouméa), others in predominantly mining areas (Kaa Wii Paa, Xârâcùù) or where Kanak subsistence agriculture remains dominant (the Loyalty Islands).

Bringing these two settler colonial societies of the Pacific—Australia and Kanaky/New Caledonia, the products of two different colonial empires—into one analysis is an attempt to liberate the academic thinking in the field from the confines of colonial empires' borders and national frameworks. It enables us to improve and sharpen our understanding of the mechanisms, polymorphism, and imperviousness of settler colonialism beyond the specificities of nationalisms and the cultural legacies of colonial empires and to better scope the possibilities to contest and destabilize settler colonialism and, ultimately, to decolonize education.

PART I

Policy and Directives

CHAPTER 2

History Curriculum Development and Reforms

On January 26, 2016, Pekeri Ruska was angry. Lawyer and cofounder of Warriors of the Aboriginal Resistance—a collective of young Aboriginal people committed to decolonization, resistance, and revival—and *Black Nations Rising* magazine, she had endured yet another Australian national holiday celebrating the invasion and genocide of Indigenous Nations. She told the press, "on this date began a war, an unsolicited occupation and the mass murder of our people. The acts of aggression committed against Aboriginal people constitute nothing short of genocide, yet many Australians choose to remain wilfully ignorant" (Ruska 2016). Ruska attributed the "wilful" ignorance of Australia Day celebrants to the school systems and explained that although she was "fortunate to be educated outside of the official curriculum," the "true nature" of colonial wars "is rarely taught in schools." She remarked that "the longer they exclude or sugarcoat the whole truth from the curriculum, the longer non-Indigenous Australians will remain ignorant" (2016). The same year, the University of New South Wales' Indigenous terminology guide incurred the wrath of Australia's conservative media and sparked another debate on the nature of the colonization of Australia. For writer, researcher, and former teacher Bruce Pascoe, that such a debate is still going on today is indicative of settler ignorance, of the imperviousness of colonial historical knowledge, and of the fact that "Australia just refuses to look at the very obvious facts of the history."[1]

What goes into the history curriculum and what is left out—whether in primary, secondary, or higher education—continues to be the subject of fierce political debate in Australia. The 2012 Australian Curriculum—its first nationwide—was contested and reviewed shortly after its implementation because conservative politicians believed that it did not make enough room for Western civilization and its contribution to Australian society. In Kanaky/New Caledonia, the history curriculum has also been an important element of the territory's politics. As part of the transfer of political powers from mainland France to Kanaky/New Caledonia, the political authority to write the history curriculum was transferred to the territory in 2000 for primary schools and in 2012 for secondary schools. The history curriculum reforms have faced both resistance (to change) and disappointment (for not meeting expectations). What do these history curricula include or leave out and ignore? What political contexts inform the curriculum reforms? What political agenda do these history curricula serve? And how do they do so?

Setting the Scene: The Languages of Instruction

Indigenous languages have been a crucial target of the colonial repression of Indigenous people and cultures and their use and revitalization a crucial objective and tool in struggles for freedom and decolonization. It is conspicuous that continuing attacks on Indigenous languages have functioned as a catalyst for Indigenous liberation struggles since the second half of the twentieth century. In Kanaky/New Caledonia, one of the key catalysts of the Kanak movement in the late 1960s was the publication of tracts against segregation written in French, Drehu, and Nengone (two of the twenty-eight Kanak languages) by members of the activist group The Red Scarves (Les Foulards Rouges) that led to the arrest of some of these activists for publishing in Indigenous languages and to subsequent popular uprisings. In another settler colonial society, South Africa, the language of instruction sparked the 1976 Soweto uprising, when the South African government made Afrikaans and English compulsory in black schools (Ndlovu 2006). Writing from yet another settler colonial society, the United States, Malathi Iyengar demonstrates that colonial language policies have been fundamental to the logic of elimination of Indigenous people in settler colonial societies (2014). The languages of instruction are an essential tool of settler colonial power and remain in both Australia and Kanaky/New Caledonia a matter of contention between the settler colonial polity and Indigenous advocates of decolonization.

Given this, the first question to ask oneself, as several teachers reminded me, before asking what is taught is "in what language is it taught?" In both Australia and Kanaky/New Caledonia, instruction continues to be mostly carried out in the language of colonization (English in the former and French in the latter). This is despite Indigenous peoples' and linguists' fighting for many decades to implement schooling in Indigenous languages, especially in areas where Indigenous languages continue to be widely spoken. What is at stake is not just the instruction of languages but the languages of instruction.

Christine Nicholls, who has worked with Warlpiri people for more than a decade, explained that "at the sheer level of practicality . . . it's very important."[2] None of the children where she was living knew any English when they came to school and it alienated them to speak in English. For these reasons, bilingual education was put in place and the schools had two sets of teachers, Warlpiri speakers and English speakers. Before that, no pupil was becoming literate and many of them did not even come to school because they were alienated. She considered that instruction in English only was "a total recipe for failure for most children." Bilingual education, on the contrary, proved successful. At best, they had 97 percent attendance at Lajamanu, whereas since bilingual education has been scrapped, attendance is apparently only 40 or 50 percent.[3]

Nicholls pointed out that although bilingualism in schools was very hard won (people in the community had fought and petitioned politicians for several decades) and recently scrapped (in 2008), multilingualism or at least bilingualism is the norm of human societies because, historically, most human beings have been multilingual. She also pushed for English to be taught as a second or a foreign language but, she said, "no authorities in the Northern Territory would accept that. They say 'they're Australians.' They called these Aboriginal kids Australians when it suited them."[4] Nicholls also deplored the fact that, even when bilingual education was implemented, it was never symmetrical bilingualism, according to which the whole curriculum alternates between the two languages. Instead, the model in the Northern Territory was decidedly conservative. It worked on a transfer model that consisted in starting off 100 percent in Warlpiri and gradually reducing until grade five, when the entire curriculum was in English. According to her, this was problematic because it made the Warlpiri language "look like a kind of baby language" because "you stop speaking it when you get a bit older."

Similarly, two teachers in Paakantyi Country spoke in interviews of a "crying need" to teach the Paakantyi language. For many years, the school taught German as a second language and many Indigenous children lost their languages (Paakantyi, Ngiyampaa, or Wiradjuri). A few years ago, the school principal agreed to change from teaching German to teaching Paakantyi. This change, however, did not happen without a struggle, especially from settler parents and Indigenous parents from other Indigenous nations:

> We had this big drama going "why should my kid learn Paakantyi language when we're not Paakantyi?" We also had other language groups coming and saying "my kids are not Paakantyi so why are they learning Paakantyi." I said to them, "at the end of the day, you're on Paakantyi Country, you respect the Country you're on, regardless if you're from here, Ngiyampaa or Wiradjuri."[5]

Nicholls warned in an interview that Indigenous languages will die out if they are "just treated like rubbish and not used in the school." The relentless challenges and attacks on bilingual programs continue to minoritize and marginalize Indigenous languages and people, further affecting the fraught relationship that many experience in the school system.

A similar issue has been raised in Kanaky/New Caledonia. When pro-independence politician Jean-Marie Tjibaou became head of the government in 1984, he repealed laws forbidding instruction and publication in Kanak languages. In the aftermath of the 1984–1988 war, the 1951 Deixonne Law—which officially recognized regional languages in France, allowing their inclusion in school curricula and exams, allowing teachers to use them in class to facilitate students' learning—was applied to Kanaky/New Caledonia in 1992.[6] The law included only four of the twenty-eight Kanak languages: Ajië, Drehu, Nengone, and Paicî. The same year, the Northern and Island Provinces implemented the teaching of these languages. The Southern Province did so only in 2005. The 1998 Nouméa Agreement set up the institutional framework for the teaching of Kanak languages and granted the latter "the status of languages of instruction in the same way as French." In 2012, nineteen Kanak languages were taught in primary schools and about ten in secondary schools (Vernaudon 2013, 116).

The teaching and status of Kanak languages, however, remain precarious. Kanak languages continue to be optional and are only offered if parents express an interest (through a survey) in their children's learning them. In a 2017 televised debate on the place of Kanak languages in public schools, National Education Inspector and Manager of the Service for the Teaching of Kanak Languages and Cultures Yves Kartono explained that Kanak languages continue to be optional and minimal as a language of instruction because "we don't force a pupil to choose a language, it's the pupil . . . who chooses." The French language, however, does not abide by this rule and, regardless of the pupil's choice, is de facto the language of instruction. The current place and status of Kanak languages in the school system therefore does not abide by the 1998 Nouméa Agreement, which stipulates that Kanak languages are, with French, official languages of instruction. Despite the political agreements, and despite linguists emphasizing during teacher training the benefits of learning in one's native language, this mandate is not followed through by the institution. One study concludes that "even freed from the 'Parisian' constraints, the New Caledonian school system continues to disseminate a monolingual ideology" and the non-European epistemologies are only rarely taken into account (Colombel and Fillol 2009, 3).

Such policies contribute to the continuing erosion of Kanak languages. Today, fifteen of the twenty-eight Kanak languages are classified by the UN Educational, Scientific and Cultural Organization as in danger (Moseley 2010). Fluency in French, meanwhile, has dramatically increased in recent decades. In 2000, 70 percent of school children spoke French as a first language whereas only about 30 percent of their parents did (Vernaudon 2013, 117). The continuing erosion of Kanak languages and the steady increase in French are the result of two systemic and conjectural factors. First, the school system and urbanization (two-thirds of the population lives in Greater Nouméa) favor the use of French over Kanak languages. Second, the 2018–2022 referenda for independence have loomed large in general attitudes to teaching and teaching in Kanak languages. The linguist Jacques Vernaudon observes political resistance and a hardening of positions according to a pro-independence/loyalist split (2013, 116). Loyalist politicians are reluctant to support measures that would be seen by their electorate as "compromising with the pro-independence adversaries." Some teachers agree that the continuing marginalization and optionalization of Kanak languages is political. One teacher observed, for instance, that if Sonia Backès, the member of parliament in charge of the education and research portfolio from 2009 to 2014, increased the teaching of English, it "wasn't innocent because the more you teach English, the less you teach Kanak languages." Kanak languages, according to one interviewee, are also minoritized by being made optional and therefore less important in that physical education is compulsory but Kanak languages are not.[7] According to other teachers, the optionalization of Kanak languages reflects a reluctance on the part of the institution and is a way of "making precarious, shaky the teaching of Kanak languages over twenty or thirty years of agreements."[8] To date, except for one pilot project at the Kuru raa (Coula) school where teaching is carried out in both French and Ajië, no policies of bilingual education have been put in place in Kanaky/New Caledonia. Instruction in Kanak languages remains precarious even though most political powers concerning the matter have been transferred from mainland France to the territory, which benefits from unmatched institutional resources relative to France's other overseas territories (Vernaudon 2013, 117).

The lack of appreciation for Kanak languages from within the institution is seen as a major impediment to the effective implementation of Kanak language curricula. According to some teachers interviewed, the Education Office advisors in charge of implementing the teaching in Kanak languages are not speakers of any Kanak languages themselves. Some teachers shared anecdotes about a particular advisor from the Education Office of New Caledonia (Direction de l'Enseignement de la Nouvelle-Calédonie) who, when coming to the classroom, would declare that they were "discovering the teaching of Kanak languages." On another occasion, a different advisor declined an offer from the teacher to participate in the teaching because she could not understand any of the Kanak languages. Looking back, a teacher saw a clear gap, in that the advisors are "not on the same page" and "don't have the same interests" in Kanak languages being taught in schools.[9] The Education Office advisors' lack of understanding and appreciation, as well as prejudices, reveal the tokenistic nature of such initiatives.

Thus linguistic exclusion was and remains common because Indigenous non-native speakers of the dominant language continue to be forced, by coercive laws and practices, to learn primarily in the dominant settler language in both Australia and Kanaky/New Caledonia. The language of instruction is a key factor not only in linguistic terms but also in terms of the pupils' social and educational development and achievements. Forcing a foreign language as a language of instruction can marginalize Indigenous people who are native speakers of another language from the start and impair their educational and emotional fulfilment. One teacher in Kanaky/New Caledonia observed that continuing inflexibility regarding the language of instruction or the level of literacy ultimately affects students' educational achievements. As an example, that exams are designed in France for a French native-speaking audience suggests that the level of literacy is another hurdle for students' achievements. One history teacher reported that as soon as the exam papers come in, they already know which questions their students will fail. The use of one particular word, one adverb, can make the exam questions unintelligible to the students. Such practices, he thought, automatically discriminate or make a selection between the European and the Kanak student.[10]

Yet research in linguistics and neurology has demonstrated that learning in one's mother tongue helps the development of neural pathways and the emotional development of the individual. These aspects, however, are not a priority for the settler colonial polity of these two societies. Indeed, it seems that the intention might well be the opposite. The skepticism of some teachers as to the willingness within the education institutions to bring Indigenous students to academic success echoes the conclusions of several studies in sociology, education, and politics that suggest that in settler colonial contexts, the same logic of elimination and replacement through assimilation persists (Iyengar 2014; Geiger 2017). Malathi Iyengar argues, for instance, that the attack on Indigenous languages is "a central component of structural genocide" in the United States (2014, 53).

It seems, therefore, that the desegregation of schools and the inclusion of Indigenous students over the last few decades have translated into renewed practices of assimilation through which the use of Indigenous languages has declined even further. The school institution continues to marginalize Indigenous languages and people, which may set in motion an already fraught process for the teaching of Indigenous-settler history.

History Curriculum Development and Indigenous Knowledge

The development of the history curriculum and the inclusion of Indigenous contribution varied, of course, between Australia and Kanaky/New Caledonia given the differences in both Indigenous-settler politics and history.

Australia

The Indigenous rights movement of the 1960s and 1970s and the
Aboriginal Education Policy established in 1982 (the first of its kind) set
the stage for the inclusion of Indigenous-settler history and Indigenous
perspectives in history curricula in Australia. The contested 1988 bicentenary celebrations, the 1991 Report on Aboriginal Deaths in Custody,
the 1991 Council for Aboriginal Reconciliation Act, and the 1992 High
Court Mabo decision pushed, each in their own way, for a reassessment
of Australia's historical narrative and a greater inclusion of Indigenous
perspectives in schools. The lead-up to the bicentennial celebrations
of 1988 and the growing resistance to them was the greatest catalyst
for popular reflection about Australia's colonial history. In 1988, the
lead-up to the bicentennial events witnessed a series of Indigenous-led
grassroots actions and protests, culminating in the January 26 March for
Freedom, Hope, and Justice that raised greater public awareness about
Indigenous people and Australia's colonial history. The same year, John
Dawkins, the commonwealth minister responsible for education, training, and employment, pressured the states to work toward a common
national curriculum rather than continue to develop state-specific curricula (1988). In February 1991, Minister for Aboriginal Affairs Robert
Tickner released a discussion paper outlining a strategy for achieving
reconciliation between Indigenous people and settlers. He stated that
the process would need to "educate non-Aboriginal Australians about
the cultures of Australia's Indigenous peoples and the treatment of
Aboriginal and Torres Strait Islander people by European settlers and
their descendants" (1991, 2). In 1992, New South Wales mandated one
hundred hours of Australian content (Parkes 2007, 384–385). This
included the perspectives of Australia's Indigenous people "as legitimate alternatives to the master-narratives of 'famous men' and 'pioneer-
ing settlement'" in its history syllabus (Parkes 2009, 119).[11] The Royal
Commission into Aboriginal Deaths in Custody, the National Inquiry
into the Separation of Aboriginal and Torres Strait Islander Children
from their Families and the Final Report of the Council for Aboriginal
Reconciliation all recommended the inclusion of Indigenous perspectives in school curricula.

The opening of historiography to Indigenous people, despite being
minimal, created a stir in the profession. The Mabo decision and the
subsequent Wik decision had a significant psychological impact on

settlers, especially conservative public figures who launched an ideological and political campaign against these reforms. As part of this conservative backlash, Geoffrey Blainey condemned what he considered
to be a "black armband" view of history (1993). Later, under the conservative Howard federal government, John Howard himself, conservative politicians, journalists, political commentators, the educationalist
Kevin Donnelly (2007), and the historian Keith Windschuttle (2002)
attacked the existing history curricula that they condemned as rewriting
"the nation's past . . . in the service of a partisan political cause" (Bishop
2006, 3). In his 2006 Australia Day speech, Howard called for a "root
and branch renewal" of the teaching of Australian history (Howard
2006) and his minister for education, science, and training called for a
national summit to rethink the teaching of Australian history in schools
(Parkes 2009, 118). This trend was somewhat reversed with the change
of government.

In 2007, Australian Labor Party leader Kevin Rudd became prime
minister and scrapped Howard's history curriculum. He and the subsequent Labor governments launched the drafting of a new, nationwide
curriculum policy framework. Between 2012 and 2017, state adaptations of the new Australian Curriculum were gradually implemented in
Australian public schools. The curriculum provides a national framework for praxis—not a prescription for content—on how to teach
Australian history. Today, public education remains under the authority
of states and territories and it is up to state and territorial authorities,
schools, teachers, and textbook writers to interpret and implement curriculum policies. In 2014, the Australian Curriculum underwent further
review under direction of the Liberal Party federal government, which
recommended putting more emphasis on Australia's Judeo-Christian
heritage, the role of Western civilization in contributing to its society,
and the influence of its British system of government (Donnelly and
Wiltshire 2014, 246). It is an indication of the ideological positions
attached to Indigenous-settler history teaching. It seems that teaching
more critical history was encouraged under Labor governments (Bob
Hawke 1981–1993, Paul Keating 1991–1996, Kevin Rudd 2007–2010,
Julia Gillard 2010–2013) only to be challenged by conservative governments (Howard 1996–2007, Tony Abbott 2013–2015).

Yet, regardless of which government is in charge, the Australian
Curriculum, along with the various state adaptations as well as their
reviews, has come under criticism for excluding Indigenous historians

from the curriculum development process. A former teacher interviewed for this research denounced the indifference he faced from the
History Advisory Committee when trying to contribute, as an Indigenous
practitioner, to the development of the Australian Curriculum:

> I contributed my opinion to the debate when the curriculum
> was being compiled and I was never, never interviewed about my
> opinion. . . . That's how Australia works . . . I'm sorry to say but
> that's how Australia has always worked. When it comes down to a
> crucial point, Australia will avoid the truth to come out. . . . The
> committee that considered it [the curriculum] is just biased. . . .
> I made a contribution to it and I was ignored.

He acknowledged that in the past perhaps the number of Aboriginal
historians or Aboriginal writers was not large, which made it difficult to
assemble a team to address those issues; he stressed, however, that it was
not impossible. He pointed out that now that this is no longer an issue,
that this is still not being done, and that the curriculum is "still a colonial
tool." In his view, "whenever anything is decided about Aboriginal people. . . , it's always done without Aboriginal consultation. . . . So, when they
want to rewrite the curriculum, do they bring in any Aboriginal editors,
writers, philosophers? No. They bring in the white historians."[12] The continuing marginalization of Indigenous contribution to curriculum development and review has also been observed in the review of the Australian
Curriculum in 2014, which did not include any Indigenous historians:

> The decision is now in the hands of the review panel, comprised
> of six history teachers and three academics—Professor Kate
> Darian-Smith, Professor Richard Broome and Dr Rosalie Triolo.
> With the exception of Professor Broome, none of these teachers
> or academics has recognised specific expertise in Aboriginal his-
> tory. And given that Broome is not Indigenous, there appears to
> have been no Indigenous perspective on the review panel. (Foley
> and Muldoon 2014)

The lack of Indigenous contribution to curriculum development has
also been raised as a crucial issue by the education scholars Kevin Lowe
and Tyson Yunkaporta, who strongly urge the Australian Curriculum,
Assessment and Reporting Authority to "establish a panel of Indigenous

academics with demonstrated expertise in curriculum design and development, cognitive development, and Indigenous epistemology and ontology, to undertake a thorough re-appraisal of the national curricula" (2013, 12). For Luke Pearson, the changes to the Australian Curriculum are "about celebrating whiteness and celebrating an imaginary white only history, in the hopes of maintaining a white dominant future. In simple terms, it is racism" (2015). The lack of consultation is happening at all levels of schooling. A preschool teacher in Victoria deplored the lack of consultation with Indigenous people when creating curricula. She remembered that

> When the people that had written the National Early Years Framework came to speak to us at the Practitioners' Advisory Group, I asked them why there was no Indigenous content in it. She said, "oh because it's just too difficult, because, they've got their own Wannik strategy." And I said, "but isn't that ghettoizing it?" "Oh, oh, no," was basically all I got.[13]

Such attitudes reflect an assumption that Indigenous content is relevant only for Indigenous students, an attitude I also faced when contacting potential participants in the early stage of the project, as mentioned. Another teacher believed that "there is an element of racism in Australia" and that Indigenous people's histories are generally not valued as much as some other histories.[14] Such assumptions indicate a practice of ignorance that pervades history education beginning at the curriculum development stage. Such practice was made even more obvious when that preschool teacher replied to the institutional representatives that "the Wannik strategy is great for Koori people, but I am not talking about educating Koori people. I am talking about educating ignorant white people. Everyone in the room just went 'Oh!' But it's still now white people interpreting what they think Indigenous people feel."[15] Thus, in addition to political antagonism holding sway over history curricula, consultation with Indigenous people in curriculum development in Australia seems to still be wanting at all levels of schooling.

Kanaky/New Caledonia

In Kanaky/New Caledonia, the 1984–1988 war and the school boycott precipitated changes in curricula. Beginning in 1985, a small group of history teachers started to reflect on the reform of history curricula. In 1986, the Territorial Mission for Training (Mission Territoriale à la Formation), directed by André Wenehoua, called for the adaptation of history curricula. Following the Matignon-Oudinot Agreements of 1988 that put an end to the armed conflict, educational institutions recognized the importance of having locally designed and adapted history teaching in the school system. The political urgency of the war and the lingering resentment of its aftermath tremendously accelerated the reform of history curricula and teaching practices for New Caledonian schools. The 1988 law sets as a goal the adaptation of education "to the particularities of the territory" through grants, teacher training, adapting curricula, and teaching local languages (Journal Officiel de la République Française 1988). In 1989, an Office of Pedagogical Adaptation (Bureau d'adaptation pédagogique) was created for primary school education. In 1989–1990, the History Committee, under the leadership of Frédéric Angleviel, oversaw the adaptation of secondary school programs and the publication of the first history textbook adapted to New Caledonian history. These changes, however, were a fraught process for those involved. A former teacher and member of the History Committee remembered that

> The years 1987 to 1990 were difficult years because New Caledonia was going through the Events (1984–1988) and people who talked about adapting the programs were seen by most of their colleagues as pro-independence or people close to the pro-independence side. With a public opinion, which was quite traumatized, what we were doing met with disapproval.[16]

This small group of history teachers would organize weekly public conferences in country towns to invite the population at large to reflect on the adaptation of history curricula. The thinking behind these conferences was to exchange ideas. A former teacher recalls that on one of their visits in Pwêêdi Wiimîâ (Poindimié), the group was followed and spied on by a delegation from the educational institution, the Vice Rectorate. History curricula were the source of a deeply political and divisive debate. This teacher explained that "the problematic at the time was that talking about Kanak history was automatically seen as being on the pro-independence side and taking part in the independence debate. It remains a tricky issue today, less intense, but still tricky."[17]

Gradually, history curricula were adapted at the primary and secondary levels of education. Looking back, a key actor in the adaptation of curricula remembered that the institution was ambivalent and only supported the initiative because "considering the political demands in the country, they had to do it." In addition, she noted an "absolutely important conservatism" from history teachers and the inspectors that slowed down and contained the process of adaptation of the history curricula. The high school history curriculum was adapted for year 10 in 1996, for year 11 in 2004, and for year 12 in 2008. It was a twelve-year process to adapt history curricula throughout the high school years. Several history teachers recalled that "it wasn't a forgone conclusion."[18]

According to many history teachers, the adaptation of history curricula was achieved with the crucial support of Michel Lextreyt. Lextreyt took on the position of academic inspector and regional pedagogical inspector in 1990 in French Polynesia, but he became very much involved in educational policies in Kanaky/New Caledonia. The history teachers interviewed for this research told of how Michel Lextreyt's conviction and struggle for the adaptation of the curricula continuously faced resistance within the institutions. "We need to put all our energy into adapting these curricula," he once said, "because we know very well that as soon as we relax our attention we will fall back into the common pot of national curricula" (2010).

In January 2000, political authority over primary schooling was transferred from mainland France to Kanaky/New Caledonia, which was then free to adapt the curriculum to the local social-historical realities. The pro-independence politician Charles Washetine was in charge of the education and research portfolio between 2004 and 2009 and finalized the preparation of the primary school curricula. The curricula were adopted by the Congress in 2005 and put into practice in 2006. The transfer of political authority over secondary schooling followed in 2012. Mainland France, however, has maintained authority over staffing, examinations, and national curricula. The transfer has therefore been partial. New Caledonia adapts the national curriculum, and this adapted curriculum is then approved by an institution in mainland France, the General Management of School Education (Direction générale de l'enseignement scolaire). Since 2012, the Vice Rectorate of New Caledonia is both an institution from the French mainland and a New Caledonian institution.

In 2012, with the reform of the French high school curriculum, the history curricula moved from adaptation to contextualization. The Northern Province observed a clear retreat, which is paradoxical given that it happened when the political authority over secondary schooling was transferred to New Caledonian institutions (Province Nord 2013, 24). In 2010, Michel Lextreyt had warned history teachers that "the battle ha[d] been won, but for how long?" considering that the General Inspection had just decided to stop the adaptation of history curricula in secondary schools (2010). A few teachers observed that since political authority was transferred, the New Caledonian government has not continued the work of pushing for the adaptation of history curricula.

Thus, in Australia and Kanaky/New Caledonia, the politicization of history teaching has translated into backlashes, institutional feebleness, and the optionalization of Indigenous-settler history in the curriculum.

Indigenous-Settler History in the Curriculum

When looking at the allocated time dedicated annually to the subject of history in the Australian Curriculum, primary years spend proportionally less time (2 to 4 percent) than secondary years (5 percent). Within history as a subject, Indigenous-settler history can be touched on from foundation to year 3 as an understanding of the pupil's local environment. The early colonial period is addressed in years 4 and 5, and Australia's twentieth century in year 6. The history curriculum from foundation to year 6 focuses mainly on local and national Australian history. At the secondary level, aspects of Indigenous-settler history are addressed in year 9 (in "The Making of the Modern World") and year 10 (in "The Modern World and Australia") only. Teachers in Australia held a range of views about the Australian Curriculum. Several teachers considered it to be a step forward. Some found it very flexible and observed an emphasis on Indigenous perspectives. Yet many interviewed for this research voiced their disapproval. Several teachers conceded that much work remained. Two teachers in New South Wales found that the Australian Curriculum offered far less than the previous state curriculum did. One teacher was disappointed because it was essentially optional, whereas the New South Wales syllabus it replaced had a real focus.

Another criticism was that many aspects of the curriculum remain optional or unclear. A Melbourne-based primary school teacher observed that the curriculum is not specific, "all very grey and vague" about what to teach, with only three or four sentences that one can interpret any way they want.[19] At the secondary level, several teachers pointed out that Indigenous-settler history is not woven through the curriculum. Instead, it is segmented and therefore marginalized within the Australian history subject. One secondary school teacher in the Northern Territory found that the curriculum is "at points superficial" and thought that if it were more mandated it would be more effective.

In Kanaky/New Caledonia, history is included as a school subject from cycle 3 (year 4 to 6). In cycle 3, the 2019 curriculum allocates seventy-two hours per year to history, geography, and civics, which is a decrease from seventy-eight hours in the 2012 curriculum. Of these, seventy-two hours, eighteen hours would be dedicated to history, that is, a half hour per week. Postcolonization New Caledonia history is taught in year 5. In that year level, all three units touch on that period, and six of the eleven key focus points on Indigenous-settler history. At the secondary level, Indigenous-settler history is included in the last two years of middle secondary school (years 8 and 9), and the last two years of high school (years 11 and 12). History makes up 4.5 percent of the curriculum in year 8 and 5.3 percent in year 9; these figures are comparable to the time allocated to the subject of history in Australia. The proportion dedicated to Indigenous-settler history today, however, is smaller than in the 2000s. It has been halved in year 9, for instance. It fell from 24 percent (2011 curriculum) to 8 percent (2012 curriculum), and rose again slightly to 12.5 percent in the 2020 curriculum. In year 11, it dropped from 22 percent (2007 curriculum) to 11 percent (2012 curriculum) in the year 11 economics and literary studies streams, and from 28 percent (2007 curriculum) to 13 percent (2013 curriculum) for the year 11 science stream. In the 2020 curriculum, both streams follow the same curriculum and the proportion of Indigenous-settler history rose again slightly to 16 percent, but remained lower than in 2007. The proportion of the history subject dedicated to Indigenous-settler history is more or less stagnant (around 10 percent) in year 8 and year 12.

The 2007 curriculum in use until 2012 was more fully developed and detailed than the 2012 curriculum and those in use in 2021. The latest history curricula are more sparse. The time allocation in the middle secondary school curriculum, for example, has shifted from being given in hours before 2012 to percentages in the 2012 curriculum to none at all in the 2020 curriculum.[20] Some teachers considered that

Indigenous-settler history is fragmented and "does not have coher-
ence" in the curriculum, and that "it is complicated to find a balance."[21]
Several secondary school teachers—especially those who started teaching after the 2012 curriculum was implemented—thought that the time
allocated to the histories of mainland France, Kanaky/New Caledonia,
and the world is quite balanced. However, many other teachers—especially those who went through the curricular changes—observed a clear
reduction in the time dedicated to New Caledonian history and were
"extremely disappointed." They felt that very few hours are dedicated
to New Caledonian history under the latest curricula. Some thought
not only that the proportion dedicated to Indigenous-settler history in
the curriculum is inadequate, but also that within this minimal proportion Kanak people are marginalized, inasmuch as it is in addition to the
national curriculum. They found the 2012 curricular changes "illogical"
and "paradoxical," "very dominated by France," and "still a Western view
cast onto the Pacific."[22] Since contextualization has been implemented,
teaching Indigenous-settler history has for many teachers become ad
hoc because they lack the systemic, infrastructural support to which they
had access when the educational system was officially implementing an
adapted program.[23] Many teachers found the adaptation of the history
curricula "timid," "disjointed," "a sprinkling," or as just scratching the
surface and tokenistic. One saw it as a "puppet curriculum" "to appease
political demands." As a result, only the "easier" and more accessible
episodes are taught: the two world wars, the protectorate, and the Kanak
uprisings.[24] Another felt that a curriculum that states that "one will mention the case of New Caledonia" clearly does not emphasize or advocate
Indigenous-settler history. Still another pointed out that teaching New
Caledonian history also suffers because teachers will not "be rapped on
the knuckles" by the inspection if they do not teach it.[25]

These views are not universal. One teacher educator, for example,
disagreed with views that he saw as excuses and instead suggested that
the new curriculum offers considerable flexibility and huge possibilities
for teaching local history. He observed a common local attitude that if it
is not written in stone, people will not teach it; he believes that ultimately
the issue in Kanaky/New Caledonia is not what one can do but what
one wants to do.[26] Such an argument is relevant inasmuch as the withdrawal of adaptation in favor of a lighter contextualization in Kanaky/
New Caledonia does not mean that teachers can no longer teach within
a contextual framework. As one teacher pointed out, "There's the

curriculum and then what you actually do with it."[27] These changes do mean, however, that it is acceptable not to teach it, to ignore it. What this means in practice is that the curriculum can no longer be used as a point of reference for students or parents who want to see Indigenous-settler history addressed. This is indeed problematic, especially in a context in which no process of truth about history and justice has been undertaken since the 1984–1988 war, which ended with an amnesty, and at a time when the history subject remains extremely controversial.

Six main possible factors explain this retreat from teaching Indigenous-settler history in recent years.

First, it might be a pedagogical choice to simplify the teaching process because having an adapted curriculum involved extra work preparing adapted exams.

Second, Michel Lextreyt, who played a key role in the adaptation of history curricula retired in 2010. His personal battle against institutional conservatism, according to interviewees, seems not to have been taken up by his successors.

Third, that New Caledonian history was included in the 2010 and 2011 baccalaureate provoked resistance from some parents and students (some of whom demonstrated in the streets of Nouméa) who feared having a debased diploma (commonly referred to as a "Coconut baccalaureate" [*Bac cocotier*]). One teacher interpreted such resistance as coming from the Nouméan bourgeoisie who want their children to have exactly the same education as students in mainland France and for them to be able to pursue further education in mainland France.

Fourth, several teachers believed that New Caledonian politicians are not sufficiently involved in education matters, "lacked vigilance," and "did not lift a finger" when the adaptation of the curriculum was abandoned. The education system, one suggested, is a lower order political priority than issues such as the political status of the territory, independence, or nickel mining.[28] In the lead-up to the 2018–2022 referenda, the struggle for independence largely focused political efforts and concerns on the economy, especially mining. Nickel mining is a cornerstone of the independence project and is used to testify to the economic viability of Kanak independence. In comparison, education is a lesser concern for local politicians and thus less political pressure has been placed on the government to drive a greater local focus in school curricula. One teacher explained that, depending on people's understanding of what the decolonization process entails, the focus is likely to be directed toward politics, the economy, or education: "The pillar of culture is education, the school and, for me, that's the main challenge. . . . I have talked to other pro-independence people who say that we must first decolonise politics and the economy, and that education will follow."[29] Another teacher and textbook author observed that local politicians, whether for or against independence, are withdrawn from educational matters and what may actually end up in history textbooks: "No one ever met with me or asked me what we were doing within these curricula." She also noticed that when history teachers complained to local politicians that programs were not sufficiently adapted to local history, none of them—whether pro- or anti-independence—used their political position and power to influence decisions in mainland France.[30] Another teacher believed that loyalist politicians "don't want to see, don't want to know," suggesting a mixture of indifference and a fear of seeing Kanak people take more and more place.[31] Pro-independence politicians, for their part, are wary of an institutional version of the history and do not necessarily go out of their way to push for the adaptation of history curricular either.

Fifth, this retreat from New Caledonian history may be the result of political decisions in mainland France. The latency between the ministerial changes in France and their impact in Kanaky/New Caledonia may explain that the apogee of the adapted curriculum (2008–2010) are policies developed under the Chirac government (1995–2007) later scrapped under the Sarkozy government (2007–2012). Another teacher recalled that inspectors have on several occasions and again recently reminded history teachers in Kanaky/New Caledonia to not fall into a history of communities and identities that could challenge national unity.

Finally, history curricula are subject to political bipolarization and adapting curricula is seen as one more step toward independence. According to one teacher, the beginning of the 2010s saw a shift in popular consciousness in the realization that the deadline for the referenda for independence was getting closer and may have led to a conservative backlash. As a result, another felt, political ulterior motives may explain the retreat from the adapted curriculum in 2012.

What Is Included and What Is Ignored

The history curricula for primary and secondary education in Australia and Kanaky/New Caledonia cover first contacts, religious missions, the involvement of Indigenous people in the two world wars, political evolutions in the second half of the twentieth century (land rights and movements for Indigenous rights in Australia and the statutory evolution of the territory in Kanaky/New Caledonia) and recent policies of reconciliation (closing the gap policies in Australia, the peace agreements in Kanaky/New Caledonia). They also mention aspects specific to their respective history: the protectorate and the Stolen Generations for the history curriculum in Australia, and the Kanak uprisings for the curriculum in Kanaky/New Caledonia. An analysis of history curricula and interviews with history teachers reveal that three aspects are ignored from the history curriculum in both Australia and Kanaky/New Caledonia: Indigenous—non-European settler relations, the word "war" to refer to colonial conflicts, and the question of Indigenous sovereignty. Additionally, history curricula in Kanaky/New Caledonia also exclude the interwar years and the pro-independence movement that culminated in the 1984–1988 war.

Indigenous and non-European settler relations. The current history curriculum for primary and secondary education does not include relations between Indigenous people and non-European settlers. Teachers interviewed in Australia and Kanaky/New Caledonia confirmed these observations. Further, current history curricula do not include a great diversity of perspectives. Accounts from Indigenous people and non-European settlers remain limited to a small section on the "experiences of non-Europeans in Australia prior to the 1900s (such as the Japanese, Chinese, South Sea Islanders, Afghans)." Some teachers thought that it does not encourage a plurality of experiences and that "a real lack of resources surrounds those perspectives."[32] Likewise, in Kanaky/New Caledonia, non-European settlers are barely included in the history curriculum. Indigenous-settler history is, as one teacher remarked, "centered on the Kanak/Europeans dichotomy."[33] One teacher thought that the experiences and history of non-European settlers are not really part of the curriculum and that this is "a huge lack." "We sometimes put the Melanesian population first at the expense of other populations in New Caledonia," she said. Although she understood the political effort, she thought it would be good to expand.[34]

Indigenous-settler history is depicted (almost) exclusively as relations between Indigenous people and European settlers. Such articulations reaffirm settler colonial power and continue to marginalize colonized peoples and non-European populations. These groups are each represented only in relation to the settler colonial polity, as they come into contact with it, first Indigenous people and then the successive waves of non-European migration. Writing from other conflict-filled contexts, Michalinos Zembylas and his colleagues condemn this as an "additive approach" that leads to the "compartmentalisation" of curricular guidelines (2009, 419).

The colonial wars. History curricula in Australia and Kanaky/New Caledonia do not use the term "war" to refer to colonial conflicts between Indigenous people and settlers from the early colonial period to more recent conflicts. Curricula mention revolts, uprisings, massacres, and conflicts, but not colonial wars. A former history teacher in Australia who would later write history content for education institutions remembered the censorship he faced. He mentioned, for instance, that the reviewing committee "refused point blank to allow [him] to use certain words in the text" and "refused any direct language about the war or direct language about the economic achievements of Aboriginal people." Such attitudes had the detrimental effect of further alienating Indigenous people from educational institutions. He decided to leave those committees and stopped writing for the institutions. He maintains that such incidents reflect common attitudes in the wider society:

> Australians have a lot of trouble with the W word. They can't bring themselves to talk about the war against Aboriginal people and they can't bring themselves to talk about Aboriginal resistance to the occupation. Nor do they bring themselves to acknowledge Aboriginal achievement.[35]

Indeed, the history of colonial wars is not explicitly mentioned in the curriculum. The year 9 curriculum, for instance, directs the teaching to "the extension of settlement, including the effects of contact (intended and unintended) between European settlers in Australia and Aboriginal and Torres Strait Islander Peoples," giving the example of massacres, although the word "war" is never mentioned. Likewise, history curricula in Kanaky/New Caledonia mention Kanak revolts and uprisings but do not use the word "war" to define colonial conflicts between Indigenous people and settlers. In addition, the 1917 war that was included in the year 9 curriculum for several years was removed in 2018.

The interwar years (Kanaky/New Caledonia). A period largely over-looked in history curricula in Kanaky/New Caledonia is the interwar years, which teachers also observed. Yet, Bouda Etemad asserts that "the height of contemporary colonial empires was situated during the inter-war years" (2012, 83). Colonialism was not an easily won case in the French centers of power but instead a gradual victory over various politi-cal groups: the centrists and radicals in the 1880s, the socialists at the beginning of the twentieth century, and the communists in the interwar years (Aldrich 1988, 31). This was mostly achieved through the zealous militant work of the lobbying Colonial Party (*le parti colonial*) and the French Oceania Committee (Comité de l'Océanie française)—the lat-ter specifically focused on France's colonies in Oceania.[36] The French Oceania Committee reached its heyday in the 1930s, encouraging set-tler migration to New Caledonia and supporting Albert Sarraut's pro-grams of "enhancement" (*mise en valeur*) (Aldrich 1989). The interwar period coincided with the emergence of the notions of "enhancement" and "development" of France's overseas colonies (Etemad 2012, 110, 91). It is also in the interwar period that a self-proclaimed "humanist colonialism" emerged that defended the possibility of a democratic colonialism through reforms. Etemad tells us that this period also coin-cides with a colonial romanticism that fixed the categories of "tradi-tions" and "modernity," between preservation of the cultural identity and penetration of Western capitalism according to which colonized peoples always remain in an in-between position (Etemad 2012, 85). These notions endure today.

The work of the Colonial Party and the French Oceania Committee pushed critical debates on colonization into oblivion. It is on this willed oblivion that twentieth-century French colonial politics could continue to flourish. Pro-colonial support was mostly won on the basis of popular apathy, images, and myths (Marseille 1986). The colonial project was continuously promoted to influence French public opin-ion, which remained largely uninterested in the colonial question (Bancel, Blanchard, and Vergès 2007, 18). Rather than a grand design, colonialism was therefore a continual, gradual process of exploitation that—supported by strong colonial propaganda and loose networks of influential people—provided its own justifications and saw its greatest support in the interwar years, culminating in the Colonial Exhibition of 1931.[37] Colonialism became a mass cultural phenomenon (exhibitions, human zoos, circus, and so on) that used discourses of racial superiority to legitimize colonial domination. The committee stopped its activities in 1940 and resumed only in the 1980s. Robert Aldrich notes that in the context of Asia's economic boom, movements for independence in Melanesia, and the 1984–1988 war in Kanaky/New Caledonia, the oceanic lobby regained its influence, and pressure groups demanded France's continued presence in the Pacific (1989, 155).

In light of these colonial logics, the eclipse of the interwar years in the history curriculum can be understood as either a serendipitous absence or as the willful effacement of contemporary colonialism that originated during that period and continues today. It seems reasonable to wonder whether the lack of curricular focus on the interwar years stems from a fear that students might realize this colonial continuity.

The pro-independence movement (Kanaky/New Caledonia). Another episode of Indigenous-settler history not touched on in the current secondary school history curriculum in Kanaky/New Caledonia is the pro-independence movement that culminated in the 1984–1988 war. Surprisingly, although these themes were included in the history curriculum in the late 2000s, they were removed after 2012 when the political authority over secondary schooling was transferred to New Caledonian institutions. For instance, the year 9 curricula of 2007 and 2011 addressed pro-independence but did not after 2012. The 2007 curriculum, in the unit titled "New Caledonia since 1945," suggests addressing the following questions: How did New Caledonia grow out of its colonial status? (1945–1957). How did the experience of autonomy lead to the emergence of a pro-independence movement? (1957–1981). How did New Caledonia move from the Events to the Matignon Agreements? (1981–1988). In what ways is the Nouméa Agreement the achievement of a "consensual solution"? (1988–1998). Likewise, the 2011 curriculum mentions "attempts for autonomy, the emergence of a pro-independence movement and the taking over of the situation by the state," "the rupture that marks the period of 'the Events,'" "how the Ouvea tragedy led to the negotiation of the New Caledonian question with the Matignon Agreements," and "the search for a consensual solution and its achievement with the Nouméa Agreement and the organic law of March 19, 1999." However, in the 2014 curriculum the unit is titled "The Fifth Republic put to the test" and recommends, succinctly, studying "the evolution of New Caledonian society during this period," "the 1988 Matignon Agreement," and "the 1998 Nouméa Agreement." The 2020 curriculum mentions only "the evolution of New Caledonia's political statuses and the reactions they elicited."

Several teachers observed that although the Matignon and Nouméa Agreements are taught, the 1984–1988 war "goes out the window." One secondary school teacher noted that the Vice Rectorate puts considerable emphasis on the two world wars, "but New Caledonian history is just not that." It is also, the teacher continued, about "gauging the reactions to the Matignon Agreements, to the assassination of Jean-Marie Tjibaou" but "all this period, is completely ousted."[38] Another explains that because they have fewer teaching hours than in mainland France and because the topic is not included in the examinations, teachers usually "speak very little about this period." Many also considered that the new curricular format, which contextualizes rather than adapts, makes it impossible to talk about the 1984–1988 war. Several believed, however, that it is part of the history and students need to know. Still another secondary school teacher found it a pity that the topic is barely included, if at all: "it clearly shows that we don't take responsibility for that part of the history." "It may be time," she believed, "to take responsibility for our history and for our past."[39] Another history teacher observed that "no one dares saying it but today New Caledonian history is very politicized" because this is a time of self-determination.[40]

The question of Indigenous sovereignties. In both Australian and New Caledonian history curricula, the question of Indigenous sovereignties is ignored. It is neither mentioned nor problematized. In both societies, the politicization of history teaching has produced conservative reactions, a retreat from Indigenous-settler history in the curricula, and the removal altogether of the most polemical or controversial aspects of those histories. It seems, therefore, that the recent evolution of history curricula testifies not to decolonization but instead to a subtle recolonization, or at least the continuing colonization, of Indigenous-settler relations.

Variables Behind Curricular Choices

Two sets of variables are significant in curricular choices. The first is schools and teachers, the second examination and testing.

Schools and Teachers

The Australian Curriculum, Assessment and Reporting Authority specifies that "decisions relating to the organisation and delivery of the Australian Curriculum, including such matters as time allocation, rest with education authorities and schools" (ACARA 2012, 8). Indeed, several teachers at both the primary and secondary levels feel that they have considerable autonomy and scope about what they are teaching, and that ultimately the implementation of the curriculum is up to the discretion of the teacher and the school principal. One secondary school teacher reported, for instance, that topics such as Indigenous rights and protests had never been taught in the school where he worked and, had he not pushed the school to teach these subjects, it would still not be doing so, regardless of the evolution of the curriculum. In that school, history as a subject is optional from year 8, which means that many students at that school will have stopped studying history in year 7, having only studied ancient times.[41] Teachers play a crucial role in influencing the curricular choices made by the school. Such observations also appear in an Indigenous media report:

> Currently, a school student's access to knowledge and understanding of Aboriginal and Torres Strait Islander histories, cultures and perspectives depends entirely on the commitment, enthusiasm and energy of the individual school, principal and teacher. Depending on the enthusiasm of the school and teacher, a student's engagement with Aboriginal and Torres Strait Islander cultures and perspectives range anywhere from a quick screening of Rabbit Proof Fence to a comprehensive program and learning on country with the local mob. (Mokak 2017)

Likewise, in Kanaky/New Caledonia, the history curriculum states that it is up to the teacher to choose what aspects they wish to emphasize and how much time they want to dedicate to each. Several teachers acknowledged that they are relatively free to interpret and adapt the content of the teaching. One observed that in some schools little emphasis, or even none, will be placed on New Caledonian history, but that in others it will be more valued. Another teacher declared that "there are as many ways to teach, as there are teachers."[42]

The Weight of Examination and Testing

The impact of examinations and testing on curricular content and implementation is also an issue raised by history teachers, and even more so in Kanaky/New Caledonia. Indeed, although no end-of-course exam is in place at the end of middle/junior secondary school in Australia, in New Caledonian schools, such an exam, called the *Brevet*, is taken at the end of year 9. The only end-of-course exam in the Australian state and territory school systems is at the end of high school in year 12. Considering that years 11 and 12 are not included in the analysis of history teaching in Australia because history at those levels is no longer included as a core subject in the curriculum, the content of history examinations does not affect the crafting or implementation of the history curriculum from foundation to year 10.[43] However, in both these societies, the government push for numeracy and literacy (through the National Assessment Program – Literacy and Numeracy testing in Australia, for instance) does affect the amount of time a teacher can spend on history as a specific subject, especially in primary school.

At the primary school level, the same observation is made in both Australia and Kanaky/New Caledonia: the time nominally allocated to history tends to crumble away in favor of the fundamental subjects, namely, English (in Australia) or French (in Kanaky/New Caledonia) and maths. A primary school teacher who previously worked in Darwin did not remember teaching much Aboriginal history there. He stressed that the fact that he could not remember teaching any Aboriginal history probably says something. Much of it was more literacy and numeracy focused. For him, that meant the politics of public education. School subjects that are less easily quantifiable—and therefore less pliable to statistics, which have become a key tool in assessing the efficiency of educational policies—are less valued: "I suppose that's our culture. We want to know what number everybody is on." Teachers believe that teaching history is important, but political priorities are aligned with the government desire to prove the efficiency of its educational policies rather than on the acquisition of knowledge per se. This situation is not peculiar to the Northern Territory. The same primary school teacher observed that even in a progressive school like his current one in Melbourne, "it's numeracy and literacy first, and everything else after that."[44]

In Kanaky/New Caledonia too, history is considered the poor relation of the primary school curriculum. As a result, another primary school teacher educator observed, "there isn't much time left to do research in history or to do history differently."[45] In secondary schools, that examinations touch at best only lightly on New Caledonian history further minimizes the time and emphasis that teachers will grant to Indigenous-settler history in years 9 and 12 (levels with examinations). Teachers said that they will put more emphasis on the units that may be in the exams—that is, French and global history—at the expense of New Caledonian history because more is at stake. When New Caledonian history is included in the exams, it usually touches on predictable topics such as the involvement of New Caledonia in the world wars. Indigenous-settler history is often included only in the Spatial and Chronological Points (Repères chronologiques et spatiaux). The more polemical issues pertaining to Indigenous-settler history, such as the 1984–1988 war or the political agreements, have never been a topic in the *Brevet*. In 2011 and 2012, New Caledonian history was included in the baccalaureate exam with a focus on "the political evolution of New Caledonia since 1945," and the demand for better treatment by Kanak sharpshooters in the Battalion of the Pacific, respectively. Since then, such topics have been removed from the exams.

One teacher thought that these episodes "haven't been digested well yet" so are usually avoided.[46] A few teachers mentioned that the exam requirements deter teachers from dedicating time to an aspect of history not included in the examinations. For instance, because New Caledonian history is excluded, teachers and students tend to prioritize the content about mainland France instead. Another teacher believed that examinations have a crucial impact on how Indigenous-settler history fare in the history curriculum: "no matter how much one changes the educational policies, so long as the content of examinations remains unchanged," the adaptation of the history curriculum will just be "decoration."[47] The weight of examinations in steering teachers' practices has also been observed in the North American context by the education scholar Wayne Ross. He argues that the "primary instruments used in the . . . enforcement of official knowledge have been the creation of state level curriculum standards paired with standardized tests, creating bureaucratic accountability systems that undermine the freedom to teach and learn" (quoted in Fanelli 2015, 407). History curricula and standardized testing therefore are the first settler colonial clutch on education that lays the foundations for settler regimes of ignorance to take hold.

The production of history curricula in both Australia and Kanaky/New Caledonia is highly political and divisive. The implementation of new curricula in 2012 spilled considerable ink. Indigenous-settler histories remain in the throes of political antagonism and vacillate between hard-won progressive evolutions and swift conservative backlashes. Regardless of political perspective, however, the process continues to exclude Indigenous languages as languages of instruction and to marginalize Indigenous people from the curriculum development process. Government language policies abide by the logic of elimination (Wolfe 2006) characteristic of settler colonialism even as history curricula and examinations seem to carefully exclude contentious aspects of the history that could reveal the polity's continuing colonial drive. These policies and practices enable settler regimes of ignorance to take hold. Teachers nonetheless have some leeway regarding the implementation of the curriculum. The curriculum is affected by three key variables: examinations, the school, and the teachers. The ways that teachers understand curricular policies, negotiate these variables, and are trained (or not) to implement them, are fundamental to their teaching. The next chapter focuses on staffing and teacher training.

CHAPTER 3

Staffing and Teacher Training

IN MANY PARTS OF THE NEW CALEDONIAN BUSH (*brousse*), and even more so in the Loyalty Islands, settlers, always a minority and often only a few, are often represented by three distinct professions: teacher, doctor, and the French paramilitary police (*gendarme*). The legacy of the three-faceted colonization of Indigenous people (to educate, to cure, and to control or punish) seems persistent. To these three professions can be added other institutional staff and birds of passage such as tourists and researchers, making up the small conglomerate of non-Kanak people in these areas. On countless occasions while hitchhiking or giving someone a ride in Kanaky/New Caledonia, I was asked whether I was the new teacher or nurse. At first bewildered that the locals would attach such sedentary positions to an unknown face, I quickly realized that these localities were characterized by a markedly high level of staff transience in such positions.

Staff transience is also characteristic of largely Indigenous-populated rural localities in Australia. It is not, however, the only characteristic. Staffing trends also vary depending on localities and teachers' certifications. As a result, the staffing policies and trends within the school system are an important factor to consider when looking at the teaching of Indigenous-settler history in Australia and Kanaky/New Caledonia. Indeed, one may suspect that these will visibly affect the ways that teaching is carried out. This chapter looks at staffing trends and teacher training in the history teacher cohort in these two societies. It and the previous chapter, on curricular development and reforms, provide a comprehensive basis for understanding the educational policies and directives of the settler colonial powers.

A White School? Staffing Trends in the History Teacher Cohort

The teacher cohort in both Australia and Kanaky/New Caledonia was for many decades composed almost exclusively of staff of European descent. Recent evolutions in staffing are slowly eroding this exclusiveness, but the marginalization of Indigenous people and the nonrepresentativeness of the teaching staff remain persistent in schools in both societies.

Australia

Since the 1980s, when the National Aboriginal Education Committee pushed to ensure that one thousand Aboriginal people were formally trained as teachers by 1990, diversification of school staff has been under way. Staff, however, is still not representative of Australia's population. No survey on the proportion of Indigenous and settler history teachers specifically in government primary and secondary schools could be located. One in 2007 on school teachers' backgrounds in Australia, however, reveals that fewer than 1 percent of teachers (working across all subjects) identified themselves as Indigenous, which is less than the actual Indigenous population of 3 percent. The survey also determines that the large majority of teachers were born in Australia (86 percent of primary teachers and 81 percent of secondary), meaning that the teacher workforce has a higher proportion of Australian-born people than Australia as a whole (76 percent in 2007). The survey also found that the largest group of teachers born overseas were from England (5 percent), which is close to the proportion of English-born people in the Australian population as a whole. The other countries however, generally had a lower proportion of teachers born in that country than their respective proportion of the Australian population (McKenzie et al. 2008, 20–22).

The figures have changed little since 2007. In 2013, 2014, and 2015, Indigenous teachers across primary and secondary schools represented about 1 percent of the government school staff, and Indigenous students made up 5 percent of the student population (MATSITI 2014). The large majority of Australian teachers in public schools were born in

Australia (82.8 percent), followed by those born in the United Kingdom (5.5 percent), New Zealand (1.5 percent), the United States (1 percent), and South Africa (0.9 percent). The proportion of teachers who spoke a language other than English at home (8.9 percent) was much lower than for the Australian population as a whole (23.2 percent).

In rural areas, the lack of representativeness among school staff is more dramatic. In 2010, more than 95 percent of teachers in the Northern Territory's remote schools were hired from interstate (Milburn 2010). Although the situation is slowly changing and an increasing number of local Indigenous practitioners achieve certification, the country schools in which I carried out interviews, especially those in the Northern Territory, continue to be staffed by teachers coming from interstate. These schools also experience a high teacher turnover.

Demographic factors such as these have noticeable repercussions on the reputation of the school system as a white school, on the relations between the school and the local community, as well as on the content of the teaching. When an educator reflected on his teaching experience, he explained that his unfamiliarity with the local history, environment, and people was an obstacle to his teaching:

> As a starting teacher—I think the turnover of teachers in this school is quite high—it does take a long time to learn about the community. I think I came quite naively thinking I'd learn everything in six months but now I've been here a year and a half and I've learned all this stuff for this unit but I still feel like I don't know much at all.

This teacher observed that the connections the school has with its community remain weak today. Interactions between Indigenous parents and the school often come down to meeting with the principal for matters concerning students' behavior. He added,

> There is a history of political mistrust within the Australian education system when it comes to Indigenous and non-Indigenous relations, in my opinion. If you think about the ways in which Indigenous people fought in the 1970s. Their access to the mainstream school system was so low. . . . There is also this interpretation in the community that the school is a non-Indigenous school.[1]

These weak connections between the school and the community are a factor that, for some teachers, explain both why schooling remains an alienating experience for many and why some Indigenous people mistrust the school system. For many, the school system does not seem to respond to their current aspirations either, and Indigenous and non-Indigenous people have different understandings about what a non-Indigenous education offers. Despite desegregation of the school system, changes in the history curriculum and current efforts from schools to engage with Indigenous people, the continuing marginalization of Indigenous contributions, the nonrepresentativeness of the teaching staff, and the feelings of mistrust impair the relationship between many schools and local Indigenous people in Australia.

Kanaky/New Caledonia

In Kanaky/New Caledonia, teachers were for a long time largely recruited in mainland France. As one retired history teacher remembered,

> In 1977, I was the only teacher born in New Caledonia at the Poindimié High School.[2] Everyone else came from mainland France. They were skilled and dedicated to their work but they knew the local environment to a far lesser extent.[3]

According to several interviewees, until the 1990s, the territory's teaching staff was almost entirely from mainland France and most teachers held very conservative views. Such staffing and educational provision patterns received growing criticism and fed the Kanak nationalist movement. Following the 1984–1988 war, awareness grew about the importance of staffing and teacher training. In 1991 the Association of History and Geography Teachers of New Caledonia was created to help New Caledonian teachers pass competitive teaching examinations and began a trend toward developing and favoring New Caledonian teaching staff.

Today, teachers from the French mainland are appointed only when no local teacher is available to fill in the position on a two-year contract renewable for another two years. People from all backgrounds are found in the history teacher cohort, but when it comes to certified teachers, one educator explained that Kanaky/New Caledonia has at most only four or five Kanak specialist history teachers. To date, the certified teacher cohort remains mainly European.[4] In 2010, Vice

Rectorate Officer Danielle Guaenere initiated a mentorship program (*dispositif d'accompagnement aux concours*) to encourage and support Kanak people to become certified secondary school teachers. By 2016, the number of Kanak certified teachers across all disciplines in secondary schools had doubled, from twenty-nine to fifty-eight of 1,800 across the territory. They thus make up about 3.2 percent of the teaching staff, which proportion is much lower than that of Kanak people (39 percent) in the territory's population as a whole (Lassauce 2016; Perron 2016).

In both Australia and Kanaky/New Caledonia, the lack of representativeness among teaching staff remains an important issue. The difficulty of attracting potential Indigenous teachers to teaching courses is also important. Luke Pearson, an Indigenous teacher who "left the job in less time than it took [him] to get the degree," explained that no strategies were put in place by the Department of Education to ensure that, once certified and hired, Indigenous teachers would want to stay. Focus was on recruitment more than retention. During the teaching course, many "struggled to be heard within a Eurocentric curriculum and, once in the position, Indigenous teachers are given responsibility for anything relating to Indigenous people, without the adequate support and training" (Pearson 2016a). According to Luke Pearson, Indigenous representation among school teaching staff is "much more than a numbers game" and necessitates "processes of decolonising and Indigenising practices."

Teachers' Educational Background

A few teachers reported having been taught about colonial history at school. One in Australia, for instance, went through school from 1992 to 2004 and remembered learning about colonization and Indigenous perspectives. The majority of teachers in both Australia and Kanaky/New Caledonia, however, reported not learning much or even "absolutely nothing" about it. Surprisingly, whether teachers went through school decades ago or quite recently, many said they had not been taught about Indigenous-settler history. In fact, several who did their schooling in the 2000s reported not learning about it, but one who attended school in Australia in the 1960s said that she did. A young teacher recalled just having one lesson about the Myall Creek massacre in year 9. Another reported learning nothing at all about colonial conflicts and wars. Likewise, in Kanaky/New Caledonia, one early-career teacher observed that people from her generation do not know anything about New Caledonian history and or why September 24 is a public holiday.[5] Another Kanaky/New Caledonia teacher believed, however, that such educational lack is not necessarily an impediment but can also be seen as an opportunity to innovate and "not stay within old educational constraints."[6]

Considering the educational deficiencies that many teachers experienced in their primary and secondary school education, several teachers in Australia saw university as a turning point in their education. Many had never been taught about their country's colonial history, and not until they were at university were they taught otherwise. Likewise, university education seems to have played a crucial part in the raising of awareness of history teachers in Kanaky/New Caledonia. For one former history teacher, it was when she went to a "left wing" university in Paris in 1975 that she "discovered another vision of history." It was also there that, coming from an old European settler family in Kanaky/New Caledonia, she was called a "colonialist" by her fellow students. This experience made her more aware, and she decided to research land issues in Kanaky/New Caledonia at a time of growing Kanak political demands for land rights.[7]

Another important factor in teachers' educational backgrounds is family influence. A few teachers believed that their family had a significant impact on their education and their approach to understanding and teaching Indigenous-settler history. Christine Nicholls, the former teacher who worked in Warlpiri Country, admitted that her upbringing was instrumental in shaping her approach to history teaching. She said in an interview that she had acquired through her parents a sensitivity that went beyond folkloric information. She considered that "it's really the luck of the birth in a way." Conversely, for another teacher in Kanaky/New Caledonia, her grandfather's deeply colonialist view that "'Europeans came to bring civilization and history because the territory had no history" explained how she initially neglected New Caledonian history. Only after a formative university education in mainland France, moving to Pwêêdi Wiimîâ, marrying a politically active pro-independence person, and witnessing the growth of Kanak political demands "right on her doorstep" in the 1980s did she try to understand and then become involved in researching the history of the territory.[8] Yet another teacher explained that coming from a racist, anti-Kanak family who have "dug their heels in" in regard to that history and "don't necessarily have the openness to consider a more positive development," she had to shed this inheritance to approach her work more objectively. The heightened sensibility of having lived through the 1984–1988 war can be an obstacle to talking about this period.[9]

Many if not most of the teachers interviewed in both Australia and Kanaky/New Caledonia are also to some degree self-trained or have learned on the job. One primary school teacher took part in a short program in the early 2000s, outside his teaching degree course, to go to the Indigenous community of Amata for a month. This experience, he explained, reformed him as a person. Teachers reported learning by talking with people, by working with students and Elders, by traveling, by reading the media and searching the internet, during cultural events, through their political activism, and going on class field trips. A few teachers acknowledged that teaching history was also a learning process for them.

Qualifications and Training

To qualify as a secondary teacher in Australia, teachers must have completed a third-year degree level in at least one subject and have taught methodology in that subject. Nonetheless, several teachers interviewed in Australia did not have a graduate degree in history. A mismatch between teachers' educational backgrounds and their allocated teaching position is not unusual in Australian schools. Many teach outside their field in subject areas where they do not necessarily have expertise. This is especially so in "remote" country schools:

> A lot of us out here teach outside our subject areas. In larger schools, you have an English Department, a History Department, whereas here you're in a Secondary Department and we all teach either English, history, geography, visual arts, Ab[original] Studies, wood tech, food tech.

Such observation is consistent with the literature. A 2013 survey showed that about one-quarter of history teachers in Australian secondary schools were out of their field (Weldon 2016, 4). These figures vary according to the location: 21 percent in New South Wales, 32 percent in Victoria, and 40 percent in the Northern Territory (Weldon 2016, 12). A report in April 2017 also found that out-of-field teaching is far more prevalent in less affluent schools (Singhal 2017).

In comparison, the phenomenon of out-of-field teaching in Kanaky/ New Caledonia seems almost nonexistent and was not observed among the teachers interviewed. In this territory, a bachelor's degree and a certificate of primary teaching are required for a person to become a certified primary school teacher. A master's degree and the CAPES certification are required for certified secondary or high school teaching.[10] Teachers only teach in the subject in which they specialized during their university education. Several of the teachers interviewed had also earned a PhD in their field.

Australia and Kanaky/New Caledonia have very different training practices. In Australia, all teachers reported that training to teach Indigenous-settler history is lacking. Some declared that Australia's colonial history was not even taught in their teaching degree course. One teacher in the Northern Territory reported that the region she worked in organized a half-a-day induction course on Indigenous perspectives and content. She believed that "it could be included for a much longer time, like a week" and that preservice training during the undergraduate degree "can't hurt." Another primary school teacher, in Melbourne, believed that Indigenous history should be part of the mandated professional development for teachers. A former teacher and current university professor observed a problem with preservice training because students at university may only take electives about Indigenous history, cultures, and languages. As a result, many who start teaching "may have very idealistic views about certain things" and may "not actually know anything much very concrete." The same teacher believed that this is problematic because if one generation of teachers does not know about Indigenous-settler history, then "they can't pass it on to the next generation" and the students learn nothing about it. The lack of adequate education and training feeds a "conspiracy of silence" that results in transgenerational ignorance.[11] Like knowledge, ignorance is passed down from teachers to students and from parents to children. It is all the more problematic in that this lack of critical engagement with Indigenous history in university teacher preparation courses can make (especially settler) teachers race illiterate and therefore ill equipped to address racist practices in their classrooms and their teaching (Schulz 2017, 210).

Yet one teacher mentioned that international training possibilities for history teachers could be adapted and applied to the local Australian context. For instance, offers of training and research fellowship on the Holocaust for Australian teachers (which include a field trip to Germany) are advertised for history teachers. No equivalent exists for teacher training about the Australian context even though, this teacher pointed out, "we have a similar thing on our backdoor step":

> Why is there nothing in Australia where you can sign up as a teacher and get paid to learn about Indigenous history and be able to teach it in your class and in your context, and be able to communicate with Indigenous people and be able to network and find people in your community who really matter? Why does that not exist?

It seems that the questions of wars and genocide are ignored in both the history curricula and in teacher training. The same teacher, who was part of the Teach for Australia program, also remarked that the New Zealand version of the program offers an induction about Māori culture for two weeks, but that the Australian version has no comparable course.[12] A teacher in Australia suggested that despite all the good gestures made by educational institutions, real action to provide greater support for teachers is needed:

> If you want to put Aboriginal perspectives into the syllabus and curriculum, are resources available for teachers to learn that? Are teachers being given professional development around that? Are teachers being given the opportunity to go and learn about Country and learn about their local communities? Is funding available for schools to develop more resources or get local people in? Are teachers and local communities part of that local development? Are they part of those policies and frameworks? It's all good for them and it's about time that they're waking up and they're wanting perspectives in schools and wanting them to be taught, but there also needs to be greater support for teachers.

Similarly, the education scholar Nado Aveling argues that "unless teachers are properly prepared, "they are not likely to have the necessary skills to discuss racism in anything other than a perfunctory way" (2012a, 107). She therefore believes that curriculum development must be accompanied by adequate teacher training for it to be effective: "the inclusion of Aboriginal studies in the Australian curriculum is satisfying after 37 years of fighting for it, but we need to proceed ahead in the right way, which means providing teachers with the right training" (2012b, 56).

As mentioned, the teacher training situation in Kanaky/New Caledonia is markedly different from that in Australia. In the 1990s, newly certified teachers from mostly urban, European backgrounds had a three-month, in-course training as well as a compulsory teaching period of two years in the country. With this requirement, the institution attempted to better prepare teachers for the realities of the territory and improve their adaptability. A former history teacher recalled how, every year, she would also organize a trip around Kanaky/New Caledonia with her student teachers. Both their socialization and previous schooling had created a profound gap between their historical and political knowledge and the daily realities of the territory they lived in, and this trip seemed decisive in teachers' approach to their work:

> I often realized on these trips that a large part of my students, who were about twenty-two years of age on average, had never been further than Bourail.[13] In fact, they did not know their country. Even geographically speaking, they did not have a conception of what the entire island may look like. . . . not only did they not know it physically but they did not have the interpretative framework that would allow them to understand through its landscape the types of social relations, histories and diversities they encountered.[14]

The training of secondary school student teachers continues today. As an example, a few years ago on one of these regular trips, student teachers at the College of Teaching and Education (Ecole supérieure du professorat et de l'éducation) spent a week at the Tchamba tribe in Pwäräiriwâ, Ponérihouen, North Province, to better understand Kanak cultures and the social milieu of students living on tribal lands (Poigoune 2017).

Primary school student teachers have three three-week placements and are required to work in Country schools or on the islands at least once. One primary school teacher also took student teachers to the reception center of the Southern Province in Poé every year to encourage them to teach beyond the classroom and engage local communities in teaching: at Fort Teremba, they talked about convict colonization and the 1878 Kanak uprising; in Bu Rhaï, they met the local representative of the Arab community; and, closer to Nouméa, they visited various museums, cultural centers, and political institutions. The situation for teachers from mainland France going to Kanaky/New Caledonia to teach was somewhat different. They received one day of training on arrival and then "they [had] to get by on their own." In these cases, several teachers from mainland France mentioned having to fall back on history textbooks at first to find their feet.

It seems, therefore, that Kanaky/New Caledonia has gone further in developing teacher training to prepare teachers for their teaching environments and to teach colonial history. In Australia, none of the teachers reported receiving adequate training before or during their teaching. This would only be the case for older-generation teachers in Kanaky/New Caledonia. It indicates that similar trends have been observed in other settler colonial societies. For example, Wayne Ross observes in an interview with Carlo Fanelli that education reforms in the United States "include a deprofessionalization of teachers, as teaching is increasingly reduced to test preparation" (Fanelli 2015, 407). Although the teacher training landscape in Kanaky/New Caledonia differs in important ways from that of Australia, it is not immune to the effects of neoliberal education reforms and to the settler colonial agenda. Indeed, teachers often spoke of the weight of examinations as greatly steering the content of their teaching; further, these examinations often avoid aspects of the history that could be polemical or detrimental to the settler colonial polity.

One manifest characteristic of the teaching staff in both Australia and Kanaky/New Caledonia is its nonrepresentativeness. The proportion of Indigenous teachers is far smaller than the proportion of Indigenous people in either society, which reinforces the image of the public school system as white and colonial. The lack or complete absence of training on Indigenous-settler history, coupled with the phenomenon of out-of-field teaching are glaring issues in Australia. The lack of adequate education and training results in transgenerational ignorance (passed down from teachers to learners), in that teachers who are ill equipped to teach Indigenous-settler history may exclude or marginalize such content in their teaching. Although Kanaky/New Caledonia seems better off in that regard, the examinations considerably constrain the scope and emphasis that teachers can give to these aspects in their teaching.

History curricula, examinations, and teacher training are therefore critical influences on the content of what is taught. All three also drive textbook production. Textbooks are the interpretation of the curriculum by few selected historians that in turn influence interpretation by history teachers who use them. Textbooks are an important historiographical and pedagogical tool for history teachers. In some cases, they are even used by some self-taught teachers to make up for their lack of training to help them find their feet. The second part of this book delves into the production (chapter 4) and content (chapter 5) of history textbooks in Australia and Kanaky/New Caledonia.

PART II

Textbooks

Teachers' Historiographical Inheritance

CHAPTER 4

Textbook Production and Authorship

HISTORY TEACHERS ARE THE INHERITORS of a historiography that may have shaped their schooling and their subsequent teacher training and may also shape their current teaching work. In the public school system, it is used, tailored, and popularized into a most accessible, pedagogical end product and teaching tool: the history textbook. Regardless of whether and how teachers use it, the history textbook is a significant element that comes into play in teachers' historical reflections and their preparatory work, if not in their daily teaching. The format and content of history textbooks is therefore part of the teacher's historiographical inheritance.

The history textbook is an interpretation of the history curriculum by editors and textbook authors. There is power in the production of textbooks, from the initial research to the writing and publishing stages. Who are the people who have been endowed with the credentials and trustworthiness to generate official knowledge in the form of textbooks, and who are those who have not? How has this authority evolved and shifted over time, in which contexts and to what effects?

Both sociopolitical and economic factors inform authorial choices in the publication of textbooks. To understand these choices in their complexities, the evolution of textbook publishing in Australia and Kanaky/New Caledonia is a crucial parameter to take into account. Recent textbooks are inscribed and shaped by longer-term processes in textbook production and publication. Before going further in analyzing these authorial choices, it is therefore important to map the broad evolution of textbook publishing and its implication for the distribution of authorial power in textbook writing.

Australian and New Caledonian history textbooks are the product of two dissimilar approaches to publishing that have noticeable consequences for authorial choices and thus for the distribution of power within the process of knowledge creation and dissemination. The aim here is not to provide a comprehensive history of the evolution of textbook publishing but instead to follow the clues that the selected textbooks give us about the political struggles that underpin textbook production. Attention has been given to information on authors, date, place, and context of publication as indicated on the title page, acknowledgments, and preface. From the information collected in those sections, I undertook extratextual research and used data from interviews with history teachers to map the broader evolution of textbook publishing in Australia and Kanaky/New Caledonia and the power relations behind the publication of the textbooks analyzed in this book.

Power Relations in Textbook Production (I): Majority Rule and Socioeconomic Determinants in Australia

In Australia, the rapid population growth and wealth from the gold rush had created a stable market for book publishing. The introduction of free, compulsory, and secular primary education in the colonies in the 1870s and 1880s offered good prospects for the development of Australia-based textbook publication. The development of such an industry thus paralleled the introduction of government school systems. This ensured that roughly from the start Australian government schools could use locally produced textbooks on Australian history. The question of whether and how these textbooks were used in the more distant past elicits only highly speculative suppositions. The sales figures found for several of these textbooks testify nonetheless to their wide circulation in several cases.[1] The objective of this chapter, however, is not to provide a historical account of how these books were used but instead to comprehend them as the historiographical inheritance that current teachers deal with in their work, in other words, to provide a genealogy of authorial power in the school system and to understand it as a significant political legacy that shapes teachers' work.

Educational publishers were in most cases locally based or else transplanted. However, they were not small, home-grown businesses but instead the product of extensive intra-imperial and international political connections, professional networks, and investments (see table 1).

Table 1. Selected History Textbooks

Year	Publisher	Author
1877	F. F. Baillière (Government)	Clarke
1880	George Robertson	Sutherland and Sutherland
1895	Turner & Henderson	Thornton
1900	A. N. Smith	n/a
1917	Whitcombe and Tombs Limited	Murdoch
1925	Oxford University Press	Scott
1936	Rigby	n/a
1941	Melbourne University Press in association with Oxford University Press	Crawford
1950	Oxford University Press	Meston
1961	Rigby	Cawte
1977	Macmillan Company of Australia	Blackmore, Cotter, and Elliott
1986	Macmillan Company of Australia	Laidlaw
1996	Oxford University Press	Schafer
2007	John Wiley	Anderson and Low
2012(a)	Jacaranda	Darlington, Smithies, and Wood
2012(b)	Jacaranda	Darlington, Jackson, and Hawkins

Source: Author's tabulation.

The publisher Ferdinand François Baillière was a descendant of a French bookselling and publishing family and had an international network with businesses in five countries (France, England, Spain, the United States, and Australia), making his family "a multinational company ahead of their time" in the nineteenth century (Clark 2000, 13). Baillière connected with and supplied important government institutions in the 1860s and 1870s: the University of Melbourne, the Public Library (now the State Library of Victoria), and the Victorian government. Marcus Clarke, an archivist at the Public Library and "the most distinguished literary celebrity of the time" according to Laurel Clark (2000, 24), was commissioned by the Victorian Education Department to write the school history textbook *History of the Continent of Australia and the Island of Tasmania (1787 to 1870)*, which Baillière published. Publisher Edward Turner arrived in Australia in 1856 and entered into partnership with William Henderson in 1871, establishing the local firm Turner and Henderson.[2] George Robertson & Co. was one of Australia's major local publishers as well as a bookseller and importer and distributor for overseas publishing houses. He had branches in Melbourne, Sydney, Brisbane, and Adelaide. William Charles Rigby, a major publishing figure, had in his youth in London worked in a booksellers' shop alongside two others, who would become the heads of two of the largest bookselling and publishing houses in Australia: George Robertson and Samuel Mullens. Staff from universities, public archives, and publishers therefore formed a somewhat close-knit cluster of people with power and influence over the production and dissemination of educational resources. The writing and publishing of early history textbooks thus depended on positional and relational sources of power within politics, education, and the media. Further, many politicians were newspapermen (Morrison 2013, 639). Several were also involved in the production of educational materials, especially until the early twentieth century. In the selection of textbooks analyzed here, publisher Arthur Norman Smith (a leading Melbourne journalist and a founder of the Australian Journalists' Association) and textbook authors Marcus Clarke, Alexander Sutherland, Walter Murdoch (a household name for his radio broadcasts and newspaper columns), and Ernest Scott were all newspaper columnists or proprietors. These two sources of power remained salient in the first half of the twentieth century.

By this time, the selection of textbooks suggests that these continued to be authored by university professors and teachers with close connections with government officials, publishers, and media outlets. For instance, Ernest Scott worked as a journalist in London and later in Melbourne until 1895. He then became a Hansard writer, first for the parliament of Victoria, and from 1901 through 1913 for the Commonwealth parliament. In 1913, he was appointed chair of history in the University of Melbourne. Functioning within these close-knit intellectual and publishing circles, authors—based on their network and reputation—were generally commissioned by publishers or their peers to write textbooks. Raymond Max Crawford had previously taught at Sydney Grammar School, lectured in history at the University of Sydney, and later at the University of Melbourne, where he succeeded Ernest Scott in taking up the chair in history when Scott retired. Crawford coordinated a group of school teachers and scholars to produce the school textbook *Ourselves and the Pacific* (1941). Archibald Lawrence Meston, an influential educationalist, worked as a primary and then secondary school teacher in Tasmania and eventually became government education officer in charge of high schools. His textbook *A Junior History of Australia* (1950) was commissioned by Oxford University Press. Frederick George Nelson Cawte was a primary school head teacher in South Australia. Rigby commissioned him to manage an educational publishing department (Page 2006, 42).

The period between Federation and World War II was less buoyant for Australia-based publishers. Economic difficulties saw the decline of educational materials. It forced the merger of George Robertson & Co. with Mullen's successors as Robertson & Mullens, for instance. Some local publishers, such as Rigby Limited, survived nonetheless. Overseas publishers took advantage of that decline to develop and increase their share in the Australian textbook market. By the turn to the twentieth century, British and foreign publishers had progressively established a studied and well-thought infiltration and domination over the Australian publishing market that would endure for several decades. The New Zealand publishing business Whitcombe and Tombs started publishing in the 1880s and developed an intra-imperial and international network with businesses in Australia, London, and New York. They opened book-shops in the main Australian cities and published many textbooks in and for Australia, supplying textbooks to schools both wholesale and retail. For their part, British publishers benefited from the British-inspired government school systems that developed in Australia. They offered discounted books to Australian resellers such as Robertson and, later, began to establish their own local branches: Macmillan in 1905 and, a few years later in 1908 its competitor Oxford. Educational sales became a key tool in their publishing markets.[3] During the interwar and war years, and even more markedly after 1945, these foreign (mostly British) companies, which managed overseas branches at a distance from the colonial centers in Europe, became rivals with Australia-based publishing companies. Ernest Scott's *A Short History of Australia* (1925), Crawford's *The Pacific and Ourselves* (1941), and Meston's *A Junior History of Australia* (1950) were all published by Oxford's Melbourne branch.

In the second half of the twentieth century, with the postwar boom years and the considerable growth of public schooling, large educational booksellers emerged and existing ones expanded. Local publishers, such as Jacaranda Press in Brisbane and Rigby Limited in Adelaide, specialized in secondary school publishing. Textbook publishing was carried out by people with publishing and bookselling experience who contracted history teachers to write textbooks. Brian Clouston, founder of Jacaranda (the leading educational publisher in the 1960s and 1970s) recalled, "You ask around until you find out who are the 'gun teachers' and you approach them to write the textbook. It helps if they are on the syllabus committee!" (quoted in Blaxell and Drummond 2006, 317). In the 1960s, publishers began indeed to employ teachers who had worked developing curricula to oversee their educational programs. Rigby expanded into educational publishing in 1947 and saw that he could make more profit from publishing its own textbooks, which led to collaboration with Frederick Cawte on the 1961 history textbook. That publisher gained a significant share of the Australian educational market and had become the largest Australian-owned book publisher by 1977, representing 35 percent of the sales of Australian-owned publishing houses. Nonetheless, British publishers continued to secure their share of the Australian textbook market through coercive legislative methods. British publishers benefited from an open market in Australia and other dominions through British legislature and the Berne convention. With the independence of India in 1947, British publishers became wary of their overseas branches becoming independent. At the same time, they predicted that India, the subsequent newly independent nations, and the rest of the Commonwealth would provide "a vast potential market, especially for school textbooks and English-language teaching materials" (Feather 1991, 211). In response, the British Commonwealth Market Agreement of 1947, which remained in place until 1976, ensured that all members of the British Commonwealth, including Australia, remained tied to the British market (211–212). Overseas publishers, especially British and American, continued to maintain a large share of the Australian textbook publishing market.

From the 1980s, and even more so since the 2000s, the market logic has intensified. Existing literature on educational publishing identifies a shift from an editorial logic (publishing as a profession) to a market logic (competition and profitability) in the 1980s (Thornton and Ocasio 1999, 803; Powel 1985; Tebbel 1987). Patricia Thornton and William Ocasio suggest that according to editorial logic, the focus of attention is on author-editor relationships and imprints, while according to market logic, sales, marketing, and finance gain more importance (1999, 818). The brief analysis here has shown that the market logic already existed at the beginning of Australian textbook publishing in the late nineteenth century. The publishing of textbooks in this selection was entirely carried out by businesses and thus the development of an Australia-based textbook market was the fruit of thorough marketing, transport, and financial considerations. It functioned through coercive legislations, competitiveness, and extensive political intra-imperial and international networks. Intensification of the market logic benefited overseas, multinational publishers, which increased their Australian textbook market share. W. H. Blackmore and colleagues' *Landmarks* (1977) and Ronald Laidlaw's *The Land They Found* (1986) were published by the Macmillan Company of Australia, Mina Shafer and Denise Brown's *Visions of Australia* (1996) by Oxford University Press. This intensification of competition and market forces reinforced the economic determinants behind textbook production. At the turn of the twenty-first century, educational publishing was worth around $500 million in Australia—that is, about a third of the entire publishing industry (ASA 2008, 3). Today, it continues to be dominated by a few multinational publishers, such as Pearson, Macmillan, Palgrave, John Wiley & Sons, McGraw-Hill, and Oxford University Press. A few Australian publishers, such as RIC Publications, also offer textbooks but remain marginal in the educational publishing market, and once-prominent Australian publishers have been acquired by multinational publishers over the last few decades. Textbook publishing in Australia is therefore currently characterized by a small number of multinational publishers dominating the sector.

Those Who Write the Textbooks

Throughout the history of government schooling, textbook publishing has been a lucrative business that has drawn entrepreneurs seeking new publishing outlets to Australia. This has had a decisive effect on the production process and the distribution of authorial power. Initially, writers emerged from relatively close-knit academic, political, and media circles. Authorial power was later gained and maintained, up to the mid-twentieth century, through extensive political and professional networks and reputations. Although its personal dimension might have frayed since the 1970s and 1980s and new marketing techniques, textbook production has changed little over time. Manuscripts continue to be acquired primarily by acquisition. Multinational publishers continue to prefer contracting history teachers with a scholarly reputation and, preferably, involved in curriculum development. Authors of the

2007 textbook *History 2,* for instance, are history teachers involved in curriculum and teacher development. Maureen Anderson has taught history for more than twenty-five years and has contributed to syllabus writing for the New South Wales Board of Studies and taught within the Teacher Education Program at Macquarie University. Anne Low has also taught history, as well as English, for more than a quarter century and has worked on secondment to Training and Development for the Department of Education.

Contracting textbook authors is intended to be financially strategic and viable rather than intellectually and politically reforming. Regardless of political evolutions within Australian society—that is the desegregation of schools, Indigenous resurgence since the 1960s, challenges to the dominant settler historical narrative, and the increasing number of Indigenous educators in the school systems—the continuity of market-oriented textbook production techniques has indeed created fairly consistent patterns in authorial power. As a result, the profile of textbook authors has remained consistent and the historical narratives disseminated in textbooks have been exclusively crafted by settlers.[4] These textbooks are either authored by a single author or by no more than four. All textbooks in this selection, it seems, are the product of settler authority and control rather than consultation and collaboration between settlers and Indigenous people. According to my personal communication with educators, it seems that, to date, no school history textbook for core history subjects (until year 10) has been authored or coauthored by an Indigenous teacher or historian. Textbook authors are also characterized by their uniformity in terms of gender identity. Authors are mostly male, though this has changed in the last couple of decades, with an increasing number of female authors.

In terms of textbook authorship, the settler domination has scarcely been challenged, and no considerable shift in power relations between settlers and Indigenous people seems evident. Interviews with history teachers reveal that in many cases this political rigidity goes hand in hand with intellectual rigidity. A former school teacher commissioned to write primary school textbooks for Macmillan education recalled that bringing reforming ideas into the content "was a struggle":

> The books didn't turn out the way I'd have wanted them to turn out because I just had to stop arguing at some point. . . . At least

I pushed to include something about Indigenous language diversity and people and so on.

In her case, the editors were primary school teachers who had been hired to do the editing job at Macmillan. Alexandra Sauvage, in her analysis of 1990s school textbooks, points out that "interpretations of the history curriculum remain in the hands of the publishing houses and the writers of the school textbooks, neither of whom are obliged to work in cooperation with Indigenous historians" (2010, 289–290). One teacher explained that

> Editors are just former primary school teachers who have got a job at Macmillan as editors. Some of them are actually more enlightened than others. But this one just wouldn't budge from what was an old racist discourse in a way. . . . one in particular just had the hegemonic view, the colonial mindset if you like about Australian history that it was all European and you put little frills on it and the frills are the Aboriginal history.

One contentious point was the editor's insistence on writing that "Captain Cook discovered Australia." The textbook author struggled to challenge the concept of discovery:

> That's when I had to fight and say . . . "Look, if you don't let me do this I'm gonna pull out" and that was near the end. . . . It takes some time for people to have that paradigm shift and they didn't get it.

Having that paradigm shift or challenging hegemonic views may be even more fraught when the economic determinants of textbook publishing do not necessarily make these a priority. Several history teachers shared their skepticism as to whether such intellectual and political shifts (in terms of textbook content and authorship) could be expected in the current publishing context. Interviewees often perceived textbooks as the product of economic pragmatism rather than of a rigorous historical inquiry. A history teacher in Shepparton saw economic imperatives as a major factor behind the persistence of a hegemonic narrative in textbooks: "I find that all widely available Indigenous-themed resources tend to be relatively generic because that's the economics of it. They're designed for as big a market as possible."[5] Considering these economic determinants, textbook publishing in Australia is determined by the majority rule, according to which settler history teachers remain the de facto go-to practitioners for textbook writing, and the dominant, simplistic historical narrative the easiest one to adopt. This argument, however, should not neglect that although economics determine many authorial choices, one teacher said, it is highly probable that the resulting exclusion of Indigenous authors is also supported by racist and colonial attitudes.

This majority rule also affects the targeted audience. A close reading of textbooks reveals how assumptions are made about their readership. Stylistic choices (such as the use of the pronouns we and they) reflect assumptions made by authors about who their readers are. The phrasing of several textbooks assumes explicitly a settler We (author + reader) and a non-Indigenous Other. For instance, in an explanation about perspective-taking in a recent textbook, authors instruct that "to find primary evidence about what it is like to be an Indigenous Australian, *we* must consult Indigenous people" (Darlington, Jackson, and Hawkins 2012, 118, emphasis added). In some cases, authors assume not only who the reader is but also how that reader thinks, such as about the reader's being a settler and holding views in favor of Australia Day celebrations: "Australia's national day, Australia Day, is celebrated each year on 26 January. What do we celebrate? Why might Indigenous Australians object to celebrating what this day commemorates?" (Darlington, Smithies, and Wood 2012, 121).

The economic determinants and the majority rule that have shaped the production of textbooks in Australia have resulted in textbooks remaining fairly impervious to broader dissemination or transferals of authorial power. Indigenous people are neglected both as potential authors and as readers. Thus the historical and political relations between Indigenous people and settlers in Australian textbooks remain and, to a large extent, narrated by settlers and for settlers.

Power Relations in Textbook Production (II): Conflicts and Consensual Politics in Kanaky/New Caledonia

The production of textbooks in Kanaky/New Caledonia reflects distinct concerns and patterns. This is partly related to the political development of the territory. Until the 1990s, history textbooks for use in government schools were those used in schools on the French mainland, produced in mainland France, and intended for a mainland France audience. Interviewed history teachers who went through school before the 1990s remembered learning about the history of the French mainland exclusively. The education of both settler and Indigenous students in government schools in Kanaky/New Caledonia was thus characterized by an incompatibility between the location of the knowledge learned at school and the local environment of the teachers and students. Until the 1980s, hardly any history teaching materials were local, and none was accredited by government. Teachers and students could use French textbooks only. In 1975, the local Association of Historical Studies published an unofficial textbook, but it was not until the early 1990s that the first government-sanctioned textbook adapted to the New Caledonian context was published.

The war in the 1980s dramatically accelerated that reforming process. War established that Kanak voices could no longer be ignored. As curricula changed, local educational institutions undertook a reform of history textbooks. Unlike textbook publishing in Australia, publication in Kanaky/New Caledonia has been supervised, funded, and published by a public educational institution: the Territorial Center for Pedagogical Research and Development (Centre territorial de recherche et développement pédagogique), later renamed the Center for Pedagogical Documentation of New Caledonia (Centre de documentation pédagogique de Nouvelle-Calédonie). Textbook publishing therefore does not abide by market logic but is the fruit of a consensual work between various institutional actors. To date, three history textbooks relevant to this analysis (on postcolonization New Caledonian history) have been published, in 1992, 2007, and 2010.

Reflecting this politics of consensus and the French textbook writing tradition of group authorship, textbooks are written by a large number of authors—between seventeen and twenty-six practitioners—and the historical narratives disseminated are the result of collaboration between settler and Kanak historians, particularly in the 1992 and 2010 textbooks. The proportion of Kanak authors (15 percent at the most across the textbooks) remains smaller than the proportion of Kanak people to the territory's total population (39 percent), however. This can be explained by political reasons as well as by the fact that very few trained historians in Kanaky/New Caledonia are Kanak. As to the ratio per gender, the male overrepresentation in authorship is less marked than in Australia, although for the 1992 and 2007 textbooks only about one-third of authors are female. The 2010 textbook, however, involves a majority of female authors. The 1992 textbook—the first to be published following the peace agreements and the implementation of a reconciliation process—gathers authors from various backgrounds and with varied political affiliations (for and against independence). A participant in the writing process explained:

> There was this willingness to work together, to overcome the trauma. . . . There was a large majority in favour of the Matignon Agreements. This consensus on achieving the objectives of these agreements was reflected in the willingness to coordinate the writing of this textbook.[6]

According to another textbook author, Frédéric Angleviel, the New Caledonian textbooks "managed to get things straight about long-known facts" and an emerging Caledonian historical school was "taking the heat off the debate to make it progress better" (Wénéhoua 1996, 32). The production of New Caledonian textbooks has indeed been presented as a process of handling and taming passions to achieve understanding and agreement. The process was based on the idea that emotions are detrimental to political relations and to consensus.

Based on this politics of consensus, the writing of textbook chapters was assigned to teachers according to their skills and expertise. The willingness authors demonstrated to abide by consensual practices throughout the writing process has been considered unquestionable, as several history teachers, either involved or not in the writing process, have testified: "Resources were the product of a consensus and I know that everything, every single word was negotiated."[7] This consensual process has influenced the content of textbooks. For instance, assumptions about readership of the kind found in Australian textbooks could not be found in New Caledonian. This may be explained by the large and mixed authorship involved in the writing process as well as the demographics of New Caledonian society: half of the student population to whom these textbooks are targeted is Kanak. Nonetheless, the historical narrative is not necessarily always unifying.

By the time the 2007 textbook was being written, it was much more difficult to gather this ethnic and political diversity around the production of a textbook. A few Kanak people took part in the production, but in the translation process, not the writing stage.[8] Indeed, several authors who had participated in the 1992 textbook pulled out for either personal or political reasons. In 2004, the loyalist movement had split and underlying divergences became more apparent. As to the pro-independence authors, they pulled out of the writing part of the process but remained involved in the reviewing. One interpreted this decision as one taken on epistemological grounds: "For them it remains a white way of doing things. It remains a historical narrative they cannot identify with, a narrative that does not meet their expectations."[9] Some perceived that the way that consensual process took place, although laudable for being a precursor, has led to a diluted historical narrative: "Is one angle more prevalent? I would say that when there is a consensus, if you keep mixing water with wine, eventually wine has become water."[10] Consultation between Kanak people and settlers remains a complex undertaking, and the crafting of a historical narrative for New Caledonian textbooks is met with skepticism and evasion from different sections of the population as well as from the institutions. According to the teachers interviewed, the lack of adequate resources remains an issue. The project of publishing new textbooks adapted to New Caledonian history seems to have been dropped around the time of the retreat of Indigenous-settler history in the curriculum around 2012. Teachers and textbook authors who were working on writing a new textbook at the time saw its publication aborted. Some history teachers and authors petitioned the government and met with local politicians to oppose the decision—in vain. The suspension of textbook production may in this case be a most effective mechanism perpetuating these settler regimes of ignorance about Indigenous-settler history.

Australia and Kanaky/New Caledonia have therefore followed dissimilar patterns in the evolution of textbook production. The economic determinants underpinning textbook publishing in Australia have maintained a consistent settler authorial power. In Kanaky/New Caledonia, however, the political urgency triggered by the 1984–1988 war called for a reformation of history teaching based on consensus politics and supported by government-funded textbook publishing.

Indigenous-Settler History in Textbooks

In his 1968 Boyer lecture "The Great Australian Silence," W.E.H. Stanner made a partial survey of history books written between 1939 and 1955 that fail to mention Indigenous people. He denounced the absence, in several books, of the history of contact and conflicts between Indigenous and non-Indigenous people, in his words, "the unacknowledged relations between two racial groups within a single field of life," an absence he notoriously named "the great Australian silence" (1991, 25). He identified the establishment of this silence as "what may well have begun as a simple forgetting of other possible views" and which "turned under habit and over time into something like a cult of forgetfulness practised on a national scale" (1974, 24–25). Stanner's notion has had a seminal impact on Australian historiography and political life. Later historians expanded his observation to encompass the whole of the late nineteenth century to pre-1960s Australian historiography.[11] This notion grew from an observation about a limited historiographical sample into a general viewpoint over Australian historiography.

Based on the sample of textbooks analyzed in this chapter, however, it seems that the evolution of historical writing is more complex. The story of Australian historiography shifting from one that largely accounts for a peaceful settlement to one that addresses the contacts and conflicts between Indigenous people and settlers "has become a little too simple" (Curthoys 2008, 235). The historian Ann Curthoys suggests that

> it is precisely because the metaphor is so striking that the too-simple narrative . . . has taken hold. Too often it is taken to imply a kind of historiographical periodisation where there was no Aboriginal history before Stanner's own lecture and an end to the silence after it. Neither half of this statement is quite true: there was neither complete silence before 1968, nor was it completely ended afterwards. (2008, 247)

The historian Mark McKenna also challenges the assumption that the great Australian silence had been ended and observes that "the struggle to end the silence is ongoing" (2002, 94). The historian Mitchell Rolls also observes in his article "Why Didn't You Listen: White Noise and Black History" that

> if attention is cast beyond the body of literature that Stanner surveyed his metaphor loses much sense of its general applicability. With a singular but important exception—that being the

absence of Aboriginal voices in the telling of their histories—it becomes apparent that what he noticed was obscured from view through one particular "window" was clearly visible through others. (2010, 14)

Findings from my research corroborate such nuances to the manifestation and periodization of the great Australian silence and build on these works. Findings show that all textbooks in this sample mention Indigenous people. The space dedicated to Indigenous-settler history has remained in the lowest quartile, oscillating between 7 and 25 percent of Australian history.[12] These textbooks were popular works, several of them going through many editions and authored by renowned historians of the time. Several are in fact mentioned by historians who have revived the term "great Australian silence." For instance, in "Breaking of the Australian Silence," Henry Reynolds quotes the preface of Murdoch's 1917 textbook *The Making of Australia* in which Murdoch advises his readers that the book tells the history of white settlers but leaves out pre-colonial Indigenous history. Reynolds concludes that this "captured the national mood" of the twentieth-century great Australian silence "phenomenon" (1984, 1–2). Yet the index of that book shows Aboriginal people mentioned on six pages, and my reading of the entire book found them mentioned on thirty-six of 238 pages. In *Why Weren't We Told?*, Reynolds briefly comments on Ernest Scott's *A Short History of Australia*. Reynolds calculates that Scott mentions Indigenous people "four times in all—three times just in passing," and once in "a brief discussion which ran to about two pages of a book of 376 pages" (1999, 16). Reynolds does not mention the edition on which he bases his observation. The one I studied, from 1925, contains 363 pages, twenty-eight of which mention (admittedly mostly in passing) Indigenous people. In the period of the supposed great Australian silence, the textbook with the least content on Indigenous-settler history is Crawford's *Ourselves and the Pacific* (1941), only six pages. The most "prolific" mention Indigenous people on more than thirty pages (1917, 1925, and 1936). The continuing marginalization of Indigenous-settler history in textbooks suggests how slow and insufficient the move away from the metaphorical "anthropological footnote" has been (La Nauze 1959). The account of Indigenous-settler history in recent textbooks is much more detailed, but these textbooks continue to articulate a white-settler-centered historical narrative that confines Indigenous people to specific chapters or units and therefore positions them at the margins of the history of their own land.

Admittedly, the content of early twentieth-century textbooks is more limited and runs only a few lines. More substantial content, when it appears, should not be confused with being "progressive." A most telling example is that Indigenous people, as contributors, have been excluded throughout the sample. The settler monopoly in that specific form of historiography still needs to be eroded. Yet, regardless of how small, exclusive, and biased the content on Indigenous-settler history is in these textbooks, such content should not be overlooked because it could provide evidence of the ways that colonial power articulated knowledge at the time and could reveal continuities with current enunciations of Indigenous-settler history. It is therefore important to not take the notion of the great Australian silence literally, to engage in a more systematic analysis of the actual textbook archive, and to avoid the pitfall of ignoring some colonial enunciations that did indeed exist.

The "Moonless Night" and Beyond in Kanaky/New Caledonia

New Caledonian historians and institutions took a long time to develop local history textbooks. It was not until the escalation of the pro-independence movement for Kanak sovereignty, which posed a consequential threat to the French government and New Caledonian settler society, that a local production of school history textbooks on New Caledonian history began. This was in the early 1990s. This lack of teaching materials led Kanak and Socialist National Liberation Front Minister Léopold Jorédié to declare—on a note somewhat similar to the "great Australian silence"—that the history of the Kanak people had remained "a moonless night" for the French people.[13] He observed,

> If throughout his schooling the young Kanak has learnt to know France through its history and geography, on the contrary, the history of the Kanak people has remained a moonless night for French people, except for a dozen Western historians and anthropologists. (quoted in Coulon 1985, 15)

As Jorédié observes, it is difficult to find French school history textbooks (which were those in use in Kanaky/New Caledonia before the production of local history textbooks) that even mention Kanak people. I carried out a search in the Territorial archives and the Tjibaou Cultural Centre in Kanaky/New Caledonia as well as in the two largest textbook archives of France, in Rouen and Lyon. I looked for French textbooks with some New Caledonian content published before the 1990s that *might* have been used in New Caledonia. I found New Caledonian content only in geography textbooks and not in history textbooks. Further, according to the teachers I interviewed, a history textbook series widely used in Kanaky/New Caledonia for several decades was Ernest Lavisse's history textbooks.[14] The editions I randomly selected (of 1913 and 1942) briefly mention the French colonies in Africa and Indochina but do not mention the Pacific and therefore omit Kanaky/New Caledonia entirely.

With the move to produce history textbooks locally in the 1990s, however, the space dedicated to Indigenous-settler history increased greatly. About 70 percent of New Caledonian history is dedicated to Indigenous-settler history in the three history textbooks that make up the New Caledonian sample.[15] The space that New Caledonian textbooks dedicate to Indigenous-settler history is in marked contrast to the Australian textbooks. Nevertheless, these findings show that as a product of a settler colonial institution inherited from colonialism, textbooks articulate a historical narrative that continues to be driven from a European settler vantage point, despite the fact that the European settler population remains a minority of the larger one (about 30 percent).

Who Has Been Telling the Story?

Trends in authorial power outlined in this chapter have given us the first hint of the textbooks' narrating voice or voices. As mentioned, authorship of textbooks in Australia is characterized by settler exclusiveness and relative gender uniformity. No Indigenous author seems to have been involved in the writing of any of the Australian textbooks, and textbook authors are mostly male (a recent increase in the number of female authors notwithstanding). By contrast, New Caledonian textbooks are characterized by greater collaboration between settler and Kanak authors as well as between male and female authors. Identifying textbook authors is key to our understanding of the standpoint or standpoints adopted in a textbook's narrative. Yet the picture would not be complete without looking at the sources these authors draw on to illustrate and complement the narrative they construct. Australian textbooks until the 1970s included settler sources or accounts exclusively.[16] This erasure of Indigeneity began to be addressed beginning in the late 1980s with the gradual inclusion of Indigenous perspectives in textbooks. In the selection of textbooks analyzed here, the first to include Indigenous perspectives was W. H. Blackmore and colleague's *Landmarks* in 1977. In textbooks that do include Indigenous accounts, the proportion of sources by an Indigenous author ranges between 11 and 13 percent.[17] The proportion has changed little over the last four decades (more or less 1 percent). The narrative of Indigenous-settler history is therefore largely supported and illustrated by settler accounts.

This imbalance in the sources is acknowledged. A recent textbook notes, for instance, that "Most of our written sources for these events, including official reports, diaries, letters and newspaper articles, derive from the colonisers. This means that for many events we have heard only one side of the story" (Darlington, Smithies, and Wood 2012, 122). Similarly, the teachers interviewed observed a continuing imbalance between settler and Indigenous accounts in the textbooks that are available to them, and that settler perspectives prevail. Considering that the teachers I interviewed did not necessarily have access to the same textbooks I analyze here, and in light of their observations, it does seem plausible that the findings from this sample are fairly representative of a more general trend in the content of Australian history textbooks, which greatly marginalizes Indigenous voices. Not only are accounts of Indigenous-settler history largely settler accounts, but the settler accounts are exclusively European or Anglo-Australian.

In Kanaky/New Caledonia, all history textbooks in the sample include Indigenous accounts. The proportion of sources by Kanak authors fluctuates between 5 percent (1992) and 19 percent (2010). The latest textbook (2010) shows a sharp increase relative to the previous ones. Indeed, the proportion almost tripled from 2007 (7 percent) and almost quadrupled relative to 1992. Nevertheless, the proportion of Kanak sources remains significantly lower than that of settler sources. Like their Australian counterparts, history teachers in Kanaky/New Caledonia were aware of this disparity and observed that textbooks provide mostly a European point of view and that very few are Indigenous accounts. Similarly, a teacher educator admitted that the colonial period continues to be taught "from the perspectives of the Europeans essentially" because "we mostly have sources from either the settlers or the colonial administration. We have very few things on the Kanak perspectives." In addition, and akin to Australian textbooks, New Caledonian textbooks do not include non-European settler sources about Indigenous-settler history. Some teachers observed that Indigenous-settler history is mostly based on European settler accounts and Kanak accounts and that non-European settler accounts are "missing tremendously."[18]

In both Australian and New Caledonian textbooks, Indigenous-settler history remains largely told and illustrated with sources taken from the European colonizer's side of the equation. Further, in comparing the Australian sample with that of Kanaky/New Caledonia, the similarities are striking. In the 1990s, 2000s, and 2010s—the three Australian textbooks in the Australian sample (1996, 2007, and 2012) relative to the three in the New Caledonian sample (1992, 2007, and 2010)—the proportion of Indigenous sources in Australian and New Caledonian textbooks are relatively similar. In the 1990s and 2000s, Australian textbooks include in fact more Indigenous sources (12 percent and 13 percent) than the New Caledonian textbooks do (5 percent and 7 percent). In the 2010s, the trend has reversed, 19 percent for the New Caledonian textbook and 12 percent for the Australian. Such findings are particularly striking when considering the tremendous demographical differences between these two societies. Although the percentage of Kanak people to the entire population of Kanaky/New Caledonia is about fourteen times higher than that of Aboriginal and Torres Strait Island peoples to the population of Australia, the marginalization of Indigenous sources in Australian and New Caledonian textbooks is comparable. These similarities may reflect a straightforward dynamic of domination: the greater the threat of being challenged (a larger colonized population), the stronger the colonial hold. In other words, the louder and larger the voices challenging the dominant narrative are, the more they are silenced.

One must be cautious, nonetheless, not to cast the argument in deterministic terms and assume that certain social positions will inevitably lead to certain epistemic positions. The decolonial thinker Ramón Grosfoguel argues that "it is important here to distinguish the 'epistemic location' from the 'social location.'" That one is socially located in the oppressed side of power relations does not automatically mean that they are thinking epistemically from an anticolonial epistemic location. Grosfoguel explains that "precisely, the success of the modern/colonial world-system consists in making subjects that are socially located in the oppressed side of the colonial difference, to think epistemically like the ones on the dominant positions" (2007, 213). Likewise, a teacher in Kanaky/New Caledonia noted in an interview that it is not necessarily because authors of sources are settlers that they occupy a colonial epistemic position as well. It seems, however, impossible to potentially decolonize the historical narrative without more prominent Indigenous viewpoints and epistemologies. In any case, the historical narratives of textbooks remain, for now, socially discriminatory.

Australia and Kanaky/New Caledonia have followed dissimilar patterns in the evolution of textbook production. The economic determinants in Australia have maintained a somewhat consistent settler authorial power. In Kanaky/New Caledonia, however, the political urgency triggered by the 1984–1988 war called for a reformation of history teaching based on consensus politics and supported by government-funded textbook publishing. These positions notwithstanding, processes in both societies have been fraught. Whether operating through the rule of the majority or consensus, settler colonial power has proved its plasticity. In both Australia and New Caledonia, the space and position of enunciation in textbooks continue to draw a settler colonial center and Indigenous margins. Power relations seem difficult to shift, and the production and content of textbooks has not gone uncritiqued or uncriticized. Teachers respond to that historiographical inheritance differently in their work. The next chapter unpacks that historiographical inheritance further and analyzes the content of Australian and New Caledonian textbooks to better identify what is at stake and to attend to the historical narratives and stereotyping endemic to the textbooks.

CHAPTER 5

Textbook Narratives and Stereotyping

THE HISTORIOGRAPHY PERTAINING to Indigenous-settler relations continues to be subject to debate in today's settler colonial societies. It is marked by issues of power and stereotyping. Stereotypes are generalized (and often erroneous) claims about an individual or a group, attributing to them specific characteristics and emotions. In defining these individuals and groups this way, these stereotypes become constitutive elements of power relations. Stereotyping entails a relation between the person producing or reproducing the stereotype and the person who is stereotyped. Stereotypes "exert control through prejudice and discrimination" and result from asymmetrical power relations (Fiske 1993, 621). These stereotypes invest us in social-political norms and positions. Meanwhile, the processes through which they are produced, circulated, and repeated are erased.

This chapter attempts to make these processes visible by undertaking an analysis of stereotyping in school history textbooks. What is at stake here is not whether or the extent to which these stereotypes are accurate, but instead the kinds of identities and power relations they create. I am therefore interested in identities based on politics rather than politics based on identity. This chapter focuses on the construction and articulation of certain identity categories that make it easy to think about Indigenous-settler history and legitimate settler colonialism.

In her analysis of power and stereotyping, Susan Fiske identifies two types of stereotypes: descriptive and prescriptive. The descriptive stereotype "tells how most people in the group supposedly behave, what they allegedly prefer, and where their competence supposedly lies." The prescriptive stereotype is even more explicitly controlling. It "purportedly tells how certain groups should think, feel, and behave." In other words, it is the emotional projection of one group toward another. Fiske concludes that "the descriptive aspect of stereotypes acts as an anchor, and the prescriptive aspect of stereotypes acts as a fence" (1993, 623).

Fiske's metaphors of the anchor and the fence provide a helpful analytical model of stereotyping for a content analysis of textbooks. Taken from a political angle, it enables us to identify the sociopolitical categorization and emotional projection at play in textbooks' narrative of Indigenous-settler history. How do political categories emerge? What are these categories? Who inhabits these categories? How do these categories relate to one another? How does this stereotyping affect what those who are thus categorized are purportedly saying? Do stereotypes act more like an anchor or a fence, or both? This chapter addresses these questions. It undertakes a long-term analysis of Australian and New Caledonian history textbooks to render visible patterns of enunciation and to understand their powerful premises. As mentioned, this long-term analysis covers different but overlapping time frames in Australia (1870s to the present) and Kanaky/New Caledonia (1990s to the present). As a result, the Australian sample comprises sixteen textbooks and the New Caledonian sample only three. This chapter therefore and logically dedicates more space to Australian textbooks.

Undertaking such a long-term analysis presupposes that Indigenous-settler history appears in the historical narrative of the selected textbooks across the period. A major finding is indeed the presence of Indigenous people and colonial wars and violence in Australian textbooks across the sample. It challenges one fundamental tenet of the Australian historiography, namely, the great Australian silence theory. It also sheds light on settler colonial epistemological logics largely overlooked so far. The structure of this chapter follows three principles I identify as characterizing the enunciation of Indigenous-settler history in Australian and New Caledonian history textbooks and as strategic to settler colonial legitimacy: externalization of colonial violence, fixed categorization, and co-opting.

Externalized Violence

Violent conflict between Indigenous people and settlers is externalized in its treatment in textbooks, its place in discourse, moral distancing, and the nature of the narrative.

Textbook Framing

The textbooks in Australia and Kanaky/New Caledonia do not shy away from addressing conflict between settlers and Indigenous peoples, and have done so from the late nineteenth century forward.

Australia. Although the period in Australia was generally characterized by a triumphalist nationalistic narrative of colonial history, historians nonetheless engaged with the questions of colonial violence. Colonial conflicts are depicted in all textbooks but one, that of 1941. Several record mentions of conflicts between twenty and forty times. Compared with other types of relations, violent conflicts are in fact the most common characteristic defining Indigenous-settler relations across all the textbooks, except for that in 1941. Such findings invalidate the invasion and massacre denialists—often identified as conservative historians and politicians upholding the "white blindfold history" (Ferrier 1999)—who consider current historiographical concerns about massacres to be a skewed interpretation of the past with contemporary eyes and a "fabrication" of history (Windschuttle 2002). Colonial violence has always been the most common characteristic of Indigenous-settler relations in Australian textbooks.

That accounts of colonial violence have coexisted with a range of political agendas is not a contradiction but instead reflects the fundamental malleability of settler colonialism and its capacity to constantly redefine its contours while concealing its inner workings. It seems judicious when attempting to identify these inner workings to ask the following questions: How has colonial violence been accounted for in textbooks? What mechanisms have enabled textbook authors to acknowledge colonial violence without destabilizing the settler colonial polity's legitimacy?

Although one could assume that earlier authors might have used more euphemistic terminology to describe colonial violence, no major shift in the language is evident. Throughout the period under examination, textbook authors have often preferred a "neutral" ter-minology (crime, attack, kill) to "lighter" (trouble, incident) or "more loaded" (war, massacre). Only a few textbooks suggest that European invasion did not meet with considerable Indigenous resistance. In addition to the 1941 textbook that does not even mention colonial conflicts, the 1900 textbook describes Indigenous people as relatively passive in the face of European colonization. Some authors also miss entire areas when reporting conflicts. Instances of textbooks failing to mention colonial conflicts or largely minimizing Indigenous resistance do exist, such as in 1900, 1936, 1941, and 1961. This suggests that, in textbooks, marginalizing colonial violence by using a racist, national-istic discourse was more acute in the period several authors identify as "the great Australian silence." Yet several other early twentieth-century textbook authors, such as Walter Murdoch (in 1917), Ernest Scott (in 1925), and Archibald Meston (in 1950), mentioned Indigenous-settler violence with less subtlety, in a manner usually more characteristic of mid- to late nineteenth-century textbook writers.

Several early textbooks do mention Indigenous resistance to European-led colonization, well before the revision of Australian history in the late twentieth century. An earlier textbook records Indigenous people's tactics of resistance, settlers' protective measures and self-train-ing in the handling of arms to counter the resistance on the mainland:

> Frequently, the aboriginal tribes united to attack the lonely farm-house and murder all its inhabitants. Hence, every settler in the country districts was well supplied with arms, and taught all his household to use them; the walls were pierced here and there with holes, through which a musket might be directed in safety against an advancing enemy. (Sutherland and Sutherland 1880, 40)

An even earlier textbook, the earliest one in this sample, accounts for resistance in Tasmania, where "reprisals by settlers and natives became numerous" and often ended in massacres (Clarke 1877, 76–77). Several history textbooks portray an extent of death and casualties, depth, inten-tions, and impact akin to genocide, though they do not use the word. Marcus Clarke records conflicts between Indigenous people and settlers in 1790, 1797, 1798, 1815, 1816, 1829, 1830, 1831, 1835, and 1836. He also records the "Black Line" as a policy akin to a military attack:[1]

Every settler was called upon to take up arms, and grants of land were promised to those who should do good service. A chain of military post was to be made across the island, the advancing forces were to drive the natives before them . . . the country was declared under martial law, and the Governor in person reviewed the little army. (77)

Clarke mentions forces of five thousand men armed with a thousand muskets, thirty thousand rounds of cartridge, and three hundred pairs of handcuffs (77). Considering the number of men and the amount of ammunition deployed, settlers' intentions can hardly be misinterpreted. Forty years later, Walter Murdoch attributed the large decrease in the Indigenous population in Tasmania to settler violence and spoke as well of the brutality of settlers in Queensland:

If a full and true account of the whole matter were ever written, it would make a very unpleasant book, a book which no one with British blood in his veins, and humane instincts in his heart, could read without feelings of shame. (1917, 176)

These early textbooks mention settlers' intent to eliminate Indigenous people and report an escalation of violence. In the 1920s, Ernest Scott argued that "no form of physical torture and moral wrong was spared" (1925, 169) and mentioned that "as settlement spread, cases of murder and outrage were frequently reported. The evidence is conclusive that the wrong-doing was on the side of the whites" (168). In response, Indigenous people resisted. Scott noted that "it was but natural that the aboriginals should at length turn upon their oppressors," but because settlers had more lethal weapons, Indigenous people "were shot in groups, as they bathed or sat round their camp-fires at night" (169). As invasion—and therefore Indigenous resistance—intensified, several authors told of free settlers—not convicts—killing Indigenous people. Practices of poisoning Indigenous people were also mentioned:

To pretend to be friendly, and in the guise of friendship to give presents of food containing deadly poison, was an act of treachery which was all too common, and for which our utmost ingenuity can find no excuse. (Murdoch 1917, 230)

Similarly, a few years later, Scott recorded the "sheer brutality and treacherous murder" that settlers committed. Governor Brisbane, he wrote, "permitted the shooting of aboriginals in batches" and "the lowest depth of mean homicide was reached by some settlers who systematically gave natives arsenic in wheaten cakes, porridge, or other food. They murdered under the guise of kindness." He also noted that "poisoning was undoubtedly one cause of the decrease of the aboriginals" (1925, 184–185).

In the decades that followed, conflicts were recorded as being more sporadic. Only from the 1990s onward did the idea of sustained conflict between Indigenous people and settlers reemerge. A 2007 textbook mentions that the Gunditjmara people "resisted European pastoral expansion by launching *guerrilla raids on settlers over several years*" (Anderson and Low 2007, 16, emphasis added). In their 2012 textbook, Robert Darlington, Graham Smithies, and Ashley Wood explain that "as Europeans spread into more distant parts of Western Australia, resistance grew and violent clashes continued *for almost a hundred years*" (143, emphasis added). These conflicts, however, are told from a particular angle without losing sight of the political stakes and with the objective of sustaining settler legitimacy. The most straightforward way this legitimation is achieved is dominance of settler sources on colonial conflicts. Sources on Indigenous-settler conflicts provide exclusively settler perspectives. Australian textbooks do not include any textual or iconographical sources made by an Indigenous person about Indigenous-settler wars and conflicts.

Kanaky/New Caledonia. In New Caledonian textbooks, colonial conflicts between Indigenous people and settlers are also widely mentioned, totaling between sixty and seventy occurrences for the 1992 and 2007 textbook. The comparatively far lesser number in the 2010 textbook (one occurrence only) is explained by its format, which makes more room for historical sources and provides only an introductory paragraph in each section as a historical narrative. In New Caledonian textbooks as well, conflicts are the most common characteristic of Indigenous-settler relations. Likewise, colonial violence is mainly described in "neutral" and "light" terms. The large-scale, systematic, and brutal forms of colonial violence are not addressed to the same extent. The violence of colonization is in some cases brushed over. Colonization is reported as a diplomatic and bureaucratic formality. Kanak chiefs are depicted signing the document stipulating that France has taken possession of the territory, implying that French sovereignty was from the outset easily accepted by Kanak people:

> [Febvrier Despointes] organised at Balade, on September 24, in company of missionaries and the local chiefs the official ceremony of taking possession . . . he explored the country and made several chiefs sign an act recognising French sovereignty and a code legislating the country's laws and customs. (Angleviel et al. 1992, 45)

In other areas, however, the process faced some resistance and when the diplomatic negotiations did not yield any results, the logic of conquest is put forward:

> French sovereignty was not always easily accepted. . . . In the region of Balade, chief Thiangoune was opposed to French presence . . . The real conquest needed to be carried out. (Angleviel et al. 1992, 45)

Dispossession is articulated as being a point of view, a perception rather than a historical fact. Frédéric Angleviel, Christiane Douyère, and Bernard Capecchi, for instance, say that "the expansion of land colonisation led to the opposition of some Indigenous chiefs who *felt* dispossessed of their land" (1992, 47, emphasis added). Further, the violence "necessary" to colonize Kanak clans is not problematized. For example, no mention is made of the military mobile columns that crossed the island to systematically and swiftly repress dissent or of the beheading of Kanak chiefs.

In addition, Kanak-settler conflicts are told from a European-settler angle and with the objective of sustaining settler legitimacy. New Caledonian textbooks do not include any Kanak iconographical sources on Indigenous-settler conflicts. These sources, however, do exist.[2] The latest New Caledonian textbook includes only one Kanak written source on Kanak-settler wars and conflicts, the testimony of Joseph Karie Bwarat from Hienghène on the 1917 war (Debien Vanmai and Lextreyt 2010, 35). It is also the only textbook providing a Kanak perspective on these conflicts.

This easily identifiable exclusionary practice aside, authors of Australian and New Caledonian textbooks also use (consciously or

unconsciously) epistemological strategies. That is, specific ways of presenting colonial violence and wars sustain settler legitimacy regardless
of the extent, form, and degree of violence acknowledged in textbooks.
I suggest that these strategies are racialist discourse (in Australian textbooks exclusively), self-distantiation, and dualistic historical narrative.
These last two strategies may be more palatable to today's reader than
earlier racialist discourse but are no less insidious in sustaining settler
legitimacy.

Racialist Discourse

Settler legitimacy is sustained in a racialist and racist discourse about
the superiority and necessity of settler colonization and the perceived
inferiority and needy quality of Indigenous people. This epistemological strategy is used in Australian textbooks from the late nineteenth
century and well into the twentieth, gradually fading away from the
1960s to the 1980s.[3] Although some authors (such as the *South Australia
History Reader*) report a supposedly logical "passing" or extinction of
Indigenous people, several authors—such as Marcus Clarke (1877) and
Walter Murdoch (1917)—account for the elimination of Indigenous
people by the number and intensity of violent conflicts and the supposed superiority of the "white race." The tone is not condemnatory
but instead reflects the scientific zeal of the time for racialist doctrines:

> The story of the gradual suppression of the aboriginal races of
> the Australian continent is full of interest. All over the world it
> has been found that where the white man takes possession of a
> country inhabited by black men, the blacks either sink into slav-
> ery or become extinct. The original inhabitants of Australia are
> not strong enough, either in muscle or in mind, to endure the
> restraints of civilisation; and as civilisation advances so the unci-
> vilised tribes die out. (Clarke 1877, 76–77)

Colonization is legitimized by the purported superiority of European
settlers. On other occasions, authors mention the inability of Indigenous
people to adapt to civilization. The narrative blames Indigenous people
themselves, and their supposed primitiveness, for their intended extinction at the hand of the settlers (Scott 1925, 184–185). These authors
wrote at a time when the Indigenous population of Australia had been

declining dramatically following the European-led colonization of their land, a demographic decline they interpreted as a validation of their racialist ideologies. These ideologies, which buttressed the settlers' self-assured legitimacy, often led to concessions on the part of the authors about the treatment of Indigenous people that are not necessarily found in recent textbooks. Early textbooks reference settlers' exploitation, ill-treatment, and killings of Indigenous people. In these accounts, it is not uncommon for authors to write of the brutality of settlers toward Indigenous people: "their retaliation oftentimes exhibited a feroc-ity and inhumanity almost incredible in civilized men" (Sutherland and Sutherland 1880, 131). Conflicts between settlers and Indigenous people in the early days of the European invasion of Queensland are recorded as follows:

> In Queensland—to the shame of our race be it said—atrocities hardly less fiendish were committed by free settlers, men who prided themselves on being clear of any taint of convictism. The settlers treated the natives as if they had been venomous snakes, which must be killed off before the country could be considered safe. (Murdoch 1917, 229)

Early textbooks often mention the savagery of the violence European settlers inflicted, the atrocities and summary vengeance they commit-ted, and the extent to which settlers had dehumanized Indigenous people in their minds. Settlers are often depicted as willfully initiating conflicts and, by their cruelties, driving Indigenous people to desperate acts (Thornton 1895, 152; 1900, 80; Murdoch 1917, 229).

Yet, according to textbook authors, the circumstantial savagery of settlers (which lies in the fearsome context of the colonial front) never surpasses the invented structural savagery of Indigenous people (which, they believed, was rooted in their biological characteristics). Thus the brutality of Aboriginal troopers for instance, when mentioned, surpasses that of settlers. Murdoch described the native police as "a mere machine for murder" (1917, 229); in doing so, he followed several of his prede-cessors who contended that "the most inhuman atrocities were commit-ted by blacks, who were employed to act as troopers" (Sutherland and Sutherland 1880, 136).

In early textbooks, conflicts are described as mostly taking place between settlers (rather than the government) and Indigenous people.

Until the 1950s, settlers are predominantly portrayed in textbooks as isolated, fearful, weak, and in danger, and Indigenous people as hostile, savage, treacherous, and troublesome. Colonial violence is excused by settlers' fear for their lives. Early textbooks represent colonial violence as inevitable and necessary to settlers' survival. The general sense of acceptance was that it was in the order of things.

Violence and massacres are therefore mentioned in textbooks. Contrary to what may be expected, the political context of the late nineteenth to early twentieth century, which condoned racialist and racist attitudes, produced a spectrum of the politically permissible in historical narrative perhaps somewhat wider than in the decades that followed and carved a place for accounts of colonial violence. Concessions were made concerning the cruelty of settlers toward Indigenous people, the widespread state of warfare and the intent of elimination, probably because textbook authors felt that less was at stake politically. Murdoch concluded in his account of colonial violence that "beyond all doubt, the white man's treatment of the black in Queensland was a crime against humanity" (1917, 230). Earlier textbook authors reported that colonial violence was widespread and known to many, as stories of massacres circulated from people to people and in the press. Murdoch wrote that "the hideous stories told by *The Queenslander* provoked fierce discussion; and men were not ashamed to defend the policy of extermination" (230).

In the following decades, however, conflicts were recorded as being more sporadic. They were represented in less racist but more subtle and vague ways. With evolutions in both world politics (condemnation of Nazism and eugenic practices, movements for decolonization) and Australian politics (demographic rise of Indigenous people, sustained and stronger activism, changes in ethnic composition of the population), the configurations of power relations changed. As a result, the boundaries of political correctness shifted, and racialist discourse and practices were drawn into question. The changes in the 1960s through 1980s were not so much a shift from "discovery and settlement" to "invasion" as suggested elsewhere (Attwood 2000, 255), but instead an epistemological shift away from racialist discourses. This does not mean that racism faded away or that it was more acceptable and widespread previously than it is now. Instead, the way that racism was woven through the historical narrative changed form. Changes in popular attitudes as well as political correctness redrew the contours of the question, and another epistemological strategy came to the fore to sustain settler legitimacy: self-distantiation.

Self-Distantiation

Colonial violence is distanced both temporally and morally in textbooks. This strategy has been used in textbooks across the sample but became more apparent when the racialist discourse was on the wane. It consists of morally distancing violence from the settlers. Colonial violence is, for instance, attributed to people of lower rank and with lower morals. Textbook authors often mention convicts as the perpetrators of the worst atrocities, a way of absolving free settlers.

Australia. In 1917, Murdoch suggested that soldiers and convicts—especially escaped convicts—"behaved like cruel and savage beasts of prey" and that in Tasmania "the worst atrocities were committed for the most part, by bushrangers and escaped convicts, the scum of the white population" (173, 229). A 2012 textbook reads that "most new arrivals were uneducated convicts and soldiers who probably feared the people whose land they had entered." Killings are mostly attributed to "gangs of escaped convicts" and squatters, and government official policy is one of conciliation (Darlington, Jackson, and Hawkins 2012, 126–132).

Alternatively, textbooks frame frontier conflicts as peripheral phenomena enacted by squatters and settlers in distant regions of the country, and beyond government control. The colonial "frontier"—marked by an absence of government control—enables the settler polity to produce a space within the boundaries of the state, yet beyond its jurisdiction. The concept of the frontier "translates the ongoing institutional exceptionalization" (Rifkin 2014, 176). Paradoxically, the inability of the settler government to produce effective surveillance and control over their population is a condition of its legitimacy.

Those involved in colonial crimes are also differentiated from the wider settler population, and settler governments are portrayed as good natured and well meaning:

> We should remember, however, that the great majority of Australians have always been against any ill-treatment of the blacks, and that some noble efforts have been made to protect them against the barbarities of civilised man. (Murdoch 1917, 176)

In the 1977 textbook, the massacre of Indigenous people in Tasmania is attributed to convicts and sealers; government officials are depicted as go-betweens, trying to appease (Blackmore, Cotter, and Elliott 1977, 56). Following conflicts, governments are portrayed in textbooks as benevolent, addressing the issue and solving the situation. That strategy of self-distantiation has been observed in other settler colonial contexts by Paulette Regan, who notes that sustaining "a comfortable intellectual, psychological, and emotional distance from the harsh realities that the system engendered enables us to retain an identity of well-intentioned, human citizens—benevolent peacemakers" (2010, 42).

Settler legitimacy is further maintained by a "good intentions/unexpected bad outcome" discourse. Several more recent textbooks suggest that although government policies may have been detrimental to Indigenous people, their intentions were morally good. When the supposedly benevolent government measures fail, the blame is more readily placed on the purported inadaptability of Indigenous people than on the values underpinning these policies (Shafer 1996, 29; Darlington, Jackson, and Hawkins 2012, 122). This discourse of benevolent settler population or government also sustains the fantasy that remedying issues is mostly a matter of making concerns known to the wider society, in other words, that political change will inevitably come from acquiring greater knowledge. Textbooks imply that as soon as it has entered popular awareness, settler benevolence changes the situation for the better. The 2012 textbook states that "growing awareness of human rights issues, specifically relating to racial discrimination, was beginning to turn the tide for Indigenous people in Australia. All the issue needed, it seemed, was a voice" (Darlington, Jackson, and Hawkins. 2012, 10). The textbook accounts for this change, this "voice," through the person of Charles Perkins. Such accounts further silence Indigenous agency by implying that before the 1960s, Indigenous people did not have a voice or use available media to articulate their claims. Having a voice and being heard are two different things.

Colonial violence is also positioned as distant in time and contrasted with the supposed fairer present: "Slowly, the lifestyle inequities Australia's first people have suffered are being changed" (Darlington, Jackson, and Hawkins 2012, 146). According to the modern linear narrative of progress, the present always transcends (and therefore absolves itself from) past injustices. Margaret Wetherell suggests that this results in an attitude whereby "accounts which most effectively justify the status quo flexibly stress the continuity of good and the discontinuity of evil" (1992, 185). Likewise, as Walter Mignolo suggests, "modernity is not a period of universal history but a European fiction to describe its own present and justify its own imperial future" (2013, 107).

In more recent textbooks, colonial violence is blamed less on settler savagery (as it was in early textbooks) and is instead framed in terms of cultural clash and incommensurability between Indigenous people and settlers. At the risk of exaggerating, making settlers more ignorant and Indigenous cultures more obscure, authors such as Robert Darlington, Graham Smithies, and Ashley Wood mention that early settlers did not comprehend Indigenous people's relation to both the human and more-than-human environment: "The seeds of conflict were sown soon after the first colonists arrived because the British authorities had no understanding of the relations between Aboriginal peoples and their land" (2012, 124). On another occasion, they contend that "these Europeans [uneducated convicts and soldiers] could not understand Aboriginal kinship systems or why they did not behave like Europeans and have farms, towns and churches" (126). Recent representations of settlers' attitudes toward Indigenous people contrast quite starkly with early accounts. Settler moral responsibility is evaded by shifting the context of colonial violence from the political to the cultural.

Kanaky/New Caledonia. In New Caledonian textbooks, colonial violence is also distanced both temporally and morally. Colonial conflicts such as the 1878 and 1917 Kanak uprisings and their repression are explained, and the 2007 and 2010 textbooks mention that the country was in a situation of war in the 1980s. Past injustices and the colonial roots of conflicts are acknowledged and, in some cases, detailed. However, as in Australian textbooks, settler legitimacy is sustained by a modern narrative of progress that depicts government actions and reforms as overcoming colonial conflicts. In the 2007 textbook authors explain that, following the 1917 war, "inspectors for the Ministry of the Colonies made an inventory of the causes of the movement, and the state would take measures to prevent it from happening again" (Jacquier, Amiot, and Terrier 2007, 105). Institutional reforms transcend past colonial injustices and therefore absolve the settler polity. The historical narrative in the 2012 textbook transitions from the situation of war in the 1980s and Kanak claims for independence to peace agreements and closing the gap policies. As Glen Coulthard argues, following conflicts, reconciliatory policies often translate into a reinforcement of settler power, as the state puts itself back "in the position where it offers some sort of recognition and gestures toward reconciliation again" (quoted in Epstein 2015). The focus is therefore on the supposed continuity of good (political initiatives and reforms to address discriminations and integrate Kanak people and cultures better) and the discontinuity of evil (colonial injustices and armed conflicts).

Dualistic Narrative

A third epistemic strategy used in textbooks in the accounts of colonial violence is the production of a dualistic narrative.

Australia. In Australia, especially since the History Wars, the narrative of Indigenous-settler history in textbooks has developed around a simplistic articulation of two standpoints: an Indigenous view of history and a white settler view. The first focuses on colonial violence, genocide, and injustices and the second on the narrative of progress of the Australian nation. In other words, it presents colonization as both beneficial and detrimental. Readers are prompted to "analyse how colonisation contributed to Australia's social, political and cultural development" and also to "evaluate the impact of colonisation on Indigenous communities and the fight for rights" (Anderson and Low 2007, 2). According to that dualistic historical narrative, Indigenous people are predominantly ascribed negative emotions and settlers are accorded positive ones. The most recent Australian textbook, for instance, records the 1938 Australia Day as being for settlers a day to celebrate and for Indigenous people a day of mourning (Darlington, Jackson, and Hawkins 2012, 120). Recent textbooks articulate a historical narrative that sits on the fence without necessarily providing greater critical thinking about the workings of colonialism and the practical implications for Indigenous-settler relations.

Kanaky/New Caledonia. New Caledonian textbooks also create a dualistic narrative of colonial, Indigenous-settler history. Whereas Australian textbooks are trying to keep a foot in both camps of the History Wars, New Caledonian books conform scrupulously to the reconciliatory dogma of "the common destiny." Since the 1998 Nouméa Agreement, New Caledonian textbooks reuse the Agreement preamble and speak of the "shadows" and the "lights" of colonial history. New Caledonian history is articulated in a morally ambivalent way between negative and positive opposites. Arguments in textbooks have moved from the benefit of coming and colonizing (bringing civilization, the fallacious claim of opening the territory to the rest of the world) to the benefit of staying on (bringing development and addressing colonial wrongs and injustices). This is articulated in New Caledonian textbooks with mentions of policies of "rebalancing" or closing the gap, projects of economic developments and the "evolution of democratic institutions" (Jacquier, Amiot, and Terrier 2007, 147–151; Debien Vanmai and Lextreyt 2010, 88, 97). Settler colonialism is supported by the idea of a double gain-benefit: that of the colonizer and that of the colonized, what Manuela Semidei calls "the two sides of the colonial argumentation" (1966, 59). The violence of colonial wars is counterbalanced with the technological "modernization" of colonized territories. Colonial history is articulated in such a way that "modernity redeems violence" (Hannoum 2010, 2). This is an epistemological strategy observed in other settler colonial contexts. Abdelmajid Hannoum speaks, for instance, of the violence of modern texts that form one side of modern violence in colonial Algeria, the other being the violence of modern armaments (2010, 8).

Thus colonial violence is presented by way of these three epistemological strategies: racialist discourse (in Australian textbooks exclusively), self-distantiation, and dualistic narrative. These strategies enable settler colonialism to coexist in a variety of contexts and with changing political agendas. These processes externalize colonial violence from the settler colonial society and polity to inscribe its legitimacy. This externalization lies in the creation of fixed political categories that tap into and feed the reconfiguration of power relations that sustain settler colonialism. The next section focuses on these categories, their political function, and the way they operate.

Fixed Categorization

Both settlers and Indigenous people are presented as fixed categories in textbooks with scant mention of relation and reciprocity between them.

Affirming the Center

Settlers are an exclusive category in textbooks. Akin to the history curricula content, the Indigenous-settler history in Australian and New

Caledonian textbooks is exclusively a history between European settlers and Indigenous people. The relations between Indigenous people and non-European settlers are not addressed. Each are represented in relation to the settler government. European settlers are characterized by their pervasive and dominant presence, which reasserts the Europe-inherited core of the settler colonial polity. For instance, in Australian textbooks, Chinese and Pacific Island people are mentioned across the selection but are represented—like other non-European settlers—solely in relation to the settler colonial power (the colony and, since federation, the nation-state). In textbooks, they exist in parallel—similarities are often drawn between their respective experiences of racism and discrimination by European settlers—but they hardly, if at all, interact. The 2012 year 9 textbook notes, for instance, that "Aboriginal people suffered greatly because of racist attitudes, and so did Chinese diggers. In the late nineteenth century, many white Australians also showed hostility to other non-Europeans, including Pacific Islanders" (Darlington, Smithies, and Wood 2012, 150). In the visual text, only two sources across the Australian textbook sample present Indigenous people and non-European settlers together. One is a drawing depicting the common discrimination they face under the White Australia Policy (Meston 1950, 115) and the other a photograph of the interfaith memorial service to commemorate the tenth anniversary of the September 11 attacks, with William Barton, Sheikh Dr. Mohammed Anas, Cardinal George Pell, and Rabbi Jeremy Lawrence (Darlington, Jackson, and Hawkins 2012, 187). As in the written text, Indigenous people and non-European settlers are again portrayed side by side, each in relation to the settler colonial polity.

Similarly, in New Caledonian textbooks, the settler category is composed of Europeans and, only on very rare occasions, of non-European settlers. Non-European settlers are portrayed in relation to the settler polity rather than to Kanak people. In the few instances where Kanak and non-European settlers are drawn together in the narrative, the latter are portrayed as economic competition to Kanak people, coworkers in their dominated position, or as allies to European settlers against the Kanak resistance (Angleviel, Douyère, and Capecchi 1992, 71, 81, 87). Non-European settlers are also mentioned side by side with Kanak people in two specific contexts: as deported convicts and as farm workers for white settlers (Jacquier, Amiot, and Terrier 2007, 96; Debien Vanmai and Lextreyt 2010, 27). Like the Australian textbooks, they bring together non-European settlers and Indigenous people within a logic of domination only, which reinforces settlers as the nexus of all social-political relations.

In addition to being white settler-centered, the narratives of the textbooks are also androcentric. In Australian textbooks, only one settler woman is ever named in the sample, and on one occasion only: Pauline Hanson, founder and leader of the far right One Nation Party, in the 2012 textbook (Darlington, Jackson, and Hawkins 2012, 138). In New Caledonian textbooks, no settler woman is ever mentioned.[4] The settler category is therefore almost exclusively male European settlers.

Textbooks also fail to record the diversity of settlers in terms of their experience of and position in regard to colonialism. In fact, settlers remain relatively emotionally unproblematized and unproblematic actors in textbooks. Settlers are largely defined with self-constituted characteristics, being predominantly characterized as farming and exploiting the land, bringing "civilization," development, and progress. The 2007 and 2012 textbooks, however, start to problematize settlers' emotive agency and raise, for the first time in the Australian textbook sample, the issue of racism. Yet such occurrences in textbooks focus on attitudes and policies before the 1970s (that is, the Stolen Generation, the racism faced by 1965 Freedom Riders in Australian country towns) and feed off the myth that racism was once more widespread or acceptable, and that it is now marginal or nonexistent.

A similar trend is visible in New Caledonian textbooks as well, where settlers are mostly defined in terms of farming, as bringing development and progress, opening up the territory through communication and trade, and bringing modernity.[5] Settlers' emotive agency and the issue of racism, for instance, are not raised in the New Caledonian sample. Across these textbooks, settlers are almost entirely defined with self-constituted characteristics. They are therefore characterized by their contemporary emotive and relational invisibility.

The Colonial Difference

Unlike the relatively consistent patterns in settler stereotypes, those of Indigenous people since colonization have changed substantially over time in Australian textbooks. Yet a similar trend across the description of settlers and Indigenous people is the marginal place given to women. In the sample textbooks, until the 1980s, the only Indigenous woman named is the nineteenth-century Truganini, a Tasmanian. Later text-books mention Indigenous female artists, athletes, activists, and so on—Cathy Freeman, Kath Walker, and Shirley Smith. Although Indigenous women fare better than their settler counterparts, they are mentioned only sporadically relative to Indigenous men.

In earlier textbooks, terms such as "natives" or "blacks" were used as catch-all categories that obscured the diversity of Indigenous people and nations and inscribed their constructed biological, social, and therefore political inferiority. The coloniality of power, Aníbal Quijano explains, was conceived together with, and buttressed by, the logics of race that classified the colonized and the colonizers as dominated and dominant. Political domination under European colonialism was mutated "in a relationship of biologically and structurally superior and inferior" (2007, 171). Decades later, Indigenous people reappropriated the term "Black" as a powerful rhetoric of Indigenous anticolonial unification and tool for the negotiation of their political rights and role. The meaning behind the use of the terms "white" and "Black" remains blurry in more recent textbooks, however. Is it referring back to a racialist categorization or to reappropriated terminology fed by Black consciousness and white critical theory? Indigenous people are also increasingly portrayed as heterogeneous groups and individuals. Nation, country, clan, and individual names have been increasingly mentioned in textbooks since the 1980s.

Until the 1980s, Indigenous people were portrayed as hostile, troublesome, and treacherous to European settlers, but eventually dying out. Indigenous people were presented as antagonists, obstacles to the European occupation of the continent. Indigenous people were for a long time depicted as heading toward extinction or assimilation. Despite the Indigenous population's taking an upward curve again from the 1930s, that the narrative of the projected extinction of Indigenous people was sustained in sample textbooks until the 1980s reflects the political fantasy of "completed settler sovereignty" and colonial completion through Indigenous elimination (Strakosch 2016, 21).[6] At the same time that Indigenous people are portrayed as adversarial and politically distinct, they are also portrayed as dying out. In other words, political distinctiveness or independence as an alternative to inclusion within settler colonial power is presented as nonviable. It reflects the "mechanism of extinguishment of political difference" that Elizabeth Strakosch observes in settler governments' responses to Indigenous land rights claims (2016, 20).

We then, however, notice a shift around the 1980s. By the time Indigenous people stop being portrayed as dying out, the main definitions of the Indigenous entity exclusively reflect relations of political and emotional dependency. Indigenous people are defined in terms of loss, as discriminated against, fighting for their rights and recognition, experiencing pain or suffering. Textbooks mention, for instance, the discrimination Indigenous people faced in the legal system (which did not allow them to testify about massacres in law courts), the discrimination that Indigenous soldiers faced during and after World War II, the segregation of public spaces, the lack of civil rights, and racism.

This marked shift before and since the 1980s in the depiction of Indigenous people can be interpreted in several ways. I suggest that it reflects a shift in enunciation from political distinctiveness and opposition to dependency relations. In both cases, the resulting configuration of power remains largely unchanged and maintains settler colonial control. The fantasy of extinction of Aboriginal sovereignty shifts from being a narrative of Indigenous people dying out to one now articulating Indigenous difference in terms of loss and disadvantage. Indigenous political difference is now absorbed into settler colonial sovereignty through policies of redress and social justice. It is a social and political difference to be overcome. The settler colonial state continues "to seek to dissolve Indigenous political difference" (Strakosch 2016, 20). In this attempt of dissolution, colonialism remains the only defining element for Indigenous people, who are exclusively framed in terms of resistance to and consequences of settler power. As Taiaiake Alfred explains, "there is a danger in allowing colonization to be the only story of Indigenous lives. . . . it limits the freedom of the colonized by framing all movement as acts of resistance or outcomes of Settler power." As a result, these strategies "offer Indigenous people only one option: dependency or destruction" (2013).

Likewise, in New Caledonian textbooks, Kanak people are predominantly described as being discriminated against and experiencing loss, acculturation, and trauma. New Caledonian textbooks mention, for instance, land dispossession, leading to acculturation, despair, and social deviance:

> the sociological and psychological crisis provoked by the loss of ancestral lands and the social and economic marginalisation of Indigenous people. This moral and social distress translated into

growing alcoholism, desperate actions and by a decrease of the birth rate. (Jacquier, Amiot, and Terrier 2007, 103)

Nonetheless, Kanak people are also portrayed as benefiting from or being compensated for colonization, as having strong culture and traditions. Indigenous cultures are portrayed as markers of distinctive identity within a settler colonial-national paradigm, of colonial difference. The old colonial tropes of irreducible cultural difference reemerge in the portrayal of Indigenous cultures as quintessentially in opposition to modernity and development.

This cultural difference translates into an emotive representation of Indigenous people around the notions of loss and lack. These notions are embedded in a modern temporal trajectory, articulated around three evolutionary stages: before (the precolonial, traditions), the between (a supposedly transitional phase between traditions and modernity, characterized by the experience of loss, discriminatory practices, and the struggle to overcome them), and after (a phase where equity and rights have been won). The notion of loss may include the loss of land and resources, of precolonial diplomatic and trade practices, the loss of cultures, people, spirituality, and dignity. In the 1996 textbook *Visions of Australia,* for instance, loss is represented as inherent to contemporary articulations and part of what it means to be Indigenous:

> Many had lost vital connections with their culture, land and spirituality. . . . The Aboriginal community generally began to acquire a new identity which recognised a common identity of European invasion and dispossession, which formed a basis for a new national Aboriginal identity. (Shafer 1996, 33)

This emotive emphasis on loss is the result of, first, traumatic experiences of colonization and dispossession; second, contemporary rejections of Indigenous claims to land and the unchallengeable legal and political superiority of settler frameworks that perpetuate dispossession and impart an added sense of loss; and, third, the persistence of the colonial notion of cultural authenticity (Shafer 1996, 37; Anderson and Low 2007, 210; Darlington, Jackson, and Hawkins 2012, 134, 138).

Another prominent characteristic attributed to Indigenous people is that of lack. Lack is characterized in textbooks by a precolonial Indigenous world that has frayed away and by an equality and equity between settlers and Indigenous people not yet attained. Indigenous people are largely defined against settler standards as lacking civil rights, experiencing social and economic inequities, and fighting for justice. Taken together, loss and lack assign Indigenous people to a fundamentally fixed, between position. Settlers and Indigenous people are accorded distinct emotive places.

Emotions are more markedly associated with Indigenous people in textbooks. They are depicted as experiencing loss, acculturation, trauma, and suffering. Scholar Sara Ahmed contends that "it is significant that the word 'passion' and the word 'passive' share the same root in the Latin word for 'suffering' (*passio*)." To be passive is to be enacted upon, to be shaped by others, to be reactive rather than active, dependent rather than autonomous (2014, 2, 3). Thus even when Indigenous people are overwhelmingly depicted as fighting for their rights and for justice, they are intrinsically represented as reactive (reacting to unjust policies) and shaped by others (the settler colonial polity that deprives them of their rights and justice). Representations of Indigenous people depend on their relations with settlers. The opposite is not the case. Settlers are largely represented with self-constituted characteristics as independent historical and political actors.

Absence of Reciprocity

Indigenous people and settlers remain fixed categories in the way that they are constituted and the way they relate to each other. In fact, at the social level, reciprocity and sexual activity between Indigenous people and settlers are little mentioned in textbooks. They therefore are largely nonporous categories. People of both Indigenous and settler descent are mentioned only sixteen times across the Australian sample (only two of which are before the twenty-first century). In the New Caledonian sample, they are mentioned four times, twice in the 1992 and 2007 textbook, respectively. The fact that the logic of colonialism rests on the elimination of reciprocity is not addressed. Neither are the ways that relationships between these groups was regulated and controlled by government institutions. For instance, in New Caledonian textbooks, intermarriage is not mentioned. Conversely, little if any reference is made to the widespread abduction and rape of Indigenous women in both Australia and Kanaky/New Caledonia. The rape of many Indigenous domestic servants while working for settler families is not acknowledged in a frank manner. For instance, a 2012 Australian textbook mentions, in passing, that "once in domestic service, many girls became pregnant" (Darlington, Jackson, and Hawkins 2012, 123). This strategy silences further discussion on the exploitative character of colonialism. The question of the forced removal of Aboriginal children from their families, the Stolen Generation, has been little addressed until recently. A noted exception is Scott's brief reference in 1925, which quotes Lieutenant Colonel Thomas Davey's denunciation of "a most barbarous and inhuman mode of proceeding, viz. the robbing of their children":

> Let any man put his hand to his heart and ask, which is the savage, the white man who robs the parent of his children, or the black man who boldly steps forward to resent the injury and recover his stolen offspring. (1925, 168)

Recent textbooks present the Stolen Generation as past policies (Anderson and Low 2007, 220), when the actual number of Indigenous children in out-of-home care in Australia has never been so high and has led to a "new Stolen Generation."

Another key aspect that may tell us more about the absence of reciprocity in textbooks is the narrative of settlers living or staying with Indigenous people. The fixed nature of Indigenous and settler categories is further enforced, and the colonial difference drawn, in the narrative of settlers interacting within an Indigenous sociality and spatiality. None of the New Caledonian textbooks mentions settlers living with Kanak people. Contact and relations always take place in the settler sociality. In the Australian context, references to this aspect of relations are more prominent in early textbooks and have been almost completely silenced in later ones.

In the case of these early narratives of settlers living with Indigenous people, the latter are represented as benevolent and determinant in the survival of settlers on their expeditions across the continent. This is important, inasmuch as a shift occurs in the power relations: the settlers become the dependent and Indigenous people those with knowledge and authority. It presents a settler figure in an Indigenous milieu. Yet this alternative to the settler colonial sociality and spatiality is debased and presented as strange, alien, and backward. The figure of William Buckley, for instance, racialized and falling into savagery after living with the Wathaurong people for more than thirty years is a recurrent theme in early textbooks (Clarke 1877, 26; Sutherland and Sutherland 1880, 70). Settler promiscuity with Indigenous people is portrayed as morally and intellectually degrading, which translates into the rejection of Indigenous people, sociality, and promiscuity (Thornton 1895, 96–97). In later textbooks, life within Indigenous sociality continues to be portrayed as impractical and undesirable (Scott 1925, 233; Meston 1950, 78). Until the 1986 textbook—which is the latest substantial narrative of settlers living with Indigenous people—these settlers are portrayed as savage. After this textbook, this aspect of Indigenous-settler relations is removed from the narrative. In Maureen Anderson and Anne Low's volume, the story of William Buckley is mentioned only in the activities section (2007, 27). Thus Indigenous sociality is first rejected by racist discourses and then by the outright silence of instances of Indigenous-settler interaction in an Indigenous milieu and under Indigenous authority. In textbooks, Indigenous people are in a double bind, where they should either be similar (and therefore disappear through assimilation) or are condemned to remain so different that their credentials to offer possible alternatives to settler colonial society and settler sociality are not acknowledged.

Thus Indigenous people and settlers remain two deeply fixed categories in the ways that they are constituted and the ways they relate to each other. The historical narrative in textbooks "immobilises peoples" (Veracini 2011b, 207). I have suggested thus far that the stereotyping of these relations is carried out through strategies of externalization and fixed categorization. Another key strategy used to sustain settler colonial power is co-opting.

Strategic Co-Opting

The strategy of co-opting consists of positioning Indigenous people as early migrants and settlers within the settler national narrative in order to assimilate them into the dominant colonial, modern project.

Indigenous People as First Settlers

The strategy of co-opting, which is more markedly present in Australian textbooks from the 1970s and 1980s forward, emerged at a time when, in the face of demographic realities, renewed confrontational protestations by Indigenous people and political recognition (the 1967 referendum) the idea of a future extinction of Indigenous people could no longer be sustained. The contemporaneity of Indigenous people and cultures could no longer be so flagrantly denied and was thus integrated into the national narrative and framed in terms of a presumed "settler society continuum," which supports the settler colonial polity and the linear modern framework. Similarity is conferred on Indigenous people as the precursors of this continuum. Settlers are defined as "the new inhabitants" and Indigenous people as "the old inhabitants," the "first immigrants," "settlers," or "explorers" (Blackmore 1977, 174; Schafer 1996, 44; Darlington et al. 2012, 110). A 1977 textbook states that "the first settlers arrived in Australia some 31,000 years ago" (Blackmore, Cotter, and Elliott 1977, 174). Two decades later, another textbook declares that "the Australian Aboriginal were the first people to discover the Australian continent. They began to settle in Australia about 75,000 years ago" (Schafer 1996, 44). Indigenous people are redefined to fit the settler colonial project. They are integrated into a colonial narrative according to which European colonization is the continuation of early migrations and settlements by Indigenous people and marks the culmination of human settlement and progress. Existing literature suggests that the repositioning of Indigenous people as early settlers on this long "settler society continuum" is not specific to Australia. The education scholar Dolores Calderón, for instance, makes a similar observation with regard to the positioning of Native Americans in US social studies textbooks:

> US history curricula have tended to frame Indigenous peoples as immigrants in order to co-opt Indigenous presence as an extension of settler nationalism. Additionally, history texts that rely on the triumph of "science"-based explanations as a key narrative device, reframe American Indians as a part of a larger immigrant-nation identity. (2014, 30)

The relationship between Indigenous people and settlers is linear. The short moment of recognition of Indigenous people by settlers is "a moment of conferral." In that moment, Indigenous people "pass the mantle of belonging to the land to the settler" (Rose 2004, 117). This co-opting of Indigenous presence as an extension of settler colonialism legitimates colonization. The narrative of modernity found in textbooks is an epistemological frame that is bound to colonialism and that works to reaffirm the settler colonial authority. In his critique of modernity and colonialism, Aníbal Quijano observes that history is conceived as an "evolutionary continuum from the primitive to the civilized; from the traditional to the modern; from the savage to the rational; from pro-capitalism to capitalism" (2007, 176). Within this continuum, settlers are the latest, advanced form of that history. This continuum remains the standard framework of the historical narrative in textbooks.

In Australian and New Caledonian history textbooks, a linear conception of time alongside stories of human progress prevails, creating a distinction between the old and the new, traditions and modernity, Indigenous and settlers. The structure of recent textbooks itself sustains this linear modern trajectory wherein Indigenous people and cultures are assigned to premodernity. Textbooks usually thread the historical narrative around the concept of progress: the colonial beginnings, the birth, challenges (wars and social movements), and the triumph of the settler colonial society (that is, political stability and opening to the world through trade). Such a narrative sustains a chronological (rather than structural) understanding of colonialism; in Australian textbooks, it confines Indigenous presence to sections on precolonial Australia (often the standard opening chapter), colonial contacts, social movements, land rights, and reconciliation or closing the gap. New Caledonian textbooks explain and frame the evolution of Indigenous-settler history as inequalities, struggle for rights, armed struggle, peace agreements, and reconciliation toward a "common destiny."

Reconciliation as Assimilation

Current representations that suggest that Indigenous-settler relations will eventually be framed by reconciliation also operate within a linear historical interpretation and assimilatory framework. Reconciliation discourses in textbooks have maintained the modern European colonial framework that sets the settler colonial concept of progress as the standard against which Indigenous people are assessed. Bruce McGuinness and Denis Walker liken the tendency to judge according to modern colonial standards of assimilation when they contend that "White people have the arrogant attitude of saying that their way of life, the white, western, straight-line way of thinking of how reality should be described is the only one. And this has in turn forced black people to conform" (1985, 50). In recent Australian textbooks, Indigenous people are represented, on the one hand, as being "behind," "lesser," negatively "different," and, on the other, as achievers or exceptions. Such representations entrench stereotypical representations of Indigenous people as either disadvantaged or as achievers or exceptions along the modern trajectory, and entrench a narrative of Us versus Them, making people who cross these boundaries difficult to account for. Although no one doubts that living conditions that deprive human beings of their dignity should be addressed, representations articulated and positioned according to a modern framework of progress tend to address the symptoms rather than the roots of the problem.

In addition, within this reconciliation framework, political relations between Indigenous people and settlers, both past and present, are narrowly defined. For instance, the textbooks analyzed for this research often exclude the US Black Power–inspired form of Indigenous activism that emerged in the 1960s. Although the Tent Embassy and the Freedom Ride are well documented in recent textbooks, these actions are presented as solely a demand for emancipation and equal citizenship rights within the Australian nation rather than a demand for liberation from ongoing colonialism. The Indigenous social movements of the 1960s and 1970s are likened to the US civil rights movement led by Martin Luther King Jr. rather than to the Black Power movement (Anderson and Low 2007). When the affiliation of many Australian Indigenous activists to Black Power ideologies is presented in textbooks, the loudest challenges to the settler colonial polity that many activists called for are omitted from the narrative. As Lorenzo Veracini observes, in settler colonial contexts, a "narrative gap contributes crucially to the invisibility of anti-colonial struggles" (2011b, 209). The Indigenous fight for sovereignty and the activism of the Black Power era are recast in textbooks as the democratization of civil rights to Indigenous people. Reviewing the year 10 component of the curriculum on "Rights and Freedoms," Gary Foley and Elizabeth Muldoon argue that "the fundamental problem is that this depth study characterises all Indigenous political struggle as a fight for civil rights, contrary to overwhelming historical evidence" (2014). In contrast, they observe that "Indigenous political struggles have for centuries been fought over rights to land and self-governance."

In regard to more current political relations, textbooks are more likely to mention popular support for reconciliation—such as the march for reconciliation over the Sydney Harbour Bridge[7]—rather than claims of continuing Indigenous sovereignty and refusals of recognition such as those by the Sovereign Union of Aboriginal Peoples of Australia and the conveners of the Aboriginal Embassy in Canberra. These relations continue to be framed in nation-building language that implicitly presents dissident Indigenous aspirations in terms of demands for civil or citizenship rights (within the settler colonial polity) rather than of human rights (beyond the settler colonial polity). This distinction is, nevertheless, of the utmost importance. The Australian sociologist Bryan Turner indicates that

> The extension of citizenship rights to peoples that have been dispossessed and subsumed by the very states that are granting these rights is simply a form of internal colonialism. Indeed, citizenship is often associated with nation building and state legitimacy and, in fact, makes no sense outside of the framework of the nation-state. Human rights, on the other hand, are extra-governmental and have been traditionally used to counteract the repressive capacity of states. (1993, 496)

Policies of "closing the gap" in Australia or "rebalancing" in Kanaky/New Caledonia are an articulation by the nation-state according to which "people closest to the future are agents of transformation; people in the rear guard are objects of transformation" (Rose 2004, 155). With these positions in place, the role of Indigenous people "is not to make but to experience the history that others have made" (155). Indigenous people are represented as struggling for recognition. Recognition by the settler colonial power—namely, the nation-state—is embedded in unequal power relations, where the call for recognition counterintuitively affirms the settler colonial center of power. Recognition is a struggle, or campaign, to be recognized and included in the settler colonial society by political agents and institutions positioned to make that decision, to recognize or exclude. The production of a colonial temporality in textbooks that present social movements, land rights, and reconciliation policies as democratic readjustments in the progress of the nation thus also serves to support and maintain the settler colonial polity embedded in place. Speaking from the Canadian context, Taiaiake Alfred argues that "'a façade of reconciliation' is being used to buttress white supremacy, pacify and co-opt Indigenous leadership" (2013).

Evidence of the continuing assimilatory framework is also found in the ways that old assimilationist practices are condoned, inasmuch as they fall into the reconciliatory dogma. In that respect, the descriptions of Governor Macquarie's policy in the 2007 and 2012 textbooks are particularly telling of such trends. The authors of the 2007 textbook contend that

> Governor Macquarie saw the Aboriginal people as a possible asset to the colony, believing that they could find a role as workers in the new Australian society. Macquarie thought he could improve Aboriginal life by encouraging settlement in one place and developing their skills as labourers, mechanics and shepherds. (Anderson and Low 2007, 16)

Macquarie is portrayed as a figure of conciliation. His policies are framed as humanitarian acts and their failure is blamed on Indigenous lifestyle or their "problematic" position between "tradition" and "modernity" (Darlington, Jackson, and Hawkins 2012, 123, 139). Macquarie himself in 1816 spoke in very different terms of the task he set for himself to assimilate the Indigenous people into the settler colonial society: "to domesticate and civilise these wild, rude people" (quoted in Inglis 1974, 160). Ms. Chalker—descendant of the Dharawal woman Giribunger, who was placed in the Parramatta Native Institution set up by Macquarie—remarked that people praise Macquarie for building a school for Aboriginal children, though he actually implemented policies to remove children from their families, policies perpetuated by later governments (Schwartzkoff 2010). In addition, one thing that textbooks fail to mention is that Governor Macquarie is known for having launched punitive actions against the Dharawal people and for giving the instructions to entice Indigenous people to surrender themselves as prisoners of war:

> If they refuse to do so, make the least show of resistance, or attempt to run away from you, you will fire upon and compel them to surrender. . . . Such Natives as happen to be killed on such occasions, if grown up men, are to be hanged up on trees in conspicuous situations, to strike the Survivors with the greater terror. (quoted in Perkins and Langton 2010, 31)

The bodies were also decapitated and their heads sent off to institutions in Europe (Organ 2014; Perrin 2015). Many of those who survived were forcibly sent to colonial institutions.

Last, the assimilationist continuum, framed by reconciliatory dogma, is suffused with the idea that the present is transcending the past and that things are changing for the better. Deborah Bird Rose observes that "within the paradigm of progress, history is a process of conflict and change . . . It puts a positive value on change, and posits that history, or society, is moving towards the resolution of conflict and contradiction" (2004, 16). The solution is often framed in textbooks in terms of financial and infrastructure provision; in other words, to a problem of human relations and (lack of) reciprocity, money is given as the solution; the sources illustrating disparities are often charts with statistical figures and images of these infrastructures (Darlington, Jackson, and Hawkins 2012, 146). Not a single source offers an Indigenous perspective on these policies and subsidies.

This distancing or transcendence between past and present is supported by a linguistic shift. Past wrongs are termed "injustices," "discrimination," or "ill-treatment"; current ones are called "challenges" and "inequities" (Darlington, Jackson, and Hawkins 2012, 116–155). This orientation toward the future, in a society built on destruction, "enables regimes of violence to continue their work while claiming the moral ground of making a better future" (Rose 2004, 15). It disregards the damage and hurt enacted in the present and deflects settlers from moral responsibility. For instance, in mid-twentieth-century Australian textbooks, no mention is made of atomic bombs at Maralinga and Yalata. In the 1990s and 2000s, mention is scant of the Northern Territory intervention, of Aboriginal deaths in custody, or of the Stolen Generation.[8] Likewise, New Caledonian textbooks do not mention the disproportionate incarceration of Kanak people, the breach to their human rights during their detention, their continuing claims for land return, and the continuing issue of rampant institutionalized racism within New Caledonian society that discriminates against Kanak people.

Empathy or Settlers' Fantasy Space

A third method of the co-opting of Indigenous people by settler textbook authors, closely connected and concomitant to the reconciliatory dogma, is empathy. Empathy is a strategy of co-opting specific to the Australian sample. As a consequence, no reference is made here to the New Caledonian textbooks. This is a crucial variation in the historical narratives between Australian and New Caledonian textbooks, and reflects the divergent power dynamics in place in these societies. The absence of empathy in New Caledonian textbooks can be explained by the political tug-of-war between Kanak people and settler power, and more specifically between pro-independence and loyalist groups within the society. Indeed, the degree of empathy of one group for another may be assessed by their perceived threat. The more a group is perceived as a threat, the less empathy it will receive. Psychological studies have shown that this perceived threat can even be associated with pleasure at the suffering of an outgroup (Leach et al. 2003). Conversely, in contexts of greater and more assured political and demographic domination, empathy is more likely to develop because, as studies suggest, it is "generally directed 'down'" toward perceived "disadvantaged targets needing support" or people "in lower power positions" (Vorauer and Quesnel 2016a, 2016b). This is the case of the historical narrative present in Australian textbooks since the 1990s.

Following the introduction of reconciliatory practices and empathy in educational guidelines and curricula, the emotional practice of empathy has been consistently promoted in history textbooks in Australia. Empathy is understood here as an "other-oriented, emotional response" that is based on one's understanding of another's emotional state or condition. It is a state of emotional arousal, which is similar to "what the other person is feeling (*or should be expected to feel*)" (Losoya and Eisenberg 2001, 22–23, emphasis added). The literature scholar Suzanne Keen suggests that empathy "can be provoked by witnessing another's emotional state, by hearing about another's condition, or even by reading" (2007, 4). Evidence of explicit empathetic practices and appeals to empathic dispositions can be found in recent Australian textbooks. Such appeals are usually found in the activities section of textbooks. Some of these activities are specifically dedicated or disposed to empathetic exercises. A specific strategy of these exercises is to foster empathetic modes of relating between settlers and Indigenous people through character identification or embodiment. Readers are encouraged to embody historical figures—both settlers and Indigenous people, although predominantly Indigenous.

Embodiment involves a relatively informed empathetic practice according to which the reader has built enough knowledge of the person or group to empathize with. These practices of embodiment take the form of role play and simulation. Activities to encourage empathetic understanding are most effectively based on real historical figures, are supported by historical accounts, and require the reader to examine the various existing perspectives within a particular context. For instance, in History Alive 10 (Darlington, Smithies, and Wood 2012, 154), a practice of embodiment suggests that the reader should

Imagine yourself on the Freedom Ride either as an Indigenous or a non-Indigenous man or woman, and be sure to detail:

- the reason for the Freedom Ride
- the towns you visited (one blog entry for each town). Note: One of the towns must be either Walgett or Moree.
- the reactions of people when you visited those towns (search for newspaper reports on the internet)
- what you want people who read your blog to do to help you
- what you hope to achieve.

It is important that you display an understanding of the event and the reasons for the Freedom Ride and place it in the context of the campaign for change and the 1967 referendum. You should also research and mention the part played by Charles Perkins in the Freedom Ride.

Such exercises encourage historical enquiry and attention to historical accuracy. However, although practices of embodiment call on the reader's historical knowledge and analytical skills, assessing the empathic accuracy resulting from such practices is difficult. Inaccuracy, fallacy, and appropriation are even more likely considering that many affective practices of embodiment found in the textbooks do not rely on precise and accurate identification but instead on the reader's subjective assumptions of broadly defined subjects and historical context. For instance, a question in the 2012 textbooks asks the reader

What do you think the men in Source 5 [a group of Indigenous people in chains arrested for stealing beef] would have thought of the kinds of ideas expressed in Source 6 [a letter in the Sydney Gazette saying that Indigenous people should be treated as any other British subject]? (Darlington, Smithies, and Wood 2012, 135)

In other instances, practices of embodiment consist of a speculative (and at times nonsensical) exercise of rewriting history by calling on the reader's partialities rather than encouraging a more complex understanding of the historical context:

> Why do you think Indigenous activists such as William Ferguson, William Cooper and Jack Patten decided to use the theme of "mourning" for 26 January 1938? How else could they have presented their protest to create a different effect? Do you think this would have been more or less effective than the protest they made?' (Darlington, Jackson, and Hawkins, 2012, 121)

Another exercise asks the learner to

> Imagine you are a nine-year-old Indigenous girl or boy and have just been taken into the custody of the state. Which do you think would be hardest to leave behind: your family, your language or your culture? Explain your choice. (Darlington, Jackson, and Hawkins, 2012, 123)

These empathetic practices may result in the reader taking his or her own interpretation at face value and failing to question whether that interpretation of someone else's feelings and experiences could be fallacious. Keen calls this "a particularly invasive form of selfishness. (I impose my feelings on you and call them your feelings. Your feelings, whatever they were, undergo erasure.)" (2006, 222). Empathy does not bring about any shift in existing power relations because the reader is already "positioned in a relative position of power by virtue of the safe distance provided by the mediating text" (Boler 1999, 166). Empathy therefore exists within a persistent structure of domination and privilege that largely articulates settler responses to Indigenous loss and suffering. At the core of empathy, therefore, lies a process of ontological detachment. This detachment is twofold. First, through the performance of embodiment, the reader obliterates his or her position and experiences detachment from self. Empathic understanding of someone else's difference or suffering does not bring the question of self and responsibility into the equation. Second, although the intention might be to foster greater understanding between settlers and Indigenous people, empathy could have the adverse effect and instead sever one's connection to the people one tries to empathize with, because empathy is an imaginary—rather than actual—mode of relating. Empathy turns into a fantasy space and the actual conversation does not take place. One particular instance of empathetic practices in a textbook illustrates how a (missed) opportunity for understanding between settlers and Indigenous people gets trapped within the settler's fantasy space. In the 2012 textbook, a practice of empathy based on a speech by the first Indigenous police officer, Colin Dillon, which mentioned the racism he faced at his swearing-in ceremony, instructs the reader to "write three questions you would most like to ask Colin Dillon about his time on the police force or his experience since. Then answer them yourself, doing your best to imagine what his responses would be" (Darlington, Jackson, and Hawkins 2012, 119). Although empathetic practices are sometimes used in textbooks to explore gaps in historical evidence and as an exercise of historical inquiry, Colin Dillon's personal accounts of his time in the police force or his experience were accessible at the time the textbook was published (Noonan 1989; Aiken 2000; Filder 2009). Such a practice of empathy therefore works through prescriptive stereotypes and translates into the further erasure of Indigenous experiences and perspectives. The forms that empathy takes in these particular texts may entrench differences and impede the coeval interior processes of self-introspection and exterior processes of self-positioning necessary to encourage conversation and debunk myths. Instead, they result in an ontological detachment that obliterates self-responsibility, severs connections, and further silences Indigenous voices within a historical narrative that continues to be told from a predominantly settler perspective. Such findings concord with studies in psychology that have observed that empathy in intergroup contexts exacerbates rather than mitigates power differentials (Vorauer and Quesnel 2016a).

Recent textbooks have begun to address the Eurocentric approach to history by including both Indigenous people in the textbook development process (Kanaky/New Caledonia) and Indigenous sources. Nevertheless, by and large, the historical narrative in textbooks continues to be a settler's epistemological space rather than a place for plural meaning-making processes. Thus textbooks continue to reproduce stereotypical enunciations of Indigenous-settler history. This stereotyping is carried out through epistemic exclusiveness and enunciation biases that sustain settler legitimacy by externalizing colonial violence, fixed categorization, and co-opting.

Settler ignorance as it manifests itself in the selected history textbooks does not consist of a mere absence of Indigenous people from the narrative (the supposed great Australian silence) or of unacknowledged, silenced colonial violence. Colonial violence is in fact present throughout the sample. Instead, ignorance lies in the capacity to externalize that violence, racially, physically, and morally. This is accomplished by three epistemological strategies: racialist discourse, self-distantiation, and dualistic historical narrative. This externalization uses fixed political categories that make it easier to think about Indigenous-settler history. Indigenous people and settlers remain two entrenched categories in the ways that they are constituted and the ways they relate and sustain power relations of domination. The centrality of the settler colonial polity is reaffirmed and Indigenous people and non-European settlers remain marginal. The resulting configuration of power remains largely unchanged. This settler-dominated epistemological space is a fantasy space in which the settler fantasy of Indigenous extinction endures. Whether this fantasy takes the form of projected racial extermination, cultural assimilation, or civic integration, it enacts that same logic of exclusion of Indigenous sovereignties. Evidence of such exclusion is apparent in the strategy of co-opting, in which the logic of replacement is framed by the reconciliatory dogma. Even the seemingly benign empathetic approach that underpins this reconciliatory framework in Australian textbooks serves only to exacerbate rather than mitigate power differentials between Indigenous people and settlers.

Stereotyping acts as both an anchor and a fence. Stereotypes are both descriptive (through externalization and fixed categorization) and prescriptive (through co-opting, especially the empathetic practices). In rendering visible patterns of enunciation in the textbooks, the intention of this chapter was to identify and examine the powerful premises of the well-told settler colonial narrative in textbooks. These textbooks constitute a key element of teachers' historiographical inheritance and a potential teaching tool. With this in mind, the next chapter looks at the ways that history teachers engage with that historiographical inheritance and the opportunities they have—or do not have—to engage critically with historical sources to influence these configurations.

PART III

Pedagogy

Teaching Indigenous-Settler History

CHAPTER 6

Compliant and Insurgent Education

AN EDUCATION SYSTEM IS MADE UP OF INDIVIDUALS, and each one responds to and acts on institutional directives and institution-sanctioned materials differently. Part 3 of this book delves into teachers' individual approaches to teaching Indigenous-settler history. It relates teachers' philosophy to their practice by addressing the following questions: What implications do official directives and teacher training have for their practice? How do teachers respond and relate to their historiographical inheritance? Do they reproduce settler colonial historical narratives or do they challenge those narratives? If they challenge the existing narratives, what strategies do they report adopting? And what are the continuing obstacles that teachers face when teaching Indigenous-settler history? This chapter charts teachers' approaches to the teaching materials they have at their disposal and the strategies they report adopting to teach Indigenous-settler history.

The respective political context of Australian and Kanaky/New Caledonia societies explains the substantial variations in teachers' approaches in each. The attention teachers give to emotions reveals their critical function when engaging with historical knowledge and addressing settler regimes of ignorance. This leads me to focus on seven teachers who displayed an attitude to ignorance distinct from that of their peers and used insurgent education methods that reveal the potential of attitudes to ignorance to destabilize those settler regimes of ignorance and initiate Indigenous-settler relations of a different kind.

Use of Teaching Materials

All the teachers interviewed reported having textbooks in the school or the classroom at their disposal. In Australia, head teachers or school committees choose the textbook materials. Teachers in the same school typically have the same textbook as their colleagues, but teachers across schools may have different sets of materials. Several of the secondary school teachers interviewed in Australia report using widely available texts such as *Oxford Big Ideas, Nelson, Retroactive,* and *History Alive.* Several teachers indicated that they tend to adopt a pick-and-choose approach. The primary school teachers reported not using any prescribed textbook because they had not come across one they considered adequate to their teaching. They relied instead on personal research and collaborative work between colleagues.

Logistical considerations are a more determining factor in Kanaky/ New Caledonia. The pool of available textbooks being so small, those on history are all the same, namely, the three analyzed in part 2 of this book. Although each student has one textbook from mainland France, several teachers report a shortage of New Caledonian textbooks and typically only one or two sets of books per level are shared among the classes. Students can access the New Caledonian textbook only during the history class.

The small range of history textbooks adapted to New Caledonian history requires that teachers do a great deal of research and pedagogical work. They often need to collect the documents and testimonies from the archives, which makes teaching New Caledonian history more difficult than teaching French or global history—for which a wealth of resources exists. Several teachers also commented that the obsolescence of the historical narrative in teaching materials is an issue and textbooks ought to be updated more often. In addition, several teachers deplored that existing school textbooks were made useless when the 2012 curriculum reform largely took away the local focus of the history curriculum. Since then, several teachers report using textbooks only occasionally or hardly ever.

Besides these logistical realities in terms of the availability and range of textbooks, pedagogical suitability plays an important role in teachers' perceptions and usage of textbooks. The gap between the literacy level of the textbooks and that of the students who use them is another factor that encourages teachers to pick and choose and adapt.

In some cases, teachers find textbooks wordy and likely difficult for some students to understand. They say that this is especially true for students whose mother tongue is not the language of instruction (that is, some Indigenous people and refugees). Textbooks, as a one-size-fits-all instructional resource, therefore contribute to further discrimination against students not in the targeted mainstream. In these cases, some teachers in Broken Hill, Tennant Creek, and Country New South Wales use textbooks primarily as a starting point, to supplement instruction, and to create resources from, rather than as a direct teaching tool. Teachers in Kanaky/New Caledonia made similar observations, especially regarding the 2006 textbook that many find quite ambitious for the age group it is directed to. Nonetheless, textbooks continue to be a useful tool in teachers' preparatory work and useful for teachers with less (or nonexistent) knowledge of their teaching environment or of their audience to fall back on, namely, substitute teachers in Australia and teachers from mainland France who have recently arrived in Kanaky/New Caledonia. Teachers' choice of teaching materials (and therefore the ways they use textbooks) also depends on the extent to which they validate the historical narrative found in those texts and they apply it in their teaching.

Favoring Settler Epistemology

A few of the teachers interviewed in Australia thought that the textbooks they used were scientifically adequate to teaching Indigenous-settler history. One claimed, for instance, that they "deal well with Indigenous and non-Indigenous conflicts" and "made huge progress in the way that they present actual colonisation and conflicts." Another explained that when focusing on the unit on the Stolen Generation, Missions, and Reserves, textbooks seemed to provide a "relatively honest history." For this teacher, the textbook addresses the policies of segregation, protectionism, and assimilation "in quite frank terms" and is not "trying to skirt around that."[1] As a result, some teachers use these texts. They nonetheless do not lose sight of the domination of settler epistemology and marginalization of Indigenous perspectives in them. As a result, all the teachers interviewed in Australia reported actively trying to at least balance out the historical sources they presented to the students, and at best, erode the domination of settler epistemology in history teaching.

The favoring of settler epistemology was more prevalent in teachers' accounts in Kanaky/New Caledonia than in Australia. Except for a few comments on the very monolithic nature of the historical narrative, teachers were more prone to readily approve textbooks. Most considered the three textbooks scientifically viable. They are generally praised for their consensual character and the scientific work behind them. The 1992 textbook, the first on New Caledonian history, has the merit of laying the foundations. The 2006 edition is praised for its multilingual content, in which some units are translated into the four most widely spoken Kanak languages. The 2010 year 11–12 textbook was well appreciated for its intellectual and scientific rigor and its pedagogical interest. Teachers found it well researched, backed by recent and well-chosen sources. One teacher explained that the chapter on the transformation of Kanak society during colonization, in which both the "positive" and "negative" sides are shown, is "a very good thing."[2] Another found this resource consensual and therefore satisfying, though he did not lose sight of his own partiality:

> But I think I have a distorted viewpoint because I know all those who worked on that textbook very well. They are my former professors. . . . so I struggle to take a step back. They taught us a specific historiography, and we consider that a text should be flavorless.[3]

Several teachers, markedly more in Kanaky/New Caledonia than in Australia, approved of this historiographical inheritance. Although teachers widely acknowledged, when asked, the overrepresentation of European settler perspectives and sources in the teaching materials available to them, they considered them satisfactory to teach Indigenous-settler history. A teacher and textbook writer contended that "the facts that are recounted are explicit enough to show the complexity of things."[4] In fact, when asked about the representativeness of the sources, a few teachers admitted that they haven't asked themselves the question. Likewise, a teacher educator did not see any political intrigue behind the overrepresentation of European settler sources, and explained that this lack of Kanak sources instead results from the limited space a textbook can offer. Considering the large overrepresentation of European settler accounts, it seems that the limited space in a textbook does not affect European sources. Ultimately, this explanation does not account for the discrimination evident in the selection of the sources, or explain why European sources are favored over Kanak and non-European settler sources.

Many teachers explained that the domination of settler perspectives and sources in New Caledonian textbooks is due to the supposed scarcity of Kanak sources. There is, they said, a lack of Kanak and non-European settler sources available to the historians in the archives and therefore a lack of Kanak and non-European settler testimonies in textbooks. They explained this perceived lack as resulting from an absence of both academic and institutional efforts, as well as opportunities to collect and critically analyze these testimonies.

Another impediment to the collection process, some teachers and textbook authors suggested, was a shortage of Kanak historians to take on the work. Some teachers explained that the historians are almost exclusively European. Few Kanak people have written the history and few Kanaks graduate in history. One teacher explained that the number of Kanak doctoral candidates, university professors, or even secondary teachers is small and that "everything reverberates, at every link in the chain, throughout the education cycle."[5]

It seems, however, that in addition to these systemic limitations, attitudes toward Kanak oral knowledge systems and historical sources also greatly influenced bias and discrimination in history teaching. The lack of Kanak perspectives in the teaching was also attributed to the oral nature of Kanak cultures. A few teachers believed that oral sources do not apply very well to historical inquiry and scientific knowledge, which are based on written culture and intellectual rigor. They therefore favored the written medium: "the issue with orality is that it is information that is passed down and, of course, the further we go back in time, the more chance there is for this narrative, which is passed down orally, to be transformed, distorted and embellished." On the other hand, this teacher educator added, "we have very precise, firsthand sources from the historical actors themselves."[6]

Although it may be true that oral culture remains a favored medium of expression, Kanak people have also substantially engaged with the written medium. Writing, for instance, has been a tool for contesting and resisting colonization, and for gaining more voice and power. The earliest Kanak writings found so far date to 1867 (Soula 2014, 72). Twentieth- and twenty-first-century Kanak viewpoints can also be found in theses, political pamphlets and essays, magazines, biographies, and so on. It seems therefore that the stereotypical representation of Indigenous people as having solely oral cultures dies hard and has a significant impact on historians' approach to their historiography. This discriminatory assumption is even more perceptible considering that none of the Kanak teachers interviewed identified a lack of Kanak material sources to teach Indigenous-settler history. As to the risk of oral knowledge transforming, distorting. and spinning facts, the same is true of written sources.

Historical actors never write from a zero-point perspective and may not write free of political interests. It is plausible that what they write may reflect not what they see, think, or believe but instead what will work in their interest. Written sources are also subject to inclusion and exclusion. The institutional process of gathering and archiving sources also influences the constituted body of knowledge. Ann Stoler, in her analysis of colonial archives and governance, suggests that an archive is "neither material site nor a set of documents." Instead, it is a "corpus of selective forgettings and collections" (2002, 94). Archives regulate what can be said. Archives order—in both the imperative and taxonomic sense—the body of knowledge to be preserved (97). The colonial archive is therefore a system that masks the structural character of colonization through a process of self-concealment that effaces its origin and purpose, which is to reflect the power of the state and become "the archived inscriptions of its authority" (96). The French philosopher Jacques Derrida once contended that "there is no political power without control of the archive" (1996, 4). Thus, for the sources to be part of these institutional archives, to be left to posterity, they may have to meet certain criteria that serve settler colonial power and do not play against it. This may explain why Kanak sources are largely excluded from these archives.

Archives may be more accurately considered documents of inclusion and exclusion, serving specific configurations of power. Just as they keep some sources, they discard others. Just as they store knowledge, they also cultivate ignorance. Although truth claims from oral knowledge are often cautiously handled or questioned in history textbooks and by teachers, written knowledge found in archives may need similar scrutiny and caution. The teacher epistemic understanding and position in regard to Indigenous accounts and epistemologies comes up in the New Caledonian context. The failure to identify bias and the mechanisms of settler colonial domination in producing and archiving historical knowledge continue to favor and legitimize a settler epistemology in the history class.

Such biases toward historical sources have two key consequences. On the academic level, settler attitudes toward orality, rigid understanding of what historical sources should look like, and what qualities a Kanak historian must have to be recognized as such, have contributed to the ongoing exclusion of Kanak accounts in history teaching. As the First Nations and Indigenous Studies scholar Daniel Justice observed in the North American context, many people have been educated to believe that Indigenous people "don't belong in this place of meaning-making, that [they] don't have anything worthwhile to contribute as Native peoples, that the intellectual traditions of [their] families and communities aren't powerful understandings of the world and her ways" (2004, 102). Miranda Fricker labels such processes "epistemic injustice" (2007). Favoring settler epistemology and the false claim to objectivity perpetuates colonizing acts, and that is what often makes academia, according to Vine Deloria, a "hotbed of racism" (2004, 18). On a fundamental human level, it continues to deprive people of their power to define their humanity. As Angela Wilson argues, after seeing Indigenous knowledge challenged by an eminent historian, "as humans we have the right to argue that our ways of knowing are equal to any on earth and we have a right to challenge colonial claims to superiority" (2004, 79).

Refusal of Textbooks: Historical Flaws and Political Bias

In Australia, the regressive language of textbooks deters some teachers from accepting the content as viable or in some cases from using them at all. One teacher described using them as practice for critical thinking, but the regressive language of some textbooks caused other teachers to simply refuse to use those texts, perceiving them to be politically biased and historically flawed. A retired history teacher said that textbooks downplay the impact of settlers' responsibility for the genocide of Indigenous people and, in doing so, legitimize colonization and perpetuate it in the present:

> Most history books will eventually blame the deaths of Aboriginal people on disease when, in fact, at least as much was a result of warfare, and an underrated aspect of Aboriginal deaths is starvation because the crop lands and their economy were completely disrupted by the taking away of their lands.[7]

Of the teachers interviewed in Australia, five adopted a "politics of refusal" (Simpson 2014) toward textbooks. They articulated their refusal to use textbooks as a political stance against the regressive and racist language or the whitewashed and sweeping historical narrative that textbooks articulate.

Several teachers pointed out that textbooks are limited inasmuch as they provide a general and uniform history but not a local lens. Australian textbooks try to cater to as large an audience as possible, and their content is therefore often broad: "I do think that with Indigenous history you really need a local lens. You need to recognize that you're dealing with about 250 traditional owner groups. Textbooks are going to struggle with that," one teacher observed.[8] In the process, Indigenous viewpoints on that history become generalized and simplified as well. "There's not going to be one perspective on colonization from Indigenous people," one teacher explained, "and I don't think that a textbook can do justice to that diversity." The inadequacy is felt even more by teachers working in schools with a large Indigenous student population. A teacher at Tennant Creek High School thought that some content is not context specific and is directed at an urban non-Indigenous audience: "They even have profiles on remote communities, for example. . . . they're not what it actually is for kids living in these communities."[9] Another teacher working in the Northern Territory recalled that at times it had been awkward to teach from the textbook because the content was quite insensitive and did not meet the needs of the Indigenous students they taught. For the same reasons, a teacher in Broken Hill preferred using history books specific to her locale than textbooks. One teacher, who had more than thirty years' experience teaching in Paakantyi Country and was a speaker of the Paakantyi language, suggested that the very format of textbooks is incompatible with Indigenous knowledge transmission, which is oral. Thus people are the ones who should be approached for Indigenous accounts of Indigenous-settler history.

In Kanaky/New Caledonia, awareness of the historical bias and flaws in textbooks has not resulted in teachers refusing to use textbooks altogether. Nonetheless, a few of them have disqualified particular teaching materials and favored other resources. For instance, the 1992 primary textbook, according to some teachers, was "very dated" and contained "disturbing comment in regard to colonization." One teacher educator explained how, for instance, placing of Kanak people into reserves at the end of the nineteenth century is described in that textbook as measures to preserve Kanak people from European civilization, to enable them to retain their identity, whereas they were in fact "mechanisms of apartheid, which completely silence the fact that if they were put into reserves, it was ultimately to steal their land."[10] As a result, two teachers preferred to use that 1992 textbook as a research tool rather than as a pedagogical one, or even not to use it at all.

In addition, a few teachers perceived bias in the historical narrative and the marginal place given to Indigenous perspectives in textbooks as the result of vested political interests. One, for instance, maintained that contentious and ungratifying topics are consciously silenced. The lack of research and absence of Kanak accounts in the historiography, one teacher remarked, are reflected in the sources found in textbooks:

> There are periods of history that are still a little bit forgotten, on which little research has been done. . . . In fact, the topics that haven't been studied are often the most sensitive. . . . There are a lot of topics that are often sensitive and that are not really studied.[11]

For other teachers, this shortage of research reflects historians' attitudes toward not only the past, but also the current political context and the future they wish for their society. For them, this shortfall is the result primarily of a reluctance to include Indigenous sources because it does not reinforce the direction of the official reconciliation policy, the "common destiny": "I think it's mostly reluctance. I think it's a choice in order to move ahead in a positive way about what is being done at the moment." Some teachers observed gaps in the narrative or aspects of history that are less well documented. For instance, few documents address the 1917 Kanak uprising and the 1931 Colonial Exhibition or non-European settlers. These teachers asserted that the positive ethos of the reconciliation policy prevents a plurality of viewpoints on Indigenous-settler history from emerging. The consensual politics is seen as the main reason why divergent viewpoints are not included in textbooks, what one teacher referred to as "the dogma of the common destiny." The same teacher pointed out that more polemical aspects of the local history—such as Messmer's letter or that Eloi Machoro was gunned down by the local police—are left out of the narrative.[12]

Instead, the teacher continued, "we are in the dogma of a plural history, there was the agreements and, bam, reconciliation."[13] Another teacher also accounted for that reluctance based on the simple fact that education remains under French domination, pointing out that "the curricula at the time are still dominated by the French government, so they assert what is dear to them and they may not wish to awaken animosities from an early age."[14] According to these teachers, the choice of sources is therefore predominantly a political choice, whether personally or institutionally motivated. The teachers who understand bias in the historical narrative as politically motivated are generally more likely to diversify the sources of knowledge in their teaching, and to actively seek to include Indigenous perspectives.

Closing the Gap in Settler Ignorance

Several teachers—more in Australia than in Kanaky/New Caledonia—have taken the initiative to bring Indigenous perspectives and voices in the history class. Australian textbooks exclude Indigenous authors entirely, which may push proactive teachers to actively seek to redress the omission. For several teachers interviewed in Australia, bringing in Indigenous voices is essential. The most common ways to include these voices are direct learning from local historical figures as well as use of videos, oral history websites, and Indigenous-produced media.[15] Several teachers reported that students show greater interest and more sustained attention when history is about people, places, or events they can personally relate to. A former teacher recounted how he always tried "to find local examples that were at odds with the history books that had been set" so that the students were "getting a different version of the history from local people." He argued that regardless of where you are in Australia, demographics cannot be used to justify the exclusion of Indigenous people in the teaching: "We are 3 percent of the population but you only have to meet a hundred people and you've met three Aboriginal people. It doesn't matter where you go, Aboriginal people are there."[16] A teacher in Shepparton said that he tried to make students realize the significance of their local surroundings. He screened videos from the Stolen Generation testimonies and included local people who identify as Yorta Yorta or Bangarang in the teaching because students need "to hear it from Indigenous people what their experience of it was."[17] Two teachers in Menindee based most of their teaching on discussions with the local communities and videos, such as the locally produced Menindee Mission.

In Kanaky/New Caledonia, the teachers who saw political bias in the historical narrative were more likely to report localizing the knowledge and bringing local perspectives into the teaching content by using Kanak publications and media as well as videos and documentaries. Only one teacher interviewed in Kanaky/New Caledonia, however, reported organizing school incursions or field trips with local Kanak people to teach Indigenous-settler history.

Some of the teachers who had not actively sought to include Indigenous accounts through school incursions or field trips so far expressed the desire to do so in the future. Three teachers interviewed in Kanaky/New Caledonia thought that engaging people from the local communities in the teaching is an interesting idea they would try to implement in the future: "Regarding school incursions, I think I'll bring that in next year. . . . It's true that it's interesting to have oral testimonies. It's a civilization with an oral tradition and they're used to hear their Elders, etc. It's a shame that I haven't done it." One of her colleagues agreed that it would be interesting and doable because even on the island of Drehu, it is "possible to find people who have been historical actors, even just for the Events."[18]

Overall Trends in Teaching Materials and Sources of Knowledge

Teachers' perceptions of history textbooks are most of the time nuanced. Several of the teachers acknowledged the logistic and pedagogical limitations or the epistemological gaps and biases of textbooks content, or both. As a result, most teachers adopt a pick-and-choose approach to textbooks. All of them supplement their teaching with, or else base it entirely on, alternative sources of knowledge, teaching materials, and media such as the internet, museums, films, books and magazines, or field trips and school incursions.

In both Australia and Kanaky/New Caledonia, teachers use the internet and films extensively to prepare and deliver their history class materials. To overcome the literacy inadequacy of textbooks, for instance, one teacher in the Northern Territory uses songs and pictures to teach some of the curriculum content, such as the 1967 referendum, the Wave Hill walk-off, and the land rights movements. In those situations, one teacher explained, the internet is also a favored medium for teachers who alter it to the needs of the students and contextualize as much as possible. Likewise, a teacher in Drehu readapted his once mostly text-based teaching to work with videos, a lively and well-appreciated medium among students. The age of the students is also an important factor in teachers' choice of teaching materials. A preschool teacher, for example, used artwork and story books—especially books by Dick Roughsey, Ginny Adams, and Sue Atkinson and another by John Marsden called *The Rabbits,* which tells the story of invasion in "a sort of safe way" for very young learners.[19]

Some variations in the media teachers in Australia and in Kanaky/New Caledonia use are notable. In the latter, teachers were more likely to use museums, for instance, and those in Australia would more readily organize field trips or incursions. In Kanaky/New Caledonia, only one teacher reported using that approach. Most did not necessarily take the initiative to actively bring in these silenced voices, whether Kanak people or non-European settlers.

When teachers attempted to bring in Kanak voices, they opted for a visit to the museum. Teachers enumerated museums in Nouméa and the Southern Province; several of those working in the bush or the islands by default mentioned their distance from the city and its museums to be a key obstacle to bringing in Kanak accounts. Kanak people and cultures continue to be museumized. These cultural institutions set the terms of recognition according to their agendas. In fact, several of the teachers' responses reveal that stepping out of the institutional mold and engaging directly with local Kanak people, regardless of Kanak people's "official" qualifications, has evidently not been considered a possibility. In these cases, the supremacy of settler epistemology and the perpetuation of settler regimes of ignorance over several generations have created a situation akin to mental apartheid, whereby one's assumptions and (unconsciously) learned behaviors systematically separate the individual from the rest of society. One teacher admitted that having people from the local community in to contribute to the teaching is "doable but more delicate" and is "not something that necessarily comes to mind."[20] Such accounts are all the more indicative of institutionally enforced mental apartheid that most of these teachers live and work in largely Kanak-populated areas, where between 75 and 99 percent of the population is Kanak. Kanak accounts seem accepted only when regulated and mediated by an institution.

A discussion with another teacher reflects this institutional bias particularly clearly. Although this teacher regarded visiting the Tjibaou Cultural

Center as "extraordinary" to learn about Kanak culture, she did not consider going to a colonial conflict or massacre site or, as she put it, "on a pilgrimage" to "reflect on someone's grave." Yet, in the school where she taught, the institution supported the creation of a year 9 "Defence" class sponsored by the army "to do history differently." The class is invited, for instance, to "every commemoration" and to meet World War II veterans.[21] Historical conflicts and their actors and victims are therefore considered differently depending on the kind of nationalism they served. The issue may not be the visit to a grave or a war monument or site per se, but whose grave it is and which historical conflict it commemorates. Although attending commemorations for wars involving the French national army seems unproblematic, pedagogically beneficial, and supported by the education institution, commemorations of conflicts that challenged French nationalism, such as Kanak nationalism during the 1984–1988 war, seem unwelcome. Such a double standard within the institution is a substantial blow to the discourse of objectivity and neutrality. A teacher educator remarked that the possibilities for field trips and engagement with Kanak perspectives are significant but conceded that excursions "mostly value colonial history through European eyes" and that "it's quite rare that people invite Kanak people to the classroom." "A whole heritage," he thought, "is completely overlooked."[22]

Thus teachers in both Australia and Kanaky/New Caledonia perceive logistic and pedagogical flaws in textbooks as well as gaps in their historical narrative. In contrast to the weight of logistical and pedagogical considerations in teachers' practices, bias in the historical narrative seems to have a lesser impact on teachers' choices. This is especially true in Kanaky/New Caledonia. The domination of settler epistemology there seems to remain an issue that most of the teachers interviewed largely do not address. Although several acknowledged the political vested interests and the sociological factors (lack of Kanak people in staffing and research) that create such discrimination, the place and credit given to Kanak oral knowledge and the ignorance of the versatility of Kanak modes of expression seem less problematized yet at the same time more problematic.

Teacher Objectives

Teacher objectives in teaching Indigenous-settler history can be distilled into four categories: allocating time and focus, encouraging political literacy, developing critical thinking among students, and combating both racism and colonialism.

Allocating Time and Focus

History teachers in both Australia and Kanaky/New Caledonia are relatively free when it comes to allocating time to Indigenous-settler history. One deplored that "there is no control." In Australia, each school adapts the state or federal curricula to its own use, so the content of history as a subject is designed by the school (a committee usually led by the head teacher). The individual teachers are then free to implement the curriculum as they see fit. Several, for example, noted substantial differences between the shape and content of their history classes and those of their colleagues. It is therefore up to the individual teachers how much time and focus they want to dedicate to Indigenous-settler history. One teacher in rural New South Wales reported always trying to include local inquiry that fits into the subject area. However, several also said that some of their colleagues might not be so proactive, adhering instead to the minimum required in the curriculum.

In Kanaky/New Caledonia, many teachers said that they attempted to "follow the curriculum to the letter" and to "never step out of the curriculum guidelines." One explained it this way:

> My job is to put this curriculum into practice. If I don't . . . I create inequalities between my pupils and other pupils. It's my duty to do it. Regardless of what I think, or how I experience things, I must bring my pupils to the same standards as all the others who follow the same curriculum in New Caledonia.

The same teacher explained that, as a result, if the curriculum does not require the teachers to talk about the 1984–1988 war for instance—a crucial period in New Caledonian contemporary history—she won't teach it:

> The basis will always be the time allocation. If I have to spend two hours on it, I won't spend an extra one. The content will also be directed by the curriculum. So, if we study the political history from 1945 to the present, and there isn't a specific focus on the Events period in the curriculum, I won't do it. It's like being a technician. I apply the national demand.[23]

Some teachers, however, always tried to include New Caledonian history in every unit whenever possible. Others also attempt to fill the gaps and make room for aspects of Indigenous-settler history that are not included in the curriculum but that they nonetheless deem important for the students to know. Students' interests for one topic or another also influence what is taught and how much. A teacher in the Loyalty Islands, for instance, remarked that although the curriculum guidelines do not explicitly include the 1931 Colonial Exhibition or the various Kanak uprisings, she decided to bring it up in a year 9 history class because they are in the history timeline and students ask why they don't learn about the Kanak political demands or even the 1984–1988 war. Students in several schools point out this silence about colonial conflicts and racist practices. A teacher in Pwêêdi Wiimîâ, who teaches classes in which 80 percent of the students are Kanak, mentioned pro-independence perspectives more often because "these are things they talk about in their homes." A secondary school teacher in Nouméa remarked that students like to learn about the 1984–1988 war precisely because sometimes families don't talk about it. A teacher in Drehu seized the opportunity provided by the inclusion of colonization in the year 9 history curriculum to focus on Kanak uprisings and the iconic Kanak leader of the 1878 insurrection, Ataï, a topic that greatly interests his students because they relate to it. He also dedicates three hours at the end of year 9 to the 1984–1988 war: one hour for the rise of political demands for independence, one hour for the war, especially the Ouvéa massacre (using films, TV news reports, and testimonies from different parts of the territories), and the last hour for the peace agreements, Caledonian citizenship and the "common destiny."

As a result of these different approaches to the curriculum, time allocated to Indigenous-settler history varies notably among teachers. Although neither in Australia nor Kanaky/New Caledonia could teachers provide an exact number because "it is hard to quantify" and "it's too mixed." Nonetheless, all teachers interviewed in Australia and Kanaky/New Caledonia reported teaching, albeit to various extents, the Indigenous-settler history of their respective societies. Such observations, however, cannot be generalized to reflect the overall history teaching trend in the two societies. As mentioned earlier, when the call for participants for this project was sent out to history teachers, several in Australia declined, saying that they did not teach this aspect of the history and were therefore not interested in participating. It is therefore quite plausible that a substantial portion of the history teacher cohort does not teach Indigenous-settler history and therefore contribute to the perpetuation of settler regimes of ignorance. In fact, even in Kanaky/ New Caledonia, where almost everyone contacted agreed to partici- pate, several interviewees reported instances in which some of their col- leagues chose not to teach Indigenous-settler history at all, even when the curriculum had allocated time for it. Based on teacher accounts, the choice to ignore this aspect of the curriculum is, in some cases, clearly political. In other instances, however, the choice may also result from the teacher's ignorance about that part of history. One former teacher and primary school teacher educator observed a few years ago that some teachers would only teach what they knew, that is, the history of mainland France mostly and a little bit of New Caledonian history, such as the beginning of colonization, leaving aside both Kanak resis- tance to it and its long-term impact on Kanak people. Another teacher remarked that when her own children went through secondary school they were not taught New Caledonian history. She interpreted this omis- sion on the grounds that it remains "complicated to teach because it hasn't been written entirely well."[24]

In those instances, the implications of teachers' historiographical inheritance and teacher training for the teaching of Indigenous-settler history are profound. Even among the proactive teachers willing to teach Indigenous-settler history in greater depth than outlined in the curriculum, some admit just skimming through because they don't have enough information or the "necessary weapons," and they would "need to know that part of history themselves" to be able to teach it in more depth.

Thus variations among the teachers interviewed are substantial in the time and focus given to Indigenous-settler history. Teachers' emo- tional response to curricular guidelines, the profile of students in their classes, and their historiographical inheritance (how much they know about Indigenous-settler history) are important factors affecting the time and focus the teachers dedicate to that history. Some prefer to put their personal perception and emotions aside and follow curricular guidelines strictly, even if that means marginalizing important aspects of Indigenous-settler history; others adapt the class content according to the interest of the learners for certain topics and always relate the his- tory content to the environment of the learners. Nonetheless, the polit- ical orientation of some teachers, and their personal ignorance, can marginalize Indigenous-settler history even more than what it already is in the history curricula.

Encouraging Political Literacy and Civic Participation

A common objective among history teachers in both Australia and Kanaky/New Caledonia is to train politically informed citizens who are aware of their position, rights, and responsibilities. One teacher in Country Victoria strove to make his students politically and historically engaged and to stress that they need to know about Indigenous-settler issues and to have an opinion on them. Likewise, in Kanaky/New Caledonia, many teachers shared "a desire to pass on a vision of this country" and an understanding of how its political institutions work. One aim is for their students to learn the history of their country to better understand the present and to become active citizens. History and citizenship overlap to an extent in a focus on topical issues. Another teacher in Drehu took the initiative to talk about topics not included in the curriculum but that she considered more relevant because of their relationship to current political affairs, such as the referenda for independence and the freezing of the electoral body. Despite its being a "subtle and delicate topic," which could in more ethnically diverse locations lead the situation to fester, this teacher decided to teach it nonetheless. So did her colleague who "bends the rules" because he thinks it will help his students in the long run. He therefore included discussions on topics such as the referendum, independence, autonomy, or the political status of New Caledonia so that students will be historically and politically better informed when the time comes to vote in the referendum. On a similar note, another teacher in Nouméa defined success as seeing these young people think about topics they will need to address in the future or when they will perhaps vote in the referenda for independence.[25]

Developing Critical Thinking

Another objective teachers often raised is developing students' critical thinking. From primary through high school, the main objective of many is to teach students "to think for themselves" and "make their own decisions and ideas" about history. A Melbourne-based primary school teacher tried to teach students to be critical about what they read. He used, to take one example, the story of William Buckley—the escaped convict who spent more than thirty years with the Wathaurong people—to "teach lots of different people's views on it and then talk about what may or may not be true, why certain histories might bend the truth or interpret things in different ways."[26] Another teacher tried to make students understand that "there isn't an absolute truth but that everything abides to a certain logic, to a will to head somewhere." To do so, he attempted to "develop a method that enables inquiry." According to him, a crucial criterion to help students develop their critical inquiry is to ensure that they are equipped with words to express their thoughts. He recalled a time this was made obvious to him:

> A young student was working on a portfolio on juvenile delinquency when he told me: "White people don't steal because their parents give them everything they want. But us, Kanak people, we don't have anything. That's why we have to steal." It's interesting because it's his words, but it's badly put and he wouldn't have the words to put it down on paper . . . but for me it means a lot because, even if he didn't express it well, he was talking about social inequalities . . . but he didn't say "it's a social inequality because most offenders are from disadvantaged social backgrounds." But he said it in his own way. . . . It was insightful but it could have gone unnoticed.

This teacher therefore considered that his job was to "give words to youth."[27] One Nouméa-based teacher believed that history teaching enables students to understand the current cultural diversity of the territory and encourages them to understand and appreciate one another better. Some teachers, with a similar desire to encourage cross-cultural understanding and appreciation through critical thinking, pursue higher aims, and seek to fight racism and colonialism.

Combating Racism and Colonialism

Some teachers see in history teaching a potential to combat racism and colonialism. This is particularly true in Australia, whereas none of the teachers interviewed in Kanaky/New Caledonia framed their objectives in such a way. One Melbourne-based preschool teacher, for instance, attempted to fight racism by raising awareness about

Indigenous sovereignty and by promoting understanding and respect for Indigenous people and cultures:

> I think it's of vital importance for non-Indigenous children to learn about Indigenous culture because the only way that the terrible racism that's present in this country is going to dissipate is if non-Indigenous people understand and respect Indigenous cultures.[28]

One primary school teacher's key objective was to "break down the stereotypes." Through drawing exercises and feedback, he attempted to raise awareness among young students about the physiological, cultural, and linguistic diversity of Indigenous people in Australia and provide them with "more alternative history" that is not present in the mass media. Another Melbourne-based teacher prioritized making students aware of ongoing Indigenous sovereignty and of the ways that colonialism continues in the present:

> I want them to be aware that this land is Indigenous land, and it has been for thousands and thousands of years. . . . it's about being aware. . . . That's the main thing that I want them to get, that there's this Indigenous history, and there's this thing colonization that happened, and that it's ongoing.

To exemplify the continuing colonialism and dispossession of Indigenous people from the land, she encouraged students to reflect on gentrification and displacement in their own surroundings:

> In the 1960s and 1970s, there were thousands living here, and they'd been pushed out. So, I think, it's something which is pretty important for them to understand. It's not like it's stopped. Indigenous people are still being oppressed. They're still being dispossessed and in kind of this refugee-within-their-own-land state.[29]

In doing so, these teachers address morality. Several reported teaching explicit ethical lessons and to promote an anticolonial, anti-racist position that engage emotive concerns and responses.

Teachers in both Australia and Kanaky/New Caledonia aim to develop their students' critical thinking, which is an expected and commonsense answer from historians. Teachers in Kanaky/New Caledonia often stressed the importance of training politically informed students who are knowledgeable about historical facts, the political institutions, and the voting process for the political future of the territory, especially in a period of referenda for independence. In Australia, several teachers pursued higher aims to fight racism and make students aware of continuing colonization, a point that was never raised in the New Caledonian interviews. As the education scholar Richard Harris observes elsewhere, whether the teaching of controversial and sensitive topics focuses on the historical questions and contexts or aims to address the underlying moral questions remains open to debate (2011, 193). It is fair to assume that these differences in teachers' objectives will influence their strategies and methods for teaching Indigenous-settler history and raising the issue of colonialism.

Teacher Strategies

Teachers in Australia and Kanaky/New Caledonia adopt varying strategies in teaching Indigenous-settler history: from seeking a neutral, de-emotionalized standpoint, to bringing emotions out and addressing trauma, and even, for a few of them, adopting insurgent education methods to reshape knowledge transmission and power relations in schools.

Teacher Neutrality

One strategy a few teachers interviewed in Australia and the large majority in Kanaky/New Caledonia adopted is a middle-of-the-road approach, presenting side by side the acknowledged two main viewpoints on colonial history: that of the settler and that of the Indigenous, or the positive and negative sides. In Australia, one teacher claimed to have framed his entire subject around that dualistic colonial history. He nuanced his approach, however, by saying that, considering the lack of institutional and curricular backing, he "would worry about the reactions of parents" if he did otherwise and said, for example, "no, this is what happened, and you need to know."[30]

In Kanaky/New Caledonia, most teachers said that they sought to "show both aspects," "that colonization has had bad and good consequences." Such an approach frames colonial history in line with a morally ambivalent positive or negative value-laden reflection. An official text often mentioned as a reference point for their teaching was the Preamble to the 1998 Nouméa Agreement, which enshrines the only two officially accepted versions of history: the Kanak and the settler perspectives. Several teachers considered the Preamble to be a good basis to work from to understand "the much-touted lights and shadows" of colonization. A teacher in Pwêêdi Wiimîâ believed that the only way for historians to teach Indigenous-settler history is to "sit on the fence and say things without shocking." This teacher shifted the focus from what he perceived to be "the stigmatization of the settlers" toward the culpability of the institutions instead: "colonization is bad but are we going to stigmatize the settlers? Shouldn't we accuse the system more than the individuals?"[31] Understanding the different dynamics between individual and institutional or systemic forms of colonization and the complex and diverse positions of settlers in regard to settler colonization is indeed crucial. Institutions or systems are, however, made up of individuals. Settlers are individuals-within-a-settler-system, regardless of whether they comply with or defy it. Thus moving our focus to institutions does not absolve settlers of their responsibilities in relation to this history. Such delegation of agency toward institutions is thus a way of evading responsibility, of blame-shifting. This form of delegation is in fact characteristic of an attitude observed in other settler colonial contexts such as Australia (Stastny, Henriss-Anderssen, and Clark 2016) and Canada (de Costa and Clark 2016).

This perceived neutrality is also reflected in teachers' morally distancing the contemporary period from the subject of inquiry to talk about colonial wars and violence. That is, the present is a break from the past and in the present lies the hope for a better future. A teacher in Kanaky/New Caledonia, for instance, explained that when teaching past colonial policies, they convey to the students "that indeed it did happen, these are facts, but today everything has changed."[32] One primary school teacher educator recalled explaining to a child who was wondering about unjust practices such as the Indigenous code that "it was just characteristic of the time."[33] This explanation falls short of understanding the intentions and reasoning behind such policies. Likewise, when a teacher in Broken Hill in Australia sought to make students aware of "how colonization and conflicts have consequences that still exist in communities today," such as "disadvantage and a lot of social issues," she represented the latter as "a consequence of, colonisation, racism and conflicts *that occurred all those years ago*" (emphasis added).[34] It is in dealing with similar assumptions of a conflictual past transcended by a fairer present and reconciliation that one teacher uses the documentary *Totem and Taboo (Totem et Tabou)*, which juxtaposes the Kanak and non-Kanak perspectives and brings a message of hope by retracing the lives of two people who were on opposite sides of the roadblocks during the 1984–1988 war and later ended up working hand in hand for the same company.

This sitting on the fence or middle-of-the-road approach is often supported by teachers' self-assumed neutrality. Most teachers, especially in Kanaky/New Caledonia, reported presenting history in a "neutral and impartial manner," "from a historian's point of view." They remarked that "we can't do politics in history," that the discipline of history is meant to be neutral and, therefore, that the "teacher must be neutral." Teachers reported that they "do not give their opinion" but only "bring out sources and testimonies." Another teacher agreed: "I don't try to say that one is more right than the other. I consider it as historical facts." One teacher believed that this impartiality will "let students' free will express itself" in the future. However, considerable limitations to this strategy come to mind. How can the teaching be neutral when most of the historical "facts" come from European perspectives and European institutions? How can the teaching be neutral when Indigenous epistemologies are not considered on par with European scientific written knowledge, and when half of humanity—women—are (almost) completely excluded from the official narratives of Indigenous-settler history?

Despite such limitations, however, the stability and safety that such a strategy offers in the current political climate seems to largely rule out the prospect of such a premise being challenged. A New Caledonian historian admits that, considering the divisive history, and because of the complexity of having both Europeans and Kanak students in the class, "taking refuge in generalities" on colonial history, as can be found in the Preamble to the Nouméa Agreement, is "a way to make the teaching easier."[35] This need for neutrality is felt even more acutely when teaching about recent political history, which is considered a more delicate task. One teacher found it all the more important that, as a Kanak teacher, she remain neutral and not show a "vengeful spirit" in front of her students.

This self-imposed supposed neutrality relies on a factualized (reducing down to a few bare facts), de-emotionalized perspective of history.

The political scientist Paul Routledge argues that "emotions have always been an important element of the practice and performance of politics" (2012, 430). When history teachers seek to be neutral and apolitical in their teaching, they take the counterpoint to that: they try to suppress emotions, to be emotionless. Indigenous-settler history is taught by the factualization, the anesthesia of that history. For several teachers, the curriculum is a safe way to approach sensitive topics, to remain factual, and not allow the subjectivity of the teacher to take over: "The curriculum is the safeguard. As long as you don't step out of it and that you don't put feelings in, there isn't any problem teaching the history of New Caledonia, regardless of how sensitive it is." Similarly, another teacher in Drehu explained that "when we take the emotional out . . . there isn't any problem. It goes very well."[36]

Most teachers in Kanaky/New Caledonia therefore opted to moderate their discourse and were cautious about what they said because some words can upset and create tensions. They admitted "not lingering on," "only lightly touching on," or "skating over" these aspects. The 1984–1988 war is even less talked about, "simplified to the maximum" in primary school, and sometimes done "very quickly, at the end of the year" in high school. One teacher educator estimated that, based on the curriculum, one hour "at the very most" in year 9 is dedicated to it across the secondary and high school years of education. It is therefore taught very "superficially." According to him, the current political and psychological context explains the continuing marginalization of this war in the history curriculum. It remains "difficult" to teach given the fear that conflicts might happen again one day. It is a history that has "not been entirely digested," that is not completely "past." First, because "people who participated in the Events, who lived through the Events are still alive"; and, second, because "the idea, which is sometimes used to instrumentalize the Events, [is] that it could happen again."[37]

In sharp contrast, one teacher in Australia considered teaching to be ineffective when it is put across simply as facts. He described, for instance, his experience in a school in Sydney's North Shore, where students were socially and emotionally detached from colonial history and the lived realities of Indigenous people:[38]

> They wouldn't care. . . . That was probably the first time they looked at an Aboriginal community when I was teaching there. . . . They would see this more as just facts, and look at

facts. . . . Because those kids are like robots. They're machines to just answer the question and provide evidence and facts. . . . When people see this they go, "here we go again, aren't they over with it yet?"

This teacher believed the message would not come across because the students did not personally relate to, and invest themselves in, the content of the teaching. He contrasted his North Shore experience with his current experience in a country school in New South Wales where 99 percent of students are Indigenous and colonization is an ongoing lived reality:

Whereas here it would be more personal I think because people live it. They see it. They see the effects of colonization every day. . . . You know, you go out on the street and you'll see it. You drive down this road, straight down you'll see it. You'll see the effects of colonization and dispossession and policies. When you live it every day, you see it.

Could it be then that the factualization of colonization, of Indigenous-settler history, is a consequence of white privilege? Is it the very position of privilege that enables de-emotionalizing colonial history and distancing oneself both from past colonial policies and practices and from ongoing injustices, discriminations, and the trauma of dispossession and dislocation? French writer Albert Camus once contended that if "French people learn without flinching about the methods that other French people sometimes use against Algerians and the Madagascans that's because they live, unconsciously, assured of our superiority over these peoples" (1947). Although written at a different time and in a different colonial context, Camus offers a pertinent reflection on the connection between emotions and perceived racial superiority, or, to be more accurate, on the connection between the absence of emotional expression and internalized perceived racial superiority.

Such a connection between settler privilege and de-emotionalized teaching was in fact identified by several teachers in Australia and a few in Kanaky/New Caledonia. One in Melbourne, for instance, criticized claims of neutrality made within state institutions by way of teaching the so-called two sides of colonial history: "It's just infuriating, their being like 'we're being so reasonable; we're showing both sides of the story.'" She believed that "this whole idea about balance" and showing both sides of the story often "just conceals the most disgusting, horrific assertion of power." She remarked that "everything about the curriculum, the fact that it's taught by, for the most part, white Australians, and within their entire cultural framework, government" demonstrates that European perspectives dominate. By presenting colonial history in such a dualistic way, being "able to show that there's dissent but it doesn't really bother you," she believed that those in power are just showing how powerful they are, yet evading their responsibilities, and in fact reasserting their power.[39] Another teacher believed that "it's a very simplified way of saying it," adding that "it's dangerous to say that there are two different sides to history."[40] The nuances and the personal stories do not come through. His point seems particularly salient considering that New Caledonian historiography is marked by the marginalization of personal and group relations in favor of a largely institutional history based on the supposed dualism of colonization. As a result, teachers critical of such a "neutral" approach reported using instead a strategy that seeks to engage the students both intellectually and emotionally and aims at making them reflect on their responsibilities and, in the case of some teachers in Australia, at openly challenging colonial attitudes and white privilege.

Talking Straight, Bringing Emotions Out, and Addressing Trauma

Teachers interviewed in Australia agreed that colonization should be talked about from preschool to high school. They generally did not think that any minimum age to start addressing these questions comes into play, but that the extent of detail would vary. In fact, a teacher who worked for many years from preschool to high school with the Warlpiri people pointed out that talking about a minimum age is already thinking from a settler privileged position because many Indigenous people grow up and live with these family stories:

> The Warlpiri people of every age knew about massacres and genocide because there had been a big massacre in 1927 and those older people . . . had a huge massacre of over a hundred Warlpiri people on Warlpiri Country. They remembered. Some of these older people were children hiding and not being shot at by this white man. So, every single Warlpiri person already knew

about the massacres. The only ones who didn't would have been these two white kids.[41]

A preschool teacher did not see the very young age of the children as a limitation to bringing up the history of colonization in the classroom. In fact, she believed it "of incredible importance to teach children simplified but accurate history" so that "that they know the truth; that this was not a peaceful settlement of Australia." She therefore tailored the content and the learning materials to the age group. Although she discussed invasion and wars, she did not mention massacres or ongoing colonial child-removal policies: "It's too horrific for little children to know that children are still being forcibly dragged away from their parents. That would give them all nightmares." She always noticed a positive and proactive response from the children: "because they haven't been part of our society for very long, they can just turn around straight away and say, 'oh, we have to fix this! How can we fix this? What do we do to fix it?'"[42]

Similarly, one teacher in New South Wales did "not hide, fabricate, or sugar-coat anything," and always debriefed. He used the same method for teaching non-Indigenous students, and observed that the way they are taught, "they never feel ashamed or guilty" and instead become "the best advocates for Aboriginal history" among non-Indigenous youth. A Melbourne-based teacher believed that making history "into this objective study" is "the worst way for kids" to learn. She strove instead to relate her students to the history and to make it "something that they experience by actually seeing different perspectives," because "they're all directly implicated."[43] Likewise, in Kanaky/New Caledonia, two teachers reported that when you personally relate to the history you teach, you will bring it out "with more affectivity" yet still ensure that the content is "clarified and well understood." Connecting the students to the history was also a strategy that a now retired history teacher who worked in Victoria adopted. The connection to that history was made physically and emotionally. This teacher noted that such strategy allowed them "to have a different kind of conversation. . . . they weren't always pleasant conversations. People got emotional, people got upset, but we have to do that because people don't change their mind if they're not upset. We change our mind after addressing trauma."[44]

Paul Routledge suggests indeed that emotions are fundamental to political action:

People become politically active because they feel something profoundly—such as injustice or ecological destruction. This emotion triggers changes in people that motivate them to engage in politics. It is people's ability to transform their feelings about the world into actions that inspire them to participate in political action. (2012, 429–430)

To achieve this, several teachers focus on localizing history, narrowing the history of colonization down to micro-history and bringing out personal, family, and community experiences. Teachers seek to engage students' emotions with the aim of opening a space for a debate. One teacher, who personally experienced the 1984–1988 war in Kanaky/New Caledonia as a young student, taps into this lived experience to encourage her students to think and talk about that history:

I'm of the generation of the Events. . . . My father had his land burned. I lived in the north back then. . . . We were a minority of young European Caldoche when the Events started at the start of the 1980s. For me, this period was a real boost, even if we experienced insecurity, doubt, and fear. They shot my eight-year-old brother. They wanted to kill him. I haven't forgotten this, but at the same time . . . it pushes us to research, to surpass oneself, to understand and question ourselves.[45]

This teacher brought this personal experience to the class and shared it with her students. She noted that everything ran well. Students are interested and ask questions. Such an approach to the teaching stirs students and encourages reflection: "I feel that they talk about it back home with their parents."[46] A teacher in Kaa Wii Paa (Kouaoua) and Xârâcùù (Canala) talked about everything even if she knew it could cause problems. Colonization, the Ataï uprising, slavery, the 1931 Colonial Exhibition, and racism are some of "the most sensitive" topics that could "upset" her students, but she decided to teach them nonetheless. Likewise, when she talked about the symbols of the French Republic and screened a French flag, "it [didn't] go down well." She noticed that

they don't feel French but that's part of the curriculum and they need to know them [the symbols of the French Republic]. . . . Some looks can be disturbing or disturbed regarding these

questions, especially when we talk about the name of New
Caledonia, and which flag we will choose. These are sensitive
questions for them. . . . I think students need to talk and need to
show who they are . . . because we hardly give them the chance to
express themselves.[47]

It is by working from students' feelings that a teacher in rural New
South Wales tried to bring out students' negative emotions and turn
them into something productive. Like the students in Kaa Wii Paa and
Xârâcùù, his Indigenous students at first felt "angry," "really sad," and
"depressed," but he then turned that energy into writing and researching more. When teaching a lesson on colonization and dispossession,
for example, he encouraged his students to think "how can I fix things
like the loss of language and culture?" This led students to go out and
"interview and record local history from Elders before they pass away,
banking all of that information and story, so it always turns into a positive
thing." Some of these teachers bring this strategy to address colonialism
and challenge dominant forms of history teaching through intellectual inquiry and emotional engagement further. They have developed
teaching practices that can be defined as insurgent education methods.

Insurgent Education: Changing the Narrative

Taiaiake Alfred notes, from the Canadian context, that "an ancestral
movement has re-emerged among some Indigenous thinkers and
Indigenous and Settler ally activists in North America: Indigenous
Resurgence" (2013). This resurgence consists of "recasting Indigenous
people in terms that are authentic and meaningful," "regenerating and
organising a radical political consciousness," "reoccupying land and
gaining restitution," "protecting the natural environment," and "restoring the Nation-to-Nation relationship between Indigenous nations and
Settlers." In teaching history in settler colonial societies, three of these
aspects are particularly relevant: "recasting Indigenous people in terms
that are authentic and meaningful" by letting Indigenous people express
and define themselves and breaking down the stereotypes; "regenerating and organizing a radical political consciousness" that challenges the
settler colonial framework and thinking critically about colonialism and
the position and responsibilities of both Indigenous people and settlers;
and "restoring the Nation-to-Nation relationship between Indigenous

Nations and settlers" by recognizing Indigenous sovereignty and epistemologies, which can lead to remolded school-community and teacher-parent relationships.

Indigenous resurgence is enabled through insurgency. Insurgency is understood as "a state of rebellion or act of rising in revolt against established authority." In that sense, insurgent education is an important part of the pedagogies of decolonization. The political scientist Jeff Corntassel explains that insurgent education "entails creating decolonizing and discomforting moments of Indigenous truth-telling that challenge the colonial status quo. It does this by questioning settler occupation of Indigenous places through direct, honest, and experiential forms of engagement and demands for accountability." These "decolonizing and discomforting moments," he says, are "teachable" moments (2011).

Insurgent education requires considering three factors: the survival of Indigenous modes of knowledge acquisition and dissemination under colonial domination despite the substantial destruction of archives of Indigenous peoples through genocide (immaterial archives of human memory, songs, and dances) and ecocide (material archives of historical traces in the land and seascape); Indigenous agency in challenging, refusing, circumventing, or turning colonial ways of doing history to their advantage; and Indigenous initiatives to reappropriate political authority in education. Insurgent education is more of an action-based than a theory-based strategy. It is defined according to what it does rather than what it is. Corntassel identifies at least four actions: it "focuses on local Indigenous struggles" rather than on faraway places and token support; it centers on Indigenous people and their relationships to homeland; it occurs both on formal and informal settings; and it "compels accountability and action to counter contemporary colonialism and to make amends to Indigenous peoples" (2011). Thus, the role of insurgent educators is to "call for new solidarity movements with local Indigenous nations and find innovative ways to assist in their resurgence efforts." Insurgency enables and facilitates Indigenous resurgence. For settler insurgent educators, it is about stepping on board the Indigenous-steered canoe and "helping with the paddling" (George Manual quoted in Corntassel 2011).

What make these seven (six in Australia and one in Kanaky/New Caledonia) teachers stand out as insurgent education facilitators is not so much the topics they teach as the way they teach them. These

insurgent educators challenge, in their own way, the dominant settler colonial discourse by raising awareness about Indigenous histories and localizing knowledge through place-based teaching. In many
respects, these educators act as "warrior[s] of the truth" (Alfred 2004,
95). Although they have each developed their own strategies in accor-
dance with where they teach, their audience, and their connections,
these strategies share themes that help delineate what insurgent education may look like. Three themes tend to recur in teachers' accounts:
acknowledgment of their ignorance (or that of their institution) and
turning it into a potential for learning and demonopolizing teaching;
an approach to history from the local to the global; and place-based
teaching made possible through community resurgence and reformulated teacher/school—community relationship that consists of consultation with local Indigenous people (insurgence of self-narrative).

**The potential of ignorance, from acknowledgment to demonopolizing
teaching.** First, these educators show a common realization of personal
ignorance and a common attitude to that ignorance. They use the
ignorance as a potential for learning and for shifting relations around
school education. Ignorance, as a lever for change, becomes part of the
solution. Several of these educators admitted, for instance, that they
did not or do not know much or enough about Indigenous-settler history or that they are not the appropriate person to talk about certain
aspects of the history. A teacher in Tennant Creek explained how "as a
non-Indigenous teacher working in this context," he had learned that
he "can't be the one teaching Indigenous perspectives." In his case,
students' agency played an important part in making him reconsider
his approach to teaching. He recalled that a comment an Indigenous
student made about colonial wars and massacres made him aware of his
ignorance of that history. That, he explained, is when he started learning everything he could: "I read really broadly at the start, and now I
contextualize my reading. I know more about the community than I
did when I came here, but it takes a long time to get to that point."[48]
Another teacher believed that Indigenous-settler history needed "to be
taught about the local people. That's the major thing to get across."[49] An
Indigenous teacher working off-country thought it to be "just a natural
thing" to consult the local community as a basis for teaching. Similarly,
a preschool teacher in Melbourne believed that it should not be white
people teaching Indigenous cultures, "it should be Indigenous people

teaching this. I think with everything there has to be consultation. . . . You can't do it in this paternalistic way of white people doing it."[50] This realization of their ignorance or of their perceived inadequate position to teach certain perspectives leads them to take a humble approach to their work, to realize that they cannot be the only transmitter of knowledge in the history class. Ignorance turns from a dominant settler colonial regime to a key to break the monopoly on knowledge in the school system.

History from the local to the global. Second, insurgent education is a matter of scale. All seven teachers challenged the settler historical narrative by adopting the opposite approach: whereas the dominant narrative starts from large trends and illustrates with specific or localized examples, insurgent education seems to rely on micro-history (individuals, families, clans) to then step back to see the bigger picture, nationwide policies, or international comparative perspectives. Thus history is used as a tool for understanding one's presence, position, possibilities, and responsibilities. Such micro-history strategies are "political-epistemic projects grounded in the histories and lived experiences of coloniality" (Walsh 2007, 234). The decolonial thinkers Walter Mignolo and Arturo Escobar make the argument "for the need to take seriously the epistemic force of local histories and the need to think theory through the political praxis of subaltern groups" (2013, 39). At stake is not the incorporation or inclusion of the Indigenous people and their histories within a settler epistemological framework but instead the creation of new learning spaces, communities, and interpretations. A teacher in Country New South Wales believed that recentering the teaching around Indigenous perspectives and narratives comes naturally to him, as an Aboriginal teacher, but also to his settler colleagues after working in mostly Indigenous populated schools. This teacher used "every chance" he had to "invite people in to tell local history, local stories." His approach consisted of not only bringing in these local voices but also in helping build his students' future by looking at the realities of where they lived, the employment possibilities, and the opportunities. For instance, he helped his students develop a business model "using what resources and local knowledge" they happened to have. One student "developed cups, mouse pads, table cloths, pillows, all from her designs." He remarked that "it's really empowering to them because they become educated about their own people, their own history . . . it's important that these kids learn about their local history so that they can maintain it and protect it for their kids."

With the same objective in mind to revitalize, protect, and pass down Indigenous historical knowledge, two teachers in Menindee always used discussions with the local community, field trips in the local area, and self-produced media to make history more real and relatable so that "it sticks in their heads." Robert Lindsay considered it to be "really good" having Kayleen Kerwin, a local Paakantyi teacher, in the class with him "for this local emphasis on history." She played a crucial role in keeping the families connected and ensuring that the local Indigenous kids know "who they are related to," "who they are and how they fit in" around the country from Menindee to Broken Hill. This is crucial in a region such as this one, where children continue to be taken away in great numbers.

In light of this reality, these teachers believe that localizing history teaching is crucial to empowering their students. It enabled them to understand where they came from, that the hurdles they faced were structural and could be fought against: "If the kids could see that colonial things, . . . that the process is still going on today then the kid can possibly fight against it, and recognise it when they see it and not think it's a fact of life."[51] Such an approach enables Indigenous people to regain authority and reappropriate their history. History teaching changes from being an exogenous, alien practice to an endogenous, identity-building experience. Such initiatives depend on consultation between the school and the community, the presence of local Indigenous staff, and non-Indigenous teachers' adaptability.

In Kanaky/New Caledonia, a former primary school teacher in a public school on coastal tribal land in Pwêêdi Wiimîâ, where most students were from the surrounding mountain and coastal tribes, adopted an approach consisted of developing surveys addressed to families and inviting local people to class. She launched two questionnaires: one based on acculturation and the evolution of Kanak customary practices across generations to help pupils understand who they are, and another based on local families' experiences of the 1984–1988 war. The first was directed to the pupils' parents, grandparents, and great-grandparents to record their life experiences. This exercise had the triple benefit of bringing in voices excluded from the official teaching materials, encouraging critical thinking, and making pupils carry out the work from the historical inquiry in their mother tongue, Paicî. The teacher also organized incursions during which parents and the tribe's chief came in to talk to the students. This survey proved particularly effective in turning acculturation into a critical tool for cultural resurgence. What came out of this project was that at a time when orality was being lost and children spent more time on new technologies than sharing time and knowledge with their families, "children paid more attention to what was happening during customary ceremonies and other exchanges within families and clans." Moreover, this strategy also enabled the strengthening of the ancestral kinship system and the resolution of tensions attributable to acculturation and modernity.[52]

The second questionnaire was also directed at the pupils' families but focused on "the Events period," a period the children did not know firsthand but their parents had experienced. The questionnaire asked about the age of the parents and their location at the time; it also asked them to tell in their own words their experiences of the war. Over the years that this teacher undertook that exercise, she observed that it brought "a lot of questioning, incomprehension and suffering" because "the parents often struggle to relate that episode" because "there had been a lot of suffering." There was "at first," "great anger" and then a need to "keep working history." One of the main objectives behind such teaching, as this teacher put it, was "mostly the need to bring to the foreground the point of view of the oppressed, which is not present in textbooks." She pointed out that "there needs to be more consultation with people from here." In fact, another aspect that arose from these forms of insurgent education is the pivotal place of local Indigenous communities in the teaching.

Place-based teaching through community resurgence and insurgence of self-narrative. Third, the relationship between the teacher or school and the local community is reformulated. This is achieved through the outward movement of the teacher or school toward the community (when the teacher is from outside the community) or from the "local" teacher taking on its responsibility to be an intermediary between the school they work at and their community. All seven insurgent education facilitators developed or nurtured strong relationships between the teacher or school and the community. Insurgent education is inscribed in place and enabled through community resurgence. It is about bringing local people, local knowledge, local resources, and local talents to the foreground, and from there facilitating a local, empowering history to unfold. One teacher—a native English speaker fluent in Warlpiri who worked in Sydney and then spent almost a decade in the 1980s and 1990s running the remote public school at Lajamanu and, on many occasions, also relieving teachers—decided naturally to include Indigenous people in the educational process. Still in Sydney, she went "through the back door" and invited the mother of two Aboriginal students in her class to come in. As a result, those two students "who had been very quiet in class began to shine," "they felt personally affirmed in their identity." Once in Lajamanu, Warlpiri Country, all her teaching was undertaken "in very close consultation with the community." To build acceptance and trust, and to integrate Warlpiri parents in the schooling of their children, she removed the spatial "boundaries" between the school and the community:

> I had this policy of bringing parents and grandparents into the school. They could come in and sit in the classes whenever they liked. They knew what was happening all the time. I could only do that because I stayed there for such a long time.

She also adapted her teaching methods and materials. She spoke in Warlpiri with the younger ones and, when helpful for learning, with the older students also. She used videos along with the contributions of the pupils' relatives and other members of the local community to teach about Indigenous-settler history. She taught of the massacres, the Stolen Generation, "and all sorts of things" because "the truth needs to be told." For instance, she once invited the mother of one of the teachers in the school who had been raped as a young woman, and therefore had a child of both Warlpiri and European descent (her colleague), to come up and talk about her experience of trying to prevent her child from being taken away by the "welfare people." She received positive feedback both from the Warlpiri parents who "felt that at last the reality was being confirmed" and her settler students, one of whom, many years later, came to her to thank her "because she had developed a different view from her parents."[53]

More recently, a teacher at Tennant Creek High School explained that even though the school did not "have many community connections," and that he never heard of teachers inviting Indigenous people to come in and speak about issues facing Indigenous people and Indigenous rights before he did, he sat down "with about six or seven

Indigenous people in the library" and "networked with them." Working from the network, he gradually built when living in Tennant Creek, he reported that he had invited five people on different occasions to talk about their personal stories, covering topics such as the Stolen Generation, Indigenous rights, and massacres. He believed that it was a "very effective" way of teaching because it was "contextualized" and remarked that students learned that a person they knew was part of the Stolen Generation, and "one student in the class actually found out that her great grandma was part of the [Coniston] massacre."[54] The cornerstone to this teaching strategy is that it uses students "as a basis for teaching." It is about having them see where they fit in the world. It is empowering for them because it makes them "feel like they are really important and they can do something about it." The teacher acknowledged that such a strategy has had a beneficial ripple effect: it empowered students; it was very instructive for him as a non-Indigenous teacher; and the people who came in to talk to the children felt recognized among their community and empowered.

The process is not necessarily one of replacing one hegemonic discourse with an alternative, but instead of introducing another approach in which the dynamic is not as much about a linear modern trajectory as about the layers and the space in between, where many voices coexist, where the land is text. Insurgent education relies on consultation between teachers and parents, the school, and the community to create a space of joint education, where knowledge is transmitted by teachers, parents, and the community. These are teaching moments when orality "rivals" European scientific knowledge "for historical authority" (Attwood 2005, 157). Place-based teaching enables the teacher and students to dismantle the modern development/progress framework, to break down the settler colonial myths, imagery, and stereotyping, and to be able to see and understand the real places with their local histories and people. Consultation happens within a remodeled school-community relationship based on community resurgence. That is, the dynamic of that relationship relies on the role of the local community as a key actor in the transmission of knowledge through a process of knowledge production that is open to epistemic diversity.

The shape and content of the teaching of Indigenous-settler history vary significantly depending on the teachers' angle and emphasis. Teachers' opinions of textbooks cover a wide spectrum from positive and more nuanced to strongly critical. The teachers who account for textbook limitations on political grounds rather than on those of historiographical lacuna are more likely to complement textbook-based teaching with, or even neglect it for, other media. As a result, teachers either adopt a selective approach or a "politics of refusal." Textbooks, as a one-size-fits-all instructional resource, contribute to further discriminating against people who do not fall in the targeted mainstream; further, they often disseminate a historical narrative that is highly biased toward European settler sources and accounts. Bias in the historical sources available to teachers is informed by history teacher staffing trends and historiographical production trends, which in turn affect the content of history teaching materials. Discrimination filters through the entire education system. Moreover, this lack of Indigenous sources in textbooks can also be explained by settler attitudes to that body of knowledge. The general skepticism about Kanak epistemologies, for example, perpetuates the exclusion of Kanak sources and settler ignorance of such perspectives.

History teachers in both Australia and Kanaky/New Caledonia are given relatively free rein when it comes to teaching Indigenous-settler history. A common objective is to train politically informed citizens who are aware of their position, rights, and responsibilities. Another objective that teachers often mentioned is developing students' critical thinking and, less frequently and only in Australia, fighting racism and raising awareness about continuing colonialism. A more problematic attitude is the settler epistemic position of several teachers, more so in Kanaky/New Caledonia, as "neutral" agents of education. This neutrality is often supported by a factual, de-emotionalized approach to history teaching. Seeing colonial history and violence as simple facts may, however, reveal a position of settler privilege and unconscious assumptions of racial superiority. Several teachers in Australia have in fact identified such a connection. They, as a result, reported using a strategy that seeks to engage the students both intellectually and emotionally and that aims at challenging colonial attitudes and at causing them to reflect on their responsibilities. Of these, seven teachers demonstrated insurgent education methods. These teachers have reported systematic efforts to reflect on their attitudes and teaching practices. In doing so, they seem to have made some earnest attempts at building decolonizing relationships and disseminating a more appropriate understanding of history. In other words, although a recipe for the status quo has been the use of flavorless texts and emotionless teaching, insurgent education aims at unsettling colonialism by using contextualized, personalized narratives that turn negative emotions and trauma into moments of empowerment. These teaching strategies have not gone uncriticized by the institution or individuals, and obstacles often either impede their sustenance in the long term within the existing educational systems or deter other teachers to walk in their steps. The next chapter analyzes these obstacles more closely and explores possible pathways toward a potential political shift.

CHAPTER 7

Further Obstacles and Possible Pathways

"WHITE MEN DON'T BRING YAMS." It is my second time on the island, and as I sit on the deck of my friend's house that adjoins the school, he updates me on some of the local educational news. Originally from the French mainland, he has worked as an educational senior advisor at the local school on Loyalty Island for several years. He knows some of the local language and is slowly putting down roots in a context of high transience of the island's institutional white staff. A few years ago, when educational regulations required him, against his will, to transfer to another school, the parents of the students at this mostly Kanak-populated school took the initiative to petition the educational institution to allow him to stay. But today he talks of a different matter.

The Educational Project of New Caledonia (Projet éducatif de la Nouvelle-Calédonie) adopted by the Congress of New Caledonia in early 2016 seeks, among other things, to promote cooperation among the school, the parents, and the institutional and customary authorities. In line with those directives, he recently paid a visit to the island's customary authorities:

> I went to see them a few weeks ago to inform them of the implementation of the Caledonian Educational Project. This project is a real step ahead in the relationship between the school and the local community. I didn't do the customary gesture with a piece of material; I did it with a yam, as it's traditionally done. I could see they were surprised to see a white man doing it with a yam. . . .

I explained to them that we, as a school, wanted to build strong relationships with the community, that the school was open to them, that customary authorities were welcome any time to take part in the education of their children. But no one has shown up so far.

His words echo those of several teachers I interviewed in both Australia and Kanaky/New Caledonia.

In both societies, the relationship between the school and Indigenous people has often been a difficult point in the educational process. Sometimes, the will and the shared sense of purpose needed to create strong bonds is lacking, and school, parents, and customary or Indigenous authorities do not necessarily meet. It is a complex legacy for today's teachers to navigate, and one that, in many instances, can impair or impede the teaching of Indigenous-settler history in schools. Despite emerging efforts to diversify the school staff, evolutions in the curricula, and teaching materials, the consequences of past and ongoing colonial policies and attitudes and current contested teaching practices weigh heavily on the work that teachers must do. This last chapter focuses on both the systemic and individual factors that affect, and in some cases prevent, the teaching of Indigenous-settler history in class. After looking at the institutional and individual factors respectively, it reflects on possible pathways for overcoming these challenges.

Institutional Rigidity and Dogmatic Teaching

The institutional factors that affect the teaching of Indigenous-settler history are based on issues of logistics (curriculum, red tape, funding) that are informed by colonial attitudes and political conservatism. Several teachers in both Australia and Kanaky/New Caledonia believed that regardless of a teacher's willingness to put a strong focus on Indigenous-settler history, "in terms of the actual curriculum, that little thing in the history is the only time Indigenous people are mentioned," which greatly constrains teachers' freedom to be more creative and proactive about their work. Other teachers found that adopting a different pedagogy, as insurgent education facilitators do, and bending the curricular rules to be "time-consuming." Likewise, a common limitation that teachers in Kanaky/New Caledonia cited is the curricular constraints they face. According to the large majority of them, the current curriculum does not allow much time to talk about these aspects. Furthermore, it is not very "explicit," which makes its implementation, as one teacher put it, "delicate."

The administrative work required to move away from standardized teaching and to organize joint-teaching sessions (incursions or excursions) between the school and the local community can be discouraging. Organizing field trips is "a really difficult thing to do because of regulations" and "the amount of paperwork that you have to do is just quite prohibitive." Some therefore opted to have incursions rather than excursions. Even the most proactive teachers thought that administrative hurdles can deter many other hard-pressed teachers from bringing Indigenous voices into the classroom. They found guest speakers difficult to organize, and that funds for field trips could be hard to obtain and were not allocated on a regular basis. Teachers often reported being "underresourced"; and schools were and are "not always equipped to cover the cost" to be able to organize incursions or excursions, whether as a one-off or on a more regular basis. In most if not all cases, schools did not have funds specifically allocated to encourage co-teaching (by the teacher and local Indigenous people) through incursions or excursions. A teacher in Nouméa mentioned at least five institutions from which she needed to ask for money, as well as to organize fundraising events in the school, to cover the cost for just one trip. A Melbourne-based teacher said that she had to pay out of her own pocket when organizing for Indigenous speakers to come into the school.

One teacher in Nouméa deplored the fact that, although the school institution was failing to support students' engagement with the local community, other cultural institutions were struggling to take over, to value initiatives to learn Indigenous-settler history, and to host students' historical and artistic works on their history. She felt that young people are not valued: "We don't speak with the young, we're not interested in youth, we don't help the young, we don't allow them to express themselves." Because of this lack of institutional support, she ended the initiative. She noted that "no one cares, by the way. . . . no one asked me why I stopped."[1] In addition to these logistical impediments, several settler teachers spoke of their ignorance of Indigenous spaces and protocols, further impairing potential cooperation with the local Indigenous community in the teaching.

Ignorance of Indigenous Spaces and Protocols

Settler colonialism depends on supplanting Indigenous societies and polities by exclusion. Although this has proved a failure, the creation of a settler colonial society and polity that function according to their own rules and practices has in many cases made settlers largely ignorant of Indigenous social and political spaces, protocols, and histories. One teacher in Tennant Creek recalled that when he first started teaching, he would leave out certain topics, such as massacres, because he was naïve and did not know the stories. Some teachers felt challenged when trying to include Indigenous narratives and perspectives because they were ignorant of local Indigenous internal politics:

> There are so many perspectives out there to really get an understanding. I still only understand a tiny fraction of what is going on in terms of the politics of Indigenous people living in Melbourne. It's so complicated, and I still feel that I'm making the wrong decisions all the time with regards to the perspectives I'm putting forward and how I am going about it. It's a huge issue.[2]

A few teachers reported that, as non-Indigenous teachers, identifying the appropriate Indigenous interlocutor who has the appropriate authority to intervene remains a complex task. They did not see a "clear point of contact." One teacher in Shepparton heard from his colleagues that many of them would not be comfortable or would not know how to approach Indigenous people or "how to connect with the community." In that case, he believed, schools should "step up and help teachers make that happen," but this did not necessarily happen because schools often did not have "a strong relationship with their community."[3]

Likewise, in Kanaky/New Caledonia, one teacher educator thought that making connections "when you don't know the tribal world" was "quite complicated" and could deter many teachers.[4] The educator Sharon Davis (2016) explains the failure of educational programs on that lack of consultation. Indigenous people, she writes, "are sick and tired of having things done TO us, rather than WITH us." The key to successful education is "consultation and engagement" with the local community. She considers, however, that current educational policies only consist of a band-aid approach, which limits the possibilities of further consultation and engagement. Findings from this research seem to confirm this observation.

Consultation and engagement are limited by the weak connection that most schools have with the community. This situation can make organizing school incursions and excursions a long process and requires considerable work. A teacher in Tennant Creek observed that the situation is further complicated by "the history of the politics of it." That the school system is marked by a "history of racism and oppression" has resulted in the ongoing "mistrust" from Indigenous people toward the schools.[5]

In fact, two teachers who have actively tried to address these issues and to build strong connections and trust with local Indigenous people have faced withdrawal of support and accusation from the school institution. The teacher who worked with the Warlpiri for many years recalled that when she and the local women agreed that they and their children would take part in and support school education, provided that she also agreed to participate in their ceremonies in return, the Education Department accused her of "dancing with the natives" and decided to sack her.[6] The Melbourne-based preschool teacher who teaches Indigenous-settler history through art and direct consultation with Indigenous people faced a parents' complaint a few years ago that had unexpected consequences. By then, she had been working in that kindergarten for thirteen years, people used to come from out of area because they wanted that particular teaching, and the local council she worked for had asked her to train all the teachers in the Indigenous content of the curriculum. Yet, despite this, the council did not stand by her when the one parent lodged a complaint about the Indigenous content and the narrative of invasion she included in her class. The case then went to the Department of Education, which investigated the case and ruled in her favor. Nevertheless, the teacher was suspended and moved to another school. Today she continues to teach Indigenous-settler history but wonders at the character of an institution that produces curricula to teach Indigenous-settler history but does not support their teachers when they do so: "There's all new documentation going out now about what we should all be teaching as far as Indigenous education was concerned, even in early childhood. . . . It's of course everything I do, and I get suspended for teaching it. It's really wild." Looking back on that incident, she feared that the lack of support from her employer "makes it very difficult for other teachers to feel safe teaching

Indigenous culture and history" and to build trust and cooperation between teachers and local Indigenous people.[7] According to several teachers, the current policies of reconciliation governments and institutions in both Australia and Kanaky/New Caledonia are pursuing do not seem to forecast any move toward addressing the institutions' racism and oppressive practices or toward building trust.

Reconciliation, or "Uniting People in Forgetting"

Among the teachers interviewed in Australia, hardly any reported supporting or taking an explicit approach toward reconciliation in their teaching.[8] In fact, several were critical of the political underpinnings that teaching history from a reconciliatory vantage point has. Some found reconciliation to be "half-hearted," "a bit weak, a bit token," or "all hell-bent on assimilation." A teacher in the Northern Territory saw reconciliation as "obliterating the racism that still exists." Reconciliation, she thought, offers "a very superficial equal opportunity" and that "the framing of Closing the Gap is a really mainstream perspective," and a negative one at that. She realized when debriefing Closing the Gap with her mostly Indigenous students that such framing further stigmatizes and attacks their self-worth. Another retired teacher in Victoria did "not bother using that word" because it connotes a feel-good settler attitude rather than the actual remediation of injustices:

> Every time I had anything to do with reconciliation committees, I've been confronted to a group of people who wanted to sugar the pill of dispossession of Aboriginal people, and declare that "we're all Australians now, and let's have a cup of tea", when, in fact, reconciliation had not really addressed the major issues of Aboriginal dispossession. . . . I think it's a forged principle.[9]

A Melbourne-based teacher argued that "reconciliation is not justice" and that it is "too soon to be talking about reconciliation." She believed that instead of having history taught to them from this reconciliatory angle, students should be encouraged to think about what it means to compensate Indigenous people for the land, for their unpaid work, and "what it means to 'pay the rent.'" She pointed out that a priority is to "deal with the actual injustice" and that in other countries, it's always truth, justice, and reconciliation.[10] Likewise, in Kanaky/New

Caledonia, one teacher believed that history teaching "comes into this dogma of the 'common destiny.'" He remarked that the way history is taught sticks to a very simplified and unproblematic understanding of the evolution of the situation, which leaves the issues of truth and justice out of the decolonization equation:

> Here, very simply, there was the events, a handshake and then there has been the "common destiny" but, in other countries of the Pacific and Africa, if you take the example of the Rwanda and the Solomon Islands, there have been truth, justice and reconciliation committees. So, they first require truth, then justice, and then reconciliation. Here we've come straight to reconciliation.[11]

Although support for the institutional policy of reconciliation is stronger among teachers interviewed in Kanaky/New Caledonia, a few were critical of the impact of such policies on their teaching. Two admitted that the "common destiny" is an "ideal" and does not reflect the sociological and political realities on the ground. Another teacher in Kaa Wii Paa and Xârâcùù said that her students "don't know what it is." She explained that "first of all, for them, we're not in Caledonia, we're in Kanaky. For them, they're not French. They're Kanak. . . . Let's face the truth, they don't give a damn about it."[12]

The social scientist Fiona Probyn-Rapsey observes that "the last two decades in Australia have produced many examples of a culture of denial being met by calls to embrace Aboriginal people, usually in the name of reconciliation. . . . But as an opposite to, or remedy for, denial, embracement is also problematic" (2013, 138). This embracing has, according to her, taken the shape of "kin-fused reconciliation where family connections are envisaged as an answer to racial discrimination" (139). Promoting family relations as a solution runs the risk of uniting people in forgetting. As Probyn-Rapsey warns, family connections may "slip into assumptions about difference (as something to be overcome) and about sharing (of land, histories and identity)" (139). In fact, one teacher in Kanaky/New Caledonia remarked that many people readily assume that biological mixing will necessarily erase tensions and lead to a common destiny. He warned that "thinking that biological mixing brings cultural mixing is a false viewpoint."[13]

Uniting people in forgetting seems indeed to occur to some extent within the school system. The institution often marginalizes or disapproves initiatives to adapt knowledge to the local historical and sociological realities and to teach about the more contentious parts of history. In Kanaky/New Caledonia, for instance, according to a former teacher and textbook writer, the educational institutions have largely promoted a "highly technical discourse" and have often shown reluctance and resentment toward teachers who attempt to localize the teaching of history to fit the sociological realities of their students. It was difficult because this sort of "openness" has been "sensed as political positioning" in favor of independence.[14] Similarly, another teacher on the Loyalty Islands recalled that when one of her colleagues asked the school for permission to take students to the Ouvéa cave (where the 1988 massacre happened), the request was rejected. According to her, the school refused in fear of reprimands from higher up in the institutional hierarchy.

When opposition or disapproval does not come from the educational institution itself, students' parents can hold a substantial lever for action that may virtually push the teacher into inaction. A teacher in Shepparton (Victoria) observed that the attitudes of parents can affect whether and how Indigenous-settler history is taught and "can also be a bit of a challenge." Even if only a few parents are involved, such an experience often "taints the whole thing" and might be enough to deter an already challenged teacher from organizing an incursion or an excursion to meet local Indigenous people and learn history from them. Such resistance, he remarked, is more likely to come from older settler families, who will see prioritizing an Indigenous perspective as a challenge to their concept of what should be happening in the school.[15]

School institutions in both Australia and Kanaky/New Caledonia continue to show some rigidity and reluctance when it comes to addressing the contentious relationship between the school and the community and supporting those teachers who strive to fully and truly engage with Indigenous-settler history and with local Indigenous people and knowledge. To these institutional obstacles are also added individual complications.

Individual Complications

The main individual factors that impair the teaching of Indigenous-settler history in Australia and Kanaky/New Caledonia are teacher transience, teacher legitimacy, and student disengagement.

Teacher Transience

Teacher transience, "the 'come and go' syndrome" (Hall 2012), is an issue raised by several teachers interviewed in rural or desert areas in both Australia and Kanaky/New Caledonia. This transience affects settler teachers working in predominantly Indigenous schools. A teacher in Menindee, who has worked in that area for several decades and is a speaker of the local Paakantyi language, observed that when he used to work in Wilcannia, "every year, we used to see half of the staff being replaced." Where he now works in Menindee, "it's not so bad . . . because it's a three-year school (you've got to stay here for three years before you can ask for transfer), but most teachers move on at the end of that period." He explained this high transience of teachers on the grounds that most teachers are career driven and not necessarily interested in bonding with the place or the local community:

> They see their career as a career and they've got to move on in order to do different things and to gain promotion. They don't have any great commitment to the place either, so they just see this as a temporary appointment where they go to, do their job, and then they can go to another school, and do their job.[16]

These findings echo similar observations in the literature, which suggest that such a pattern is neither uncommon nor new. A 2005 study at a "remote rural state school in an Aboriginal community" mentions that the local Aboriginal community describes such a pattern as "tourist teaching" and teachers as "two-year tourists." This same study observes that teachers use this two-year "tour of duty" as a career stepping-stone to be able to pick their job locations later on and become principals more readily in the future (Hickling-Hudson and Ahlquist 2004, 69). The former teacher who worked in Lajamanu (Warlpiri Country, Northern Territory) for many years also observed that teachers "don't stay for a very long time" and usually work in "remote" schools for one or two years. She remarked that the transience of teachers greatly reduced the potential for establishing connections with the local community, which in turn affected the effectiveness of their teaching.[17]

In fact, in both Australia and Kanaky/New Caledonia, the division between Indigenous social groups and settler social groups remains entrenched. The "logical" behavior seems to be for a settler person to remain in the mainstream; and the mainstream is a whitestream. Christine Nicholls, who worked at Lajamanu for many years, saw it as "a sort of Us-and-Them situation" in which "most of the non-Aboriginal people, even if they were a very, very small number, would only interact with each other. They would not interact with Aboriginal people. They loved talking about them but not with them, which is very indicative." She also recalled in an interview that the Education Department at the time in the Northern Territory was so racist that when she bonded with the local Warlpiri people, she was called a "boong mother" and "nigger mother." As she pointed out, slur words and other terminologies are commonly used to label settler people who bond and live with Indigenous people. In Kanaky/New Caledonia, a person is said to "Kanakize themselves" (*s'enkanaker*). According to that logic, the workings of settler colonialism normalize the fact that some settler teachers ignore the protocols to interact with Indigenous people or find the appropriate interlocutor in the Indigenous community or tribe, after respectively 232 years and 167 years of European presence on Indigenous lands. Indigenous social groups remain in many cases, the Other.

In Kanaky/New Caledonia, where the posting of new teachers for their initial two-year period is at the discretion of the institution, the reaction from new teachers who are assigned "to the bush" is quite telling of such processes of Othering and depreciation of Kanak societies. A former teacher educator observed that most of her students who were posted to schools in the bush "went into survival mode" for the two years they had to spend there and after that "came back to their original milieu as soon as possible." Although a few found a vocation, most "made the minimal efforts to cope for two years, often at the cost of return journey between the city and the bush on weekends with their belongings in their cars."[18] One teacher I interviewed also recalled "the great fear" she had and how "she cried like anything . . . for an afternoon" when she got the news she had been posted to Xârâcùù. Her colleagues had warned her that she would be "bullied" and "beaten" by her students. After arriving there, and with the hindsight she has today, she realized that these warnings were far from the truth.[19] Nonetheless, the stereotypes and racist assumptions that continue to circulate in society impact on teachers' approaches to their workplaces and audiences. Working in largely Indigenous classes remains in many cases a default choice and compulsory (in the case of Kanaky/New Caledonia) albeit a temporary stint. In some cases, teacher transience can also be linked to another challenge teachers face in teaching Indigenous-settler history: their legitimacy to teach it in the eyes of the students and their parents.

Teacher Legitimacy

A few settler teachers in both Australia and Kanaky/New Caledonia experienced a "legitimacy crisis" when it came to talking about colonial history and Indigenous people. One teacher in the Northern Territory felt that "there have definitely been times that have been awkward," especially when teaching, that "there was so much racism in Australia, even ingrained in the system of government, and telling students that, as a white teacher. It doesn't sit, it's just not easy to do." This awkwardness may tell us more about the ways that Indigenous people continue to be treated. The awkwardness might indeed arise from the fact that racism continues unabated and that distancing oneself from that history is less of an option.

In Kanaky/New Caledonia, teaching Indigenous-settler history may be not only awkward but also conflictual. A history teacher on the east coast contended that in pro-independence and ethnically exclusive discourses both the students and the parents question the legitimacy of the non-Kanak teacher. Teaching Indigenous-settler history was for him, therefore, difficult at first, and teachers are cautious about the words they use because France is still considered "a colonialist country." He recalled an incident when one parent complained about what he was teaching in class. The teacher defended himself by saying that he had "nothing to do with what happened two hundred years ago," to which the parent replied, "yes, but you are the colonial representative. You sustain the system."[20] Another retired teacher and teacher educator in Kanaky/New Caledonia felt that "in some milieu, especially Kanak, only Kanak people or people sympathizing with the Kanak cause can have a reliable discourse on the history of this country." It is a tendency, she noted, that used to exist within European circles as well (that only people living in New Caledonia could talk about New Caledonian history), and therefore may be interpreted as "a stage in an identity process and within a political framework."[21] Similarly, yet another teacher in La Foa has also heard his non-Kanak colleagues say that for them, as non-Kanak teachers, it is more difficult to teach because the students "make them feel that they're not from the country."[22]

The lack of legitimacy that some settler teachers experience is also exacerbated by the fact that some are career driven and may show less interest in building connections with the local community. Giving priority to their career may encourage them to comply with institutional directives rather than to seek to challenge them and teach history differently. One retired teacher and teacher educator conceded that it was "a very hierarchical, structured system in which . . . career progress depends on how you are evaluated by the inspection." As a result, at the time she was teaching, from the 1970s to 2008, it "didn't push many people to be original." Her typical student teachers were often young women "who aspired to a job that would enable them to have kids, a well-paid job, a safe and stable job." She observed that the "technical functioning of the institution" suited them well because "they didn't want to ask themselves too many questions." In such an institutional situation, asking difficult questions would have been "personally demanding."[23]

The lack of legitimacy that settler teachers experienced in their work, however, was shared by some of their Kanak colleagues, though for very different reasons. One Kanak teacher explained that the colonial mentality students develop growing up in a society where the type of work you do and your qualifications still run very much along color lines can discredit some Kanak teachers. He mentioned, for instance, how his year 8 students once told him that they would ask to change teachers because he wasn't qualified to teach. He believed that, being a Kanak, he was less respected because "since they are very little, when they go to the doctor, it's always a European . . . , when they go to the post office, to the bank, it's a white person. So, unconsciously, that's the image that stays in their mind." This teacher, from Drehu, also felt that divisions internal to Kanak societies and inherited from colonization continue to run deep and affect his teaching. On a few occasions, his students on the main island have disrespected him for being from the Loyalty Islands and called him *planche à voile* (windsurfing board), a derogatory term used by some Kanak of the Grande Terre (main island) to talk about Kanak people from the Loyalty Islands. He explained that because the Kanak from the Loyalty Islands, and especially Drehu, were the first to be Christianized and therefore to read and write, many served as auxiliaries to colonization, by working in the administration, for instance. They are therefore sometimes still "perceived as a symbol of neocolonization."[24]

Considering that the school system continues to be seen by many as sustaining the colonial system, teachers—both settler and Indigenous— are in some cases discredited in the eyes of the Indigenous students and their parents. From history teachers' accounts, a difference between teachers in Australia and Kanaky/New Caledonia is apparent in the way this issue was brought up and experienced. In Australia, this "crisis" of legitimacy seems to be more the fruit of settler teachers' self-reflection on whiteness, historical representation, and Indigenous agency. In Kanaky/New Caledonia, however, challenges to their teachers' legitimacy arise from points of contention between the teachers and the students or their parents. Students, in fact, may play a crucial part in the ways that teachers choose to teach Indigenous-settler history. Although many teachers reported that teaching Indigenous-settler history "goes well" and talked about the positive and interested attitude of their students, other teachers face students' disengagement from, or refusal of, the teaching.

Student Disengagement and Refusal

In some cases, teachers felt that the attitudes of their students—either Indigenous or settler—make teaching some topics difficult, if not almost impossible. The reasons for student disengagement differ, depending on whether the student is Indigenous or settler.

A few teachers spoke about the attitudes of settler students to their teaching as impeding the learning process. Some settler students refused, for instance, to hear anything to do with colonial history and Indigenous cultures. One teacher in Australia remembered a work experience in a small farming community in New South Wales, "where everyone was white" except for one Indigenous student, and where teaching Indigenous-settler history was difficult because "everyone was racist." They were "less open-minded," "very religious, very Christian," and "proud to call themselves a WAS [White Anglo-Saxon] [sic] community." He recalled that it was "really hard for a history teacher, trying to teach tolerance, because their families are all culturally very anti-Indigenous."[25] More often than not, however, this settler refusal is not necessarily voiced but instead reflected in the behavior of the students through an obvious nonengagement (looking away, pretending to sleep, self-involvement, acting bored). One teacher in Kanaky/ New Caledonia recalled that when he screened the movie *Selma* on the

US civil rights movement as an international entry point into debating the local history in Kanaky/New Caledonia, one European settler student was either deliberately sleeping or showing no interest and looking away. This teacher interpreted that student's behavior as a "not wanting to see" and reflecting "unease."[26]

Settlers' ignorance (refusal to know) of the teaching content seems to arise from students' racism, unease, and complacency with their position of privilege. As a result, ignoring and being self-involved seemed to them a better option. At the heart of this is an incapacity to acknowledge one's involvement in that history and one's responsibilities. This withdrawal is a political statement and provides little scope for a fundamental political change. One teacher in Australia observed that today "the racism is different." In her eye, "people are so self-involved now, they don't care," whereas previously racism was "a bit more overt." Self-involvement, she said, is a more difficult form of racism to challenge: "If something is overt, you can actually mount an argument against it. You can contest it. But if it's just ignoring this happening, there's no way. You just don't contest it. It goes back into the silent category again."[27]

Several teachers believed that family background has a major impact on how the students will receive their teaching. One interviewee pointed out that teachers deal with students who also "hear things at home," which makes teaching that history complex and sensitive, "like walking on eggshells."[28] Teachers believed that "the majority of the influence on a child comes from the home," and that home education can overweigh the influence of the school education. One teacher in Kanaky/New Caledonia, working with classes in which 90 percent of students are Kanak and 10 percent are European, observed the influence of his students' families on their behaviors. He noticed, for instance, that many students (both European and Kanak) do not wish to talk about it and claim that they already know:

> I feel like it's not the students that we have in class but the parents. It's the parents with the same comments, whether it be one side or the other. . . . There is an unease. . . . It's as if the current generation inherits what happened before. . . . It's divisive. One part will listen and another part won't.[29]

Teachers pointed out that "behind one pupil there are two parents" and observed that "today's generation inherits what happened before" so that "they lose any capacity for analysis." Teaching Indigenous-settler history, they remarked, remains divisive and difficult in a politically fractured context: "There isn't really any exchange" and "everyone holds their position."

Another phenomenon among students that two teachers in Nouméa observed was "islandness" (*îléité* in French). "Islandness" is the psychological attitude specific to small islands that prompts islanders to belittle or denigrate their surroundings and hold foreign lands in higher esteem, aspiring to escape there. These two teachers declared that, as a result of some settler students' islandness, many students reject the history of Kanaky/New Caledonia as a whole.

As for Indigenous students, issues of their nonengagement were not mentioned in interviews with teachers in Australia. In Kanaky/New Caledonia, however, a few teachers on the east coast of the main island did raise the issue, whether their lack of engagement with, opposition to, or refusal of the way that Indigenous-settler history is taught. One teacher educator observed that in some places in Kanaky/New Caledonia, especially on the east coast of the main island, "anything related to the study of colonisation is rejected by the pupils." "There is a kind of rejection of this history, a refusal to talk about it" because "it's too painful," and "can bring back sufferings" and stories heard at home.[30] Another teacher who worked in Xârâcùù said that indeed certain topics relating to colonization "remain taboo or difficult to talk about" because Kanak students refuse the way it is taught in the classroom.[31] These attitudes can be interpreted as outright refusal of a settler colonial interpretation of history (epistemic domination) that further alienates their experience of that history, or that it is taught by a settler teacher as well. One teacher in the Loyalty Islands remarked that because she was a Kanak teacher working on her island of origin, she faced less reluctance when teaching the symbols of the French Republic, for instance. In that case, Indigenous students' deliberate ignorance of the teaching can reflect self-defense from further trauma or refusal of the mode of knowledge acquisition (through school, a settler teacher, a textbook). Another former teacher accounted for the nonengagement of Kanak students with the history content by the fact that taking a Western approach to history did not "touch their sensibility, their relation to history." That teacher "had the feeling" that they experienced it as "a new misappropriation of their history."[32] Indigenous nonengagement with the teaching content (in the form of passivity or voiced refusal) as well as absenteeism therefore amount to political resistance.[33]

Such students' responses are not unique to Australia and Kanaky/New Caledonia, but have also been observed in other settler colonial societies, such as the United States, where a study shows similar distrust of a single narrative and distrust of the way that slavery is taught (Weintraub 2000). Shelly Weintraub concludes that "clearly, history is not a neutral, dry, academic topic; it can hurt" (2000, 182). Despite a significant trend in teachers' practices to handle colonial history and colonial violence in a de-emotionalized, factual way, this history is everything but "just facts" on the receiving end. The chasm between what teachers project the teaching to be and what it actually is for students receiving that knowledge is emotional. Some historical knowledge, as it is taught in schools today, appears too difficult, painful, or distressful for many Indigenous students to bear. The difficulty is not cognitive but emotional. Thus several of these students adopt strategies to cope with the ongoing trauma.

Research on intergenerational trauma among First Nations peoples in Canada argues that coping strategies "can be classified into two general types": problem-focused and emotion-focused. Problem-focused strategies aim "to manage or alter the stressor, and include problem solving, cognitive restructuring or positive growth, among others." Emotion-focused strategies aim to regulate "the emotional response" of the stressed individual and "may comprise emotional expression, emotional containment, self- or other-blame, withdrawal, denial, and passive resignation." The former is a longer-term strategy, the latter a "temporary relief" (Bombay, Matheson, and Anisman 2009, 11). The nonengagement or refusal of Kanak students leans toward emotional response for temporary relief. One teacher in Kaa Wii Paa and Xârâcùù spoke of how, when she teaches controversial aspects of the history such as the symbols of the French Republic, comments included "'We're not in France" and "I don't like white people!" They "thump the table and say, 'No, it's this way here, that's how we want it.'" That teacher also recalled that when she sometimes told her students, "we are in France. We are French. The choice will be made later," the referendum "always comes back to mind" and the discussion "goes off course."[34] It is common among teachers working in largely Indigenous schools, one said, to witness students "calling names" when colonization is talked about in class. These teachers specified that the situation has never turned to actual fights in the classroom. Yet, because teaching colonial violence remains problematic in some places, some teachers put the brakes on what they teach. One teacher in the Loyalty Islands hesitated before teaching the 1931 Colonial Exhibition, in which several local Elders had been forcibly involved, because she feared that the students would "walk out of the classroom" and confuse what happened before and what is happening now.

Some teachers also observed that this refusal or nonengagement reflects a lack of interest in, or rejection of, the school system as a whole. In some areas, school is for many students only a "compulsory stage." A teacher in Kaa Wii Paa related that a discourse she heard often from her year 9 students was that they do not like or care about school, and that most, once reaching the minimum school leaving age, plan to "stay in the tribe" and "go to the field." The school system, however, has not adapted to those sociological and economic realities. Indeed, students' lack of engagement with the content of the teaching also reflects a considerable gap between the local community's expectations of the school and what the institution wants the students to get out of it.

Thus the remaining obstacles to the teaching of Indigenous-settler history are both institutional and individual. They include continuing marginalization of Indigenous people and epistemologies, weak relations between school and community, and students' disengagement from the teaching. These are perpetuated through ignorance of Indigenous protocols, ongoing assimilationist policies (in the guise of reconciliatory attitudes), teacher transience, and the background of both teachers and students. However, the resilience and persistence of some teachers dedicated to addressing those obstacles have proved that difficult knowledge can be an opportunity for learning.

Pathways Toward a Potential Political Shift

How is the teacher to engage learners with difficult knowledge, with colonial violence, and trauma without contributing to further violence and trauma? Trauma requires testimonials, testimonials require witnessing, witnessing requires taking action to stop the cause of the trauma. Both testimonies and witnessing are crucial to learning. Yet some of these links are being broken. Some of these responsibilities are not being taken up. Indigenous student opposition to the history taught in schools has been far more prevalent in interviews with teachers from Kanaky/

New Caledonia, who reported hardly ever adopting the practice of testimonials and witnessing through school incursions or excursions. As a result, although Australian and New Caledonian histories are "littered with traumatic events and traumatic lives" (McConaghy 2003, 15), and with written, visual, and oral evidences of these traumas, the methods used to teach these histories in the school system continue to be largely inadequate apart from the individual efforts from some teachers. The Indigenous education scholar Cathryn McConaghy remarked in 2003 that teaching difficult colonial history in Australian schools often came down to presenting a simplified and sanitized narrative around opposed binaries. She believes that when controversy and trauma is erased from the teaching in such a way, "in the name of protecting children," teachers, in fact, rescue themselves "from dealing with uncomfortable knowledge and the realisation of our own ambivalences." In response, she asked whether good pedagogy and good curriculum are "only that which consoles—not that which provokes?" She argues that instead engaging with these difficult and traumatic histories, "speaking the unspeakable," and teaching histories that are "continuous" and relatable to our lives in ways that provoke and heal are pressing issues.

Settler colonialism has never depended on popular knowledge of colonial history, but instead is maintained through ignorance of it. It is the privilege of not knowing that sustains day-to-day settler colonialism. One former teacher educator in Kanaky/New Caledonia remarked, for instance, that the settler society has gone from "hostility to polite indifference," to then a "growing interest," but more "with opportunistic aims than out of a real willingness to understand."[35] Knowledge follows power and control. Although settlers do not need to know, or are even required not to know, for the system of domination to endure, Indigenous people learn to know for the purpose of survival, strategic adaptation, and resistance to the very process of settler domination and assimilation.

In many respects, struggles against colonialism and colonial power are a "struggle of memory against forgetting" (Kundera 1996, 4). This struggle is all the more difficult in that knowledge is sometimes silenced by a double process of colonial forgetting for political purposes and Indigenous silencing in response to trauma. Settler regimes of ignorance can be a perverse phenomenon by which settler power is reinforced even as it is resisted. Settlers need ignorance "to shield them from knowing the realities of the injustices that undergird their privileges for their psychological well-being and for the perpetuation of privilege to remain unquestioned." Indigenous people, on the other hand, may at times use ignorance as a coping strategy, "to manage their condition within unequal power relations and keep body and soul together" (Steyn 2012, 21).

Several teachers also spoke of their students' ignorance of history, even the one closest to them. Even teachers close to certain historical events admitted not teaching them thoroughly because they lack the relevant knowledge. In their analysis of the legacy of the Holocaust on second and third generations, Victoria Aarons and Alan Berger argue, citing Henri Raczymow, that the third generation, not unlike the second generation, "is caught in something of a 'double bind,' in the abyss between the 'imperious need to speak and the prohibition on speaking'" (2017, 6). They explain that

> this "prohibition" is self-imposed, the tension between the need to bear witness to the past and the anticipated taboo against doing so creates the conditions for fraught self-reckoning and anxious expression among the third generation, and anxiety born form the awareness of their woefully incomplete knowledge and their likely transgression, a fear of intrusion and fraudulent appropriation. (6)

Such factors can also partly explain the "struggle for memory" in settler colonial societies such as Australia and Kanaky/New Caledonia. The question of the connections between trauma and historical knowledge, however, remains largely unacknowledged in these societies and unaddressed in school systems. Examples of such traumatic silence include a girl who did not know that her grandmother was involved in the Coniston massacre, children in Tennant Creek who were unaware that someone they knew well was part of the Stolen Generation, others in Broken Hill who continue to be taken away from their families and would lose sense of their identity if not for the unwavering efforts of a local Pakaantyi teacher. In all these cases, this traumatic silence has been addressed by insurgent education facilitators and through orality, that is, an act of speaking reciprocated by an act of listening.

Can the Settler Listen? Witnessing and Acting Protocols

W.E.H. Stanner claims that non-Indigenous people's inattention to Indigenous people in the historiography was "a structural matter, a view from a window which has been carefully placed to exclude a whole quadrant of the landscape" (1979, 214). Four decades later, the Australian historian Patrick Wolfe applies this critique to settler colonialism as a whole, arguing that it was "not an event but a structure" (2006, 388). The decolonial thinker Walter Mignolo, in his analysis of the irreducible colonial difference, uses a similar architectural metaphor to Stanner's:

> A room looks altered if you enter it from a different door. Furthermore, of them any doors through which one could have entered the room . . . , only one was open. The rest were closed. You understand what it means to have only one door open and the entry heavily regulated. (2002, 65)

In his efforts to explore the possibilities of decolonizing knowledge, Mignolo's interest is in the "humble recognition of the limits of continental philosophy," or what he terms elsewhere the Western epistemology (72). The findings from this research tend to agree with the need for a humble recognition of the limits of settler European knowledge of Indigenous-settler history in Australia and Kanaky/New Caledonia. The decolonial critique aims to de-monopolize Western European scientific knowledge and "to foster spaces where the listening of what has been relegated to oblivion becomes possible" (Vázquez 2012, 243). Listening becomes the critique: "It is a critique that opens, that humbles, a critique that builds understanding in and through listening" (246).

Following the renowned article "Can the Subaltern Speak?" by Gayatri Spivak, much postcolonial literature has focused on helping the voice of the "voiceless" to emerge (1988). Emphasis is on the act of speaking by those who were colonized, oppressed, and silenced. The act of speaking, however, is inseparable from the act of listening. Rolando Vázquez argues that "modernity's monopoly over representation is grounded on the negation of *listening*, that is, the negation of language as *relationality*" (2012, 246, emphasis in the original). At stake, therefore, is not necessarily the supposed absence of voices but instead the negation of listening, or what has been termed in this book settler regimes of ignorance. The focus shifts from the colonized to the colonizer. A potential destabilizer of settler regimes of ignorance is the capacity of settlers to listen. Deborah Rose explains in her *Ethics for Decolonisation* that listening is to be drawn into an ethical encounter: "to hear is to witness; to witness is to become entangled," that is, to "be in a relation-ship" (2004, 213).

In fact, several of the more proactive teachers explain that their main source of learning is listening to the people: "What I know, I know from listening and from people teaching me. . . . I would just sit and lis-ten if people were willing to share their story with me."[36] Likewise, Chris Sarra, former principal of Cherbourg School and founder of the "stron-ger smarter approach" stressed the importance of teachers listening to their students, their stories, and the stories of their communities as a way of improving the learning experience. He suggested that people should "stop being victims to the complexities" of the situation they find themselves in and "be mindful of the things that we control." For teach-ers to be the best that they can, they "need to get out there and connect with students beyond the classroom so [they] can find out more about where they're coming from . . . , what baggage they carry, and getting to know the community." He argued that "it's not quite right to think that cross-cultural training is the answer. The ultimate answer is to be in a relationship, a high-expectations relationship with children and with their community" (cited in NITV 2017).

The question of relations was at the core of this research. The question is indeed based on the assumption that to decolonize settler colonial societies, one must learn and understand the history of the relations between members of those societies, to understand how they continue to be colonial. As this research reveals, the school system's engagement with Indigenous-settler histories has little to do with rela-tions, and only a few dedicated teachers seek to bring these issues to the fore. In fact, Indigenous-settler relations have proven something almost untraceable in institutional guidelines and teaching materials because settler colonialism seeks to sever relationships and to suppress reciproc-ity and emotionality. Settler colonialism prevents us "from understand-ing that we are always already in relationship with Indigenous peoples" (Strackosch 2016, 25); and settler regimes of ignorance continue to build up, layer upon layer. Writing from another settler colonial con-text, Taiaiake Alfred speaks of the "complete ignorance of Canadian society about the facts of their relationship with Indigenous peoples and the willful denial of historical reality by Canadians" (2009, 181).

In view of such observations, to build and "be in a relationship" might be a possible pathway out of these settler regimes of ignorance. Surprisingly, the answer to the research question lies in the question itself. Attitudes to ignorance are both where the problem is and where the solution lies. Settler regimes of ignorance are a problematic mechanism that contribute to sustain settler colonialism. Yet, a person's attitude to their own ignorance has the potential to destabilize these regimes, build relationships, and shift power differentials between Indigenous people and settlers.

Decolonizing Knowledge and the Curriculum

In shifting power differentials between Indigenous people and settlers, the aim is not to discard Western epistemology altogether but to remove it from its supremacy, to create exchanges with other epistemologies, and potentially to facilitate Indigenous resurgence. One aim of decolonial education is "to generate knowledge and understanding for epistemic and political liberation" and to account for the heterogeneity of the world (Mignolo 2013, 117). It centers Indigenous voices and representations that have been historically silenced and marginalized. The Indigenous education scholar Linda Tuhiwai Smith, for instance, calls for a prioritizing of Indigenous world views (1999, 39). The education scholar Johansson-Fua conceives a third space as the Motutapu, not only a place "of continuous tension and negotiation," but also "a place of rejuvenation, a sanctuary, a place to launch new journeys" (2016, 36–37). The third space, however, is not a hybrid space but a de-monopolized space delineated by Indigenous sovereign spatiality where Indigenous and non-Indigenous people renegotiate their cohabitation and build reciprocity. The third space is a space "to confront and dominate the colonialism inside" (Alfred 2011). It is a space of truth-telling and justice. Taiaiake Alfred believes that "the strongest weapon we have against the power of the state to destroy us at the core is the truth" (2004, 95). The notion of truth can be misleading. It is not understood here as a universal claim but as the opening of a demonopolized, permissive space, a practice of personal enunciation, the potential for what Walter Mignolo calls "pluri-versality." Pluri-versality is "an ethical commitment to creating a world in which many worlds could co-exist, rather than toward one world in which many worlds would sub-sist" (2005, 116, 125). It is a place of encounter and exchange. The educator Sharon Davis suggests developing "a truth, justice and reconciliation educational approach" (2016). She argues that "it is time to move beyond merely improving the old education model" and that education systems needs to transform:

"the opportunity to stop ripping the band aid off and begin by dealing with the wound is now." Findings from this research show that, indeed, what is at stake is not mere inclusion in the current school system, but ultimately transforming education to restructure the authority base of the school system, that is, by shifting power from settlers and reconstituting an authority base founded on reciprocity and Indigenous people, educators, and sovereignties as the cornerstones.

School institutions in both Australia and Kanaky/New Caledonia continue to show some rigidity and reluctance when it comes to addressing the contentious relationship between the school and the community and supporting those teachers who strive to engage with Indigenous-settler history and with local Indigenous people and knowledge. To these institutional obstacles are also added individual complications. They include ignorance of Indigenous protocols, ongoing assimilationist policies, teacher transience, and students' disengagement from teaching. However, the resilience and persistence of some teachers dedicated to addressing those obstacles has proved that difficult knowledge can be an opportunity for learning. Although settler regimes of ignorance are a problematic mechanism that contribute to sustain settler colonialism, attitudes to personal ignorance have the potential to destabilize these regimes, build relationships, and shift power differentials between Indigenous people and settlers.

I HAVE ANALYZED THE TEACHING of Indigenous-settler history in public schools in Australia and Kanaky/New Caledonia. Focusing on the key role of the history teacher, I looked at the three main elements constituting their work: policy and directives (curriculum, staffing, and teacher training), history textbooks, and pedagogy (teacher's pedagogical choices and discussion of classroom teaching). This book testifies that the teaching of Indigenous-settler history largely enacts settler regimes of ignorance. It is an institutionalized, colonial ignorance that maintains political authority and societal arrangements in abiding by the settler colonial logic of elimination whereby "wilful ignorance means purposeful erasure" (Lomawaima 2014, 352). The failure to comprehend the realities of colonialism is the social achievement of settler colonial power.

The evolution of history curricula in Australia and Kanaky/New Caledonia has been highly divisive and remains in the throes of political antagonism, swaying between hard-won progressive changes and swift conservative backlashes. Their recent evolution is characterized by a recent retreat from Indigenous-settler history and a careful exclusion of the most contentious issues so that settler regimes of ignorance can take hold. In addition, training for staff to appropriately implement the curriculum content is nonexistent in the Australian pool of interviewed teachers. Kanaky/New Caledonia, on the other hand, seems to have made more progress in this direction. Yet, surprisingly, teachers in Australia, who reported a lack of training, are much more likely than their New Caledonian counterparts who went through teacher training to go out of their way to teach Indigenous-settler history through incursions or excursions. Presumably this lack of training worked in this case as an enabler. It may indeed be the stark realization of their ignorance and the lack of institutional support that pushed these teachers to teach Indigenous-settler history differently. Although it may initially seem counterintuitive, this reveals the power of the school system to format teachers' practices into settler colonial mechanisms of erasure of Indigenous agency and epistemic domination.

Another support and teaching tool that teachers may fall back on is their historiographical inheritance in the form of history textbooks. These, however, have revealed significant limitations. Notwithstanding the dissimilar patterns in the evolution of the production of textbooks between Australia and Kanaky/New Caledonia, this process has been fraught in both societies. In both, the space, authors, and content of enunciation in textbooks continue to articulate a monolithic historical narrative that draws a settler colonial center and Indigenous margins. Recent textbooks have begun to address the Eurocentric approach to history by including Indigenous people in the textbook development process (in Kanaky/New Caledonia) and including Indigenous sources. Nevertheless, by and large, the historical narratives in textbooks continue to be a settler's epistemological space rather than a place for plural meaning-making processes. Textbooks therefore continue to reproduce stereotypical enunciations of Indigenous-settler history. I suggest that this stereotyping is carried out through epistemic exclusiveness and biases in enunciation that sustain settler legitimacy by externalizing colonial violence, a fixed categorization of political categories, and co-opting.

A major finding is to contest the theory of the great Australian silence. Indeed, colonial ignorance as it manifests itself in the selected history textbooks does not consist of a mere absence of Indigenous people from the narrative or of unacknowledged, silenced colonial violence. Colonial violence is in fact present throughout the sample. Ignorance lies in the capacity to externalize that violence, racially, physically, and morally. This is done using three epistemological strategies: racialist discourse, self-distantiation, and a dualistic historical narrative. Externalization uses fixed political categories that make it easier to think about Indigenous-settler history. Settler-dominated epistemological space is a fantasy space wherein the settler colonial fantasy of Indigenous extinction endures. Whether this fantasy takes the form of projected racial extermination, cultural assimilation, or civic integration, it enacts the same logic of exclusion of Indigenous sovereignty and exacerbates rather than mitigates power differentials between Indigenous people and settlers.

Although teachers may use these textbooks to varying degrees, they also in many cases enunciate and replicate them. This is even more frequent in the New Caledonian context, where most teachers articulate their teaching around the preamble of the Nouméa Agreement that promotes a morally ambivalent view of colonization and "forecloses Kanak sovereignty" (Mokaddem 2017). A common objective among history teachers is to train politically informed citizens who are aware of their position, rights, and responsibilities. Another often-mentioned objective is developing students' critical thinking; less frequently, and only in Australia, fighting racism and raising awareness about ongoing colonialism are cited. I suggest that a more problematic attitude is the settler epistemic stance of several teachers, more in Kanaky/New Caledonia than Australia, as "neutral" agents of education. This neutrality is often supported by a factual, de-emotionalized approach to teaching history. On the other end of the spectrum, several teachers in Australia reported taking the opposite approach and using a strategy to engage the students both intellectually and emotionally.

Seven of the interviewed teachers reported teaching methods that stood out for their approach to teaching and their effectiveness in initiating change in the power relations between Indigenous people and settlers. I suggest that these provide practical examples of what constitutes insurgent education and what decolonization may require. Although teachers may not be able to change the system in the present and by themselves, some of them have attempted to move the lines and change power relations between Indigenous people and settlers, and between the school and Indigenous people in their lived environments. These education initiatives are "insurgent coping strategies" that have challenged dominant forms of history teaching from within the school system. As such, they also need to be accompanied and followed by resurgent education to build relationships between forms of knowledge (Gaventa and Cornwall 2008). These processes could move education, and ultimately society, in the right direction.

Yet these teaching strategies have not gone uncriticized by the institution or individuals, and teachers face continuing obstacles to teaching Indigenous-settler history. Both individual and institutional factors, conditioned by settler colonial frameworks, can prevent or deter teachers from engaging in teaching practices that tend toward decolonization. Obstacles such as logistical concerns, ignorance of consultation protocols, lack of institutional support, teacher transience, and student disengagement continue to impede the teaching of Indigenous-settler history. The greatest impediment of all, however, is that Indigenous agency continues to be marginalized or ignored outright throughout. Indigenous peoples are routinely marginalized from curriculum development procedures, marginal in the teaching staff cohort, excluded from textbook production in the case of Australia, marginalized in the historical sources, and rarely consulted or included in the teaching process, with rare exceptions. The current school system can therefore teach only but so much about Indigenous-settler history.

Possible pathways out of these settler regimes of ignorance may lie in the potential of one's attitude to ignorance. Several teachers have demonstrated that self-realization of one's ignorance can initiate a change in the teacher's practices and eventually a shift in Indigenous-settler relations. In this self-realization of personal ignorance lies the capacity of settlers to listen. What is at stake is not improving history teaching or including Indigenous voices but ultimately transforming education to decolonize the authority base of the school system, that is, by shifting power from settlers (as well as French people in the French mainland in the case of Kanaky/New Caledonia) and reconstituting an authority base where Indigenous people and educators are the cornerstones. Decolonization can take many forms in the educational space, but mere inclusion in the current school systems is not one of them.

Another pattern is evident just beneath the surface of this book. The high absenteeism in some schools, the disengagement of Indigenous practitioners from curriculum development and textbook production, Indigenous students' refusal to learn a version of history imposed on them and to which they cannot relate, and the continuing reluctance of Indigenous communities and people to engage with a school system that continues to marginalize their voices, epistemologies, and political practices are all important political statements. Yet settler regimes of ignorance are consistent and resilient in their "deafness" (Maddison and Stastny 2016). In fact, a most formidable tool to sustain settler colonial power and maintain the status quo remains its regime of ignorance.

Ironically, some of the response to this project only confirms the key argument of the book. In advance of presenting the results of my research in Kanaky/New Caledonia in a series of public conferences across the territory, one of the hosting institutions requested that the term "Kanaky" be removed from the title and suggested also removing the word "oppression" when referring to past educational policies. The former turned out to be nonnegotiable. During the conferences, I was informed elsewhere by a friend who kindly volunteered to put up a few posters around a country town to advertise the conference that all the posters were torn down within a few hours. Yet, although I expected that after such disproportionate reactions, debates at these conferences would be heated, the opposite was true. It seemed that those who opposed my research intended to simply suppress the information to minimize the chance of discussion on Indigenous-settler history; they did not attend any of the conferences. As the political scientist Elizabeth Strakosch observes, the settler colonial dynamic consists of "suppressing a genuine political conversation" (2016, 21–22). Settler colonialism lies "in the desire to close down political relations between Indigenous and settler selves once and for all." In doing so, "we evacuate the space of true politics." Strakosch defines true politics as "human freedom," as occurring "in the always unpredictable and spontaneous interaction between humans in their irreducible differences." Human plurality, she explains, is "the condition of politics" (28–29). In that respect, settler colonial contexts are characteristic of the lack of politics, the lack of a genuine political debate, and the expression of human plurality. Surprisingly, settler colonial contexts are depoliticized even as they claim to be politicized. Sustained efforts and measures are therefore needed to continue pushing for genuine political debates on Indigenous-settler relations that move beyond reconciliatory dogmas and settler colonial political agendas of homogenization and civic integration, and engage instead with the ineluctable questions of Indigenous sovereignties, knowledges, and histories, and settler positions and responsibilities in regard to them.

Appendix 1. Selected History Textbooks
(in chronological order)

Australia

Clarke, Marcus A. H. 1877. *History of the Continent of Australia and the Island of Tasmania (1787 to 1870): Compiled for the Use of Schools.* Melbourne: F. F. Baillière.

Sutherland, Alexander, and George Sutherland. 1880. *The History of Australia from 1606 to 1876,* 4th ed. Melbourne: George Robertson.

Thornton, George. 1895. *School History of Australia and Tasmania.* Sydney: Turner & Henderson.

———. 1900. *School History of Australia: Being a Brief Account of the Progress of the Colonies from the Earliest Discoveries to the Year 1900.* Melbourne: A. N. Smith.

Murdoch, Walter. 1917. *The Making of Australia. An Introductory History.* Melbourne: Whitcombe & Tombs.

Scott, Ernest. 1925. *A Short History of Australia.* Melbourne: Oxford University Press.

———. 1936. *The South Australian History Reader. Grade VII.* Melbourne: Whitcombe & Tombs.

Crawford, Raymond M. 1941. *Ourselves and the Pacific.* Melbourne: Melbourne University Press.

Meston, Archibald L. 1950. *A Junior History of Australia,* 2nd ed. Melbourne: Oxford University Press.

Cawte, F. G. N. 1961. *Australia and Ourselves.* Adelaide: Specialty Printers.

Blackmore, Wes H., R. E. Cotter, and M. J. Elliott. 1977. *Landmarks: A History of Australia to the Present Day.* Melbourne: Macmillan of Australia.

Laidlaw, Ronald. 1986. *The Land They Found: Australian History for Secondary Schools,* 2nd ed. South Melbourne: The Macmillan Company of Australia.

Shafer, Mina. 1996. *Visions of Australia: Exploring Our History.* Melbourne: Oxford University Press.

Anderson, Maureen, and Anne Low. 2007. *History 2.* Milton: John Wiley & Sons.

Darlington, Robert, Graeme Smithies, and Ashely Wood. 2012. *History Alive 9 for the Australian Curriculum.* Milton: Jacaranda Plus.

Darlington, Robert, Luke Jackson, and Tom Hawkins. 2012. *History Alive 10 for the Australian Curriculum.* Milton: John Wiley & Sons Australia.

Kanaky/New Caledonia

Angleviel, Frédéric, Christiane Douyère, and Bernard Capecchi, eds. 1992. *La Nouvelle-Calédonie: histoire, CM.* Nouméa: Centre territorial de recherche et de documentation pédagogique / Hachette.

Jacquier, Yves, Isabelle Amiot, and Christiane Terrier, eds. 2007. *Histoire: cycle 3 Nouvelle-Calédonie.* Nouméa: Centre de documentation pédagogique de Nouvelle-Calédonie.

Debien-Vanmaï, Cynthia, and Michel Lextreyt, eds. 2010. *Histoire et géographie. La Nouvelle Calédonie et l'Océanie. première et terminale.* Nouméa: Centre de documentation pédagogique de Nouvelle-Calédonie.

Appendix 2. History Teachers Interviewed
(February 2016–November 2016)

Australia

Anonymous, school teacher, Sydney area, New South Wales

Anonymous, school teacher, Country New South Wales

Anonymous, school teacher, Northern Territory

Alan Aldridge, school teacher, Broken Hill, Paakantyi Country, New South Wales

Andrew Ashton, school teacher, Naarm/Melbourne, Wurundjeri Country, Victoria

Kayleen Kerwin, school teacher, Menindee, Paakantyi Country, New South Wales

Robert Lindsay, school teacher, Menindee, Paakantyi Country, New South Wales

William Lutwyche, school teacher, Tennant Creek, Warumungu Country, Northern Territory

Elizabeth Muldoon, school teacher, Naarm/Melbourne, Wurundjeri Country, Victoria

Christine Nicholls, teacher educator, former school teacher and head of school, Lajamanu, Warlpiri Country, Northern Territory

Jo Onus, preschool teacher, Naarm/Melbourne, Wurundjeri Country, Victoria

Bruce Pascoe, retired school teacher

Kara Valentine, school teacher, Broken Hill, Paakantyi Country, New South Wales

Tim Warwick, school teacher, Shepparton, Yorta Yorta Country, Victoria

Kanaky/New Caledonia

Anonymous, school teacher, Loyalty Islands
Anonymous, school teacher, Pwêêdi Wiimîâ, Paicî-Cèmuhî Country
Anonymous 2, school teacher, Pwêêdi Wiimîâ, Paicî-Cèmuhî Country
Martine Abbadie, school teacher, Noumea, Drubea-Kapumë Country
Cynthia Debien-Vanmaï, school teacher and textbook author, Nouméa, Drubea-Kapumë Country
Micheline Edmond-Olivier, teacher educator and former school teacher, Nouméa, Drubea-Kapumë Country
J. Bernard Fayard, school teacher, Nouméa, Drubea-Kapumë Country
Magulue Paul Fizin, school teacher, La Foa, Xârâcùù Country
Philippe Fortin, school teacher, Kaa Wii Paa, Xârâcùù Country
Jérôme Geoffroy, school teacher, Pwêêdi Wiimîâ, Paicî-Cèmuhî Country
Guillaume Grabette, school teacher, We, Drehu Country
Olivier Hoffer, school teacher, Nouméa, Drubea-Kapumë Country
Alison Janisel, school teacher, Xârâcùù, Xârâcùù Country
Allison Lotti, school teacher, We, Drehu Country
Stéphanie Maëda-Tardivel, school teacher, Dumbea, Drubea-Kapumë Country
Iris Maloune, school teacher, Pwêêdi Wiimîâ, Paicî-Cèmuhî Country
Stéphane Minvielle, teacher educator, Nouméa, Drubea-Kapumë Country
Morgane Monnier, school teacher, Xârâcùù and Kaa Wii Paa, Xârâcùù Country
Christiane Terrier, retired teacher educator, school teacher, and textbook author

Notes

Author's Note

1. Settler nativism, what Vine Deloria Jr. calls "the Indian-grandmother complex" in the US context (1988), is a strategy used by some settlers to evade settler identity and moral responsibility by claiming distant Indigenous ancestry or belonging to the land "while continuing to enjoy settler privilege and occupying stolen land" (Tuck and Yang 2012, 11).

2. For more details on delinking and decolonial forms of identification, see the interview of Walter Mignolo by Rubén Gaztambide-Fernández 2014.

Introduction

1. On the teaching of Pacific history and Pacific studies at university level, see Thaman 2003; Firth 2011; D'Arcy 2011; Teaiwa 2011, 2017; and Taumoefolau 2011. On decolonization and education, see Hutchings and Lee-Morgan 2016.

2. For such observations in the Canadian context, see McGonegal 2009; James 2012; and Davis et al. 2016; for the Australian, see Maddison and Stastny 2016.

3. Indigenous people, teachers, and students boycotted the bicentennial celebrations. Teacher unions threatened to boycott syllabus that did not include Indigenous perspectives. As a result, the New South Wales Education Department allowed Indigenous people to boycott some bicentennial activities (Macintyre and Clark 2004, 177).

4. For studies on knowledge and power, see, for instance, Foucault and Gordon 1980; Apple 1982; Freire 1984; and Popkewitz 1997b. For the implications of knowledge and power on decolonization, see Watson-Gegeo and Gegeo 1992; and Wilson 2004. For the relationship between Indigenous knowledge resurgence and Indigenous governance, see Alfred 1999. For foundational works on the field of ignorance studies, see Mills 1997; Sullivan and Tuana 2007; Proctor and Schiebinger 2008; Bedford 2010; and Malewski and Jaramillo 2011. The study of ignorance has recently been termed "agnotology" (Proctor and Schiebinger 2008).

5. For further analysis of emotional regimes, see Reddy 2001; and Rosenwein 2010.

6. Colonization was led by the British Crown, but colonizers were not exclusively British. As an example, the first fleet consisted of people from Britain, Ireland, the Channel Islands, Africa, North America, the West Indies, Madagascar, Holland, France, Germany, Norway, Portugal, Sweden, Bengal, and Hong Kong, among other places.

7. Kanaky/New Caledonia consists of eight Kanak customary areas.

8. It is estimated that between one thousand and fifteen hundred Kanak people were exiled to places as far as Tahiti, southeast Asia, and Africa.

9. The southeast of Australia was the most severely affected by colonization and dispossession, so much so that, for instance, today no fluent speakers of any of the thirty-eight language groups in Victoria remain (Nicholson 2016). In Kanaky/New Caledonia, for instance, the Loyalty Islands were declared Kanak reserves in their entirety. They therefore have not experienced the form of settler invasion and pastoral colonization that occurred on the main island, and they continue to be almost exclusively customary lands today. The Kanak sociopolitical structures and relations were, however, deeply affected by Catholic and Protestant missions as well as by the structural, administrative, legal, and institutional forms of settler colonialism.

10. Heather Goodall nuances the government will to control and dispossess Aboriginal people and the trauma of concentration on reserves with Aboriginal concept of independence through land under the reserve system and their use of independent reserves in southeast Australia until the early twentieth century (1990).

11. Colonialism also deeply contributed to gender domination. For instance, missions (which discriminated against Indigenous women relative to Indigenous men by implementing a male hierarchy and subjugating women to Christian notions of morality) put Indigenous women in a

double bind. Racial domination and violence doubled with gender domination and violence. However, Indigenous girls and boys alike were victims of rape by some clergymen. Admittedly, although some missionaries treated Indigenous people more humanely, they remained adamant that Indigenous people could not become civilized if they were not Christianized.

12. In 2000, about 70 percent of school students were in government schools. To date, government schools continue to be the major provider of school education in Australia, some 65 percent of school-age students enrolled being in government schools (Burke and Spauli 2001; Australian Bureau of Statistics 2001).

13. The first governor of New Caledonia, Charles Guillain, opened public primary schools across the territory and decided, thirteen years ahead of mainland France, to make education free and compulsory. His initiative, however, would not be carried on after he left the territory in 1870. Additionally, in 1862, he opened a professional school for Indigenous people in Nouméa.

14. For further reading on Aboriginal and Torres Strait Island activism in the early twentieth century, see McGregor 1993; Jones 2000; and Maynard 2005. For Indigenous activism from the 1960s onward in the Australian context, see Lothian 2005; McGregor 2009; and Foley, Schaap, and Howell 2014; for the New Caledonian, see Connell 1987; and Chappell 2003, 2013.

15. Community-run programs created in the early 1970s by Indigenous activists and inspired by Black Power forms of activism were later recuperated by government institutions in the late 1970s and 1980s. These programs became responsible to the government for their finances and for receiving funding. Therefore, politically speaking, it is self-management rather than self-determination that was achieved. Policy delivery was in Indigenous hands but policymaking remained in the hands of the government.

16. The Australian government promoted and celebrated the 1988 bicentenary with advertising and merchandising (through the Australian Bicentennial Authority) and a television program for instance. A privately funded reenactment of the first fleet also took place (Spillman 1994; White 2004).

17. The 1984–1988 war opposed those for the independence of the territory to those against it and shook the territory with the creation of roadblocks, the occupation of land and police stations, population displacements, electoral boycotts, physical confrontations, killings, assassinations, and massacres.

18. The Mabo legal case was named after Torres Strait Islander Eddie Koiki Mabo, who challenged the State of Queensland and the Australian legal system and fought for recognition of the rights of the Meriam people to the land. In 1992, the High Court of Australia overturned the notion of *terra nullius* and recognized that Aboriginal and Torres Strait Islander peoples have rights to the land. This led to the Australian Parliament passing the Native Title Act in 1993.

19. See Dodson 1996; Foley 1997; Atkinson 2001; and McNeil 2004.

20. The Technical and Scientific Cultural Office became the Agency for the Development of Kanak culture (Agence de développement de la culture kanak) after the 1988 Matignon-Oudinot Agreements. The Land Office became the Agency for Rural Development and Land Planning (Agence de développement rural et d'aménagement foncier) in 1986.

21. When Prime Minister Tony Abbott established the Council in 2013, it was made up of twelve members. In early 2017, Prime Minister Turnbull disbanded it and created another of six members.

22. The Congress is elected by the New Caledonian citizens. Political parties have to win at least 5 percent of votes to be represented in the Congress. The Congress includes fifty-four members. Seven (of fourteen) are sent by the Loyalty Islands Province parliament, fifteen (of twenty-two) by the Northern Province parliament and thirty-two (of forty) by the Southern Province parliament. Congress elects the New Caledonian government. The government seats are shared in proportion to the seats of the parliamentary groups.

23. In 2005, Kanak women mobilized and called for the inclusion of Kanak women in the Customary Senate.

24. For instance, the Stolen Generation continues to be a daily reality for many Aboriginal families. Larissa Behrendt notes that Indigenous children in out-of-home care rose from 9,070 in June 2007, the year before the apology speech, to 15,455 in June 2015 (2016). In 2007, 45.3 percent of Indigenous children in out-of-home care were placed with their own Indigenous family; in 2016, only 35.9 percent were. More Indigenous children are being removed today than at any other time in Australian history.

25. Clinton Pryor is a Wajuk, Balardung, Kija, and Yulparitja man. In 2016 and 2017, he undertook a year-long walk across the Australian continent to demand justice for Indigenous people.

Chapter 1: Settler Colonialism and Decolonization

1. The association CORAIL (Coordination pour l'Océanie des Recherches sur les Arts les Idées et les Littératures) was founded in 1987 to enable scholars working at the French University of the Pacific (now the University of New Caledonia) to share their research.

2. Several politicians, thinkers, and authors of the nineteenth and early twentieth century already held anticolonial values and condemned Western European nations' colonial practices. Many more took a stance against colonialism in one form or another throughout the colonial period. For instance, some settlers fought on the Indigenous side, some refused to take part in massacres, and others hid Indigenous people lest they be massacred by other settlers and condemned colonial practices in local newspapers. For more details on the various forms of criticism of colonialism articulated from the late nineteenth to the mid-twentieth century, see Ageron 1973; and Biondi and Morin 1992.

3. "Coloniality" is a portmanteau word of the terms "'colonialism" and "modernity."

4. The *Routledge Handbook of the History of Settler Colonialism* is a multiauthor book in which authors address various geographical locations across European colonialisms individually (Cavanagh and Veracini 2016). They do not engage in a comparative analysis across European colonialisms.

5. For examples of such collections, see Taylor and Guyver 2012; and Elmersjö, Clark, and Vinterek 2017. One recent exception focuses on a comparative analysis of decolonizing history education in two formally colonized countries (Blackburn and Wu 2019).

6. Following World War II, the Australian National University founded a chair in the history of the Pacific in 1949 and launched the *Journal of Pacific History* in 1966. Historians such as James Wightman Davidson, Dorothy Shineberg, and Bronwen Douglas engaged in the history of the Pacific islands.

7. For North America, see Smith et al. 2011; Hickman and Porfilio 2012; and Shadowwalker 2012; for South Africa, see Engelbrecht 2006; and for Aotearoa, see Openshaw 2005.

8. Anonymous, email correspondence. NAPLAN (National Assessment Program—Literacy and Numeracy) is a series of standardized tests introduced in Australia in 2008 assessing students' reading, writing, language, and numeracy.

9. This figure is nonetheless higher than the national proportion of Indigenous teachers in Australian schools (1 percent).

10. These locations do not include the workplace of teachers who chose to remain anonymous.

11. The Teach for Australia program aims at attracting high-quality candidates without a background in education to the teaching profession. It consists of a two-year employment contract in a disadvantaged secondary school, with a reduced teaching load, and a higher level of support and training. Once the placement and program of study are completed, participants are awarded a postgraduate teaching qualification.

12. This figure is nonetheless higher than the national proportion of Kanak teachers in New Caledonian schools (4 percent).

13. These do not include the workplace of teachers who chose to remain anonymous.

Chapter 2: History Curriculum Development and Reforms

1. Bruce Pascoe, author interview, 2016.

2. Christine Nicholls, author interview, 2016.

3. The Northern Territory's bilingual education programs were implemented in 1973. In 1998, the territorial government decided, without community consultation, to ax these programs on the grounds that students were performing poorly, although such evidence was not brought forward (Nicholls 2005). The government decision faced fierce objections from Indigenous people and teachers.

4. Christine Nicholls, author interview, 2016.

5. Kayleen Kerwin, author interview, 2016.

6. In 1971, local politicians had demanded that the law be extended to Kanak languages but were refused by the Vice Rectorate in 1975 (Vernaudon 2013, 115).

7. Magulue Paul Fizin, author interview, 2016. Interviews were conducted in French in Kanaky/New Caledonia. Translation of the New Caledonian interview data into English is my own.

8. Iris Maloune, author interview, 2016.

9. Iris Maloune, author interview, 2016.

10. Jérôme Geoffroy, author interview, 2016.

11. The 1982 NSW History Syllabus included a section title "The Aboriginal People" in the unit "Australia to 1914," which included the study of their prehistory, culture, and the impact of white "Settlement" (Condie 2012, 51).

12. Bruce Pascoe, author interview, 2016.

13. Jo Onus, author interview, 2016. The Wannik strategy is a Victorian government's education strategy for Indigenous students, which requires all government schools to develop an Individual Education Plan (IEP) for every Indigenous student from prep years to year 12 to improve their educational outcomes.

14. Andrew Ashton, author interview, 2016.

15. In Victoria and part of New South Wales, Aboriginal people refer to themselves as Koori when not referencing their specific Indigenous Nation.

16. This term (Events) is a common euphemistic way to label the war of the 1980s.

17. Christiane Terrier, author interview, 2016.

18. Christiane Terrier and Olivier Hoffer, author interviews, 2016.

19. Andrew Ashton, author interview, 2016.

20. As a result, for the 2018 provisional curriculum and the 2020 curriculum, I have estimated the proportion of Indigenous-settler history in the history curriculum according to the key focus points within each theme of historical inquiry. For example, in year 8, only one focus point of nine engages with Indigenous-settler history, which represents 11 percent of the history curriculum.

21. Magulue Paul Fizin and Guillaume Grabette, author interviews, 2016.

22. J. Bernard Fayard, Philippe Fortin, and Cynthia Debien-Vanmai, author interviews, 2016.

23. The curriculum in use is the French national curriculum with some contextualization to the New Caledonian and Pacific histories.

24. Allison Lotti, author interview, 2016.

25. Guillaume Grabette and Martine Abbadie, author interviews, 2016.

26. Stéphane Minvielle, author interview, 2016.

27. Guillaume Grabette, author interview, 2016.

28. Ismet Kurtovitc, J. Bernard Fayard, Cynthia Debien-Vanmai, and Olivier Hoffer, author interviews, 2016.

29. Magulue Paul Fizin, author interview, 2016.

30. Cynthia Debien-Vanmai, author interview, 2016.

31. Martine Abbadie, author interview, 2016.

32. Tim Warwick and William Lutwyche, author interviews, 2016.

33. Magulue Paul Fizin, author interview, 2016.

34. Morgan Monnier, author interview, 2016.

35. Bruce Pascoe, author interview, 2016.

36. The Colonial Party was "a loose collection of individuals, groups, and publications" with economic, political, and scientific interests in the colonies that organized meetings of pro-colonial representatives in the lower house from 1892 and in the upper house (le Sénat) from 1898 (Aldrich 1988, 31–32). The French Oceania Committee, created in 1905, gathered politicians, lawyers, academics, colonial administrators, and businessmen from the largest transport and mining companies operating in the Pacific at the time.

37. The Colonial Exhibition of 1931 was removed from the year 9 curriculum in 2018.

38. Allison Lotti, author interview, 2016.

39. Alison Janisel, author interview, 2016.

40. Jérôme Geoffroy, author interview, 2016.

41. Tim Warwick, author interview, 2016.

42. Stéphane Minvielle and Stéphanie Maëda-Tardivel, author interviews, 2016.

43. High school students can instead take electives in modern history or Aboriginal studies, for example.

44. Andrew Ashton, author interview, 2016.

45. Micheline Edmond-Olivier, author interview, 2016.

46. Guillaume Grabette, author interview, 2016.

47. Magulue Paul Fizin, author interview, 2016.

Chapter 3: Staffing and Teacher Training

1. William Lutwyche, author interview, 2016.

2. Pwêêdi Wiimîâ (Poindimié) is a town on the east coast of the Northern Province.

3. Christiane Terrier, author interview, 2016.

4. Stéphane Minvielle, author interview, 2016.

5. September 24 marks the official colonization of "New Caledonia" by France. It is a public holiday contested by a sizable portion of the New Caledonian population, which calls it a "Day of Mourning."

6. Stéphanie Maëda-Tardivel, author interview, 2016.

7. Christiane Terrier, author interview, 2016.

8. Christiane Terrier, author interview, 2016.

9. Stéphanie Maëda-Tardivel, author interview, 2016.

10. CAPES is the abbreviation of Certificat d'aptitude au professorat de l'enseignement secondaire (Certificate of Aptitude for Teachers of Secondary Education). It is a competitive examination.

11. Christine Nicholls, author interview, 2016.

12. William Lutwyche, author interview, 2016.

13. Bu Rhaï (Bourail) is a country town on the main island 150 kilometers (93 miles) from Nouméa, known for its European settler farming heritage, and one of the very few towns in Kanaky/New Caledonia where most of the population have a European settler background.

14. Christiane Terrier, author interview, 2016.

Chapter 4: Textbook Production and Authorship

1. Some materials presented in the section titled "The 'Great Australian Silence' Re-Examined" are based on Angélique Stastny, "The Fabrication of Settler Legitimacy: Managing Colonial Violence and Wars in Australian School Textbooks from the 1870s to the Present," *Postcolonial Studies* 22(3) (2019): 362–383.

Sutherland and Sutherland's *History of Australia from 1606 to 1876* sold more than 120,000 copies when first published in 1877. It was last republished in 2008 by Dodo Press. Whitcombe and Tomb's school publications were used widely in Australian schools from the late nineteenth century until the 1960s (Bradford 2001, 120). Walter Murdoch was an influential academic and political figure of his time and one of Australia's most popular and selling authors of the twentieth century. His books sold in the tens of thousands. Ernest Scott's textbook went through many editions between 1910 and 1964, meaning that a couple of generations learned about Australia's history from his textbook.

2. No further information could be obtained about this publisher.

3. For more details on the evolution of these publishers in Australia, see Muir 2006 and Tritter 2013 for Oxford University Press, and Handford 2001 for Macmillan.

4. The identity of two of the 1977 textbook authors could not be traced from their initials. Nevertheless, considering the nature of the content of that textbook and the general authorial practices of the time, it is highly unlikely that either of these authors was Indigenous. It seems highly probable that no Indigenous author has been involved in the writing of any of the textbooks in this selection and that textbooks have therefore been designed without input from any Indigenous practitioners.

5. Tim Warwick, author interview, 2016.

6. Christiane Terrier, author interview, 2016.

7. Magulue Paul Fizin, author interview, 2016.

8. The 2007 textbook is a multilingual textbook and some units are translated into a few Kanak languages.

9. Christiane Terrier, author interview, 2016.

10. Magulue Paul Fizin, author interview, 2016.

11. See, for instance, Reynolds 1984, 1992; Attwood 2005; Gunstone 2004; Macintyre and Clark 2004; and Parkes 2007.

12. The percentage of Indigenous-settler content is calculated against the total number of pages on Australian history. That is, sections of textbooks that deal with international history are not taken into account.

13. The Kanak and Socialist National Liberation Front (Front de libération nationale Kanak et socialiste) is a pro-independence alliance of political parties in Kanaky/New Caledonia created in 1984.

14. Ernest Lavisse was a prominent historian whose school textbooks became classics and were used to educate generations of French schoolchildren until the 1960s.

15. The proportion of Indigenous-settler history is 70 percent for the 1992 textbook, 71 percent for the 2007 textbook, and 69 percent for the 2010 textbook.

16. The 1877, 1880, 1895, and 1941 textbooks do not include any sources.

17. I classified the sources into three categories: "settler," "Indigenous," and "un-specified." These calculations are based exclusively on the sources found in the book sections that mention Indigenous-settler history. The sources used in the sections of the book that address Australian history but fail to mention Indigenous people are not counted.

18. Stéphane Minvielle, author interview, 2016.

Chapter 5: Textbook Narratives and Stereotyping

Some materials presented in this chapter were previously published in the journal *Postcolonial Studies*. See Angélique Stastny, "The Fabrication of Settler Legitimacy: Managing Colonial Violence and Wars in Australian School Textbooks from the 1870s to the Present," *Postcolonial Studies* 22(3) (2019): 362–383.

1. The Black Line was a military tactic instigated in Van Diemen's Land (today Tasmania) in 1830 by Lieutenant-Governor George Arthur. Arthur ordered thousands of settlers to form a human chain—what became known as the Black Line—that moved across Tasmania over many weeks to capture and relocate the remaining Aboriginal people to the Tasman Peninsula.

The plan to capture a large number of Aboriginal people failed but it increased settlers' control over the region, which ended in the "forced surrender of Aboriginal people" (Ryan 2013).

2. Nineteenth-century colonial conflicts are depicted on Kanak engraved bamboos, for instance, and Kanak iconographical archives on the 1984–1988 war exist. Macki Wéa's personal archives, which are exhibited every year during the commemoration of the 1988 Ouvéa massacre, include children's drawings of the Ouvéa crisis and massacre that were made in the Kanak Popular Schools in the aftermath of the conflicts.

3. For this reason, considering that the earliest official New Caledonian textbook dates to the 1990s, racialist discourse was not found in the New Caledonian sample. This epistemological strategy therefore does not apply to New Caledonian textbooks.

4. In the 2007 textbook are lessons on "the evolution of the status of women in the world and in Oceania" and "the evolution of the status of women in New Caledonia" but no settler woman is named in the body of the text of these lessons.

5. In the 1992 textbook, they are also described in terms of loss. Yet they are more likely to be represented as modernity and progress personified.

6. One could assume that the Native Title Act of 1993 that conceded some rights to lands for Indigenous people acted as a considerable lever for change in that respect.

7. The 2000 Walk for Reconciliation over the Sydney Harbour Bridge was one of the forms of public expression of support for meaningful reconciliation between Indigenous people and settlers in Australia. Some 250,000 people took part.

8. In the 1996 textbook, Aboriginal deaths in custody are relegated to guidelines for further study (41), and excerpts from the Royal Commission on Aboriginal Deaths in Custody (184–186) outlining recommendations for a better future do not address the institutional mechanisms and attitudes that allow violence against Indigenous people to be perpetuated.

Chapter 6. Compliant and Insurgent Education

1. Kara Valentine and Tim Warwick, author interviews, 2016.
2. Micheline Edmond-Olivier, author interview, 2016.
3. Magulue Paul Fizin, author interview, 2016.
4. Cynthia Debien-Vanmai, author interview, 2016.
5. Olivier Hoffer, author interview, 2016.

6. Stéphane Minvielle, author interview, 2016.

7. Bruce Pascoe, author interview, 2016.

8. Tim Warwick, author interview, 2016.

9. William Lutwyche, author interview, 2016.

10. Stéphane Minvielle, author interview, 2016.

11. Martine Abbadie, author interview, 2016.

12. The 1972 letter by Prime Minister Pierre Messmer to his state secretary for overseas departments and territories states France's interests in encouraging "mass migration" to Kanaky/New Caledonia to shift political power in favor of the loyalist electorate and ensure that it remains "a prosperous French territory." Eloi Machoro was one of the key Kanak figures of the pro-independence movement in the 1980s. He, and Marcel Nonnaro, were shut down by the elite police tactical unit of the French National Gendarmerie in 1985.

13. Magulue Paul Fizin, author interview, 2016.

14. Iris Maloune, author interview, 2016.

15. In Australia, the most commonly mentioned websites for that purpose are the Stolen Generations' Testimonies, the oral history website Yarnin, and Culture Victoria, which according to some teachers also have the advantage of maintaining knowledge that otherwise might have been lost with the passing of the Elders.

16. Bruce Pascoe, author interview, 2016.

17. Tim Warwick, author interview, 2016.

18. Allison Lotti and Guillaume Grabette, author interviews, 2016.

19. Jo Onus, author interview, 2016.

20. Alison Janisel, author interview, 2016.

21. Stéphanie Maëda-Tardivel, author interview, 2016.

22. Stéphane Minvielle, author interview, 2016.

23. Stéphanie Maëda-Tardivel, author interview, 2016.

24. Cynthia Debien-Vanmai, author interview, 2016.

25. Allison Lotti, Guillaume Grabette, and Jean-Bernard Fayard, author interviews, 2016.

26. Andrew Ashton, author interview, 2016.

27. Magulue Paul Fizin, author interview, 2016.

28. Jo Onus, author interview, 2016.

29. Elizabeth Muldoon, author interview, 2016.

30. Tim Warwick, author interview, 2016.

31. Jérôme Geoffroy, author interview, 2016.

32. Philippe Fortin, author interview, 2016.

33. Micheline Edmond-Olivier, author interview, 2016.

34. Kara Valentine, author interview, 2016.

35. Ismet Kurtovitch, author interview, 2016.

36. Stéphanie Maëda-Tardivel and Guillaume Grabette, author interviews, 2016.

37. Stéphane Minvielle, author interview, 2016.

38. North Shore is a socioeconomically privileged area of Sydney with a large number of elite private schools.

39. Elizabeth Muldoon, author interview, 2016.

40. Andrew Ashton, author interview, 2016.

41. Christine Nicholls, author interview, 2016.

42. Jo Onus, author interview, 2016.

43. Elizabeth Muldoon, author interview, 2016.

44. Bruce Pascoe, author interview, 2016.

45. "Caldoche" is the name given to settlers who have lived in Kanaky/ New Caledonia for several generations.

46. Cynthia Debien-Vanmai, author interview, 2016.

47. Morgane Monnier, author interview, 2016.

48. William Lutwyche, author interview, 2016.

49. Robert Lindsay, author interview, 2016.

50. Jo Onus, author interview, 2016.

51. Robert Lindsay and Kayleen Kerwin, author interview, 2016.

52. Iris Maloune, author interview, 2016.

53. Christine Nicholls, author interview, 2016.

54. William Lutwyche, author interview, 2016.

Chapter 7: Further Obstacles and Possible Pathways

1. Martine Abbadie, author interview, 2016.

2. Elizabeth Muldoon, author interview, 2016.

3. Tim Warwick, author interview, 2016.

4. Stéphane Minvielle, author interview, 2016.

5. William Lutwyche, author interview, 2016.

6. Christine Nicholls, author interview, 2016.

7. Jo Onus, author interview, 2016.

8. One exception is a teacher who understood reconciliation as "the removal of racism" and as an understanding of how inequality works. She deplored, however, that the way it was taught was "not done very well," not "authentic," and often a "textbook lesson."

9. Bruce Pascoe, author interview, 2016.

10. Elizabeth Muldoon, author interview, 2016.

11. Magulue Paul Fizin, author interview, 2016.

12. Magulue Paul Fizin; Morgane Monnier, author interviews, 2016.

13. Magulue Paul Fizin, author interview, 2016.

14. Christiane Terrier, author interview, 2016.

15. Tim Warwick, author interview, 2016.

16. Robert Lindsay, author interview, 2016.

17. Christine Nicholls, author interview, 2016.

18. Christiane Terrier, author interview, 2016.

19. Morgane Monnier, author interview, 2016.

20. Philippe Fortin, author interview, 2016.

21. Christiane Terrier, author interview, 2016.

22. Magulue Paul Fizin, author interview, 2016.

23. Christiane Terrier, author interview, 2016.

24. Magulue Paul Fizin, author interview, 2016.

25. Alan Aldridge, author interview, 2016.

26. Magulue Paul Fizin, author interview, 2016.

27. Christine Nicholls, author interview, 2016.

28. Stéphanie Maëda-Tardivel, author interview, 2016.

29. Magulue Paul Fizin, author interview, 2016.

30. Stéphane Minvielle, author interview, 2016.

31. Alison Janisel, author interview, 2016.

32. Christiane Terrier, author interview, 2016.

33. As early as the 1980s, the educator Ralph Folds described a range of Aboriginal resistance behaviors, the most effective and widespread of which was absenteeism (1987, 455).

34. Morgane Monnier, author interview, 2016.

35. Christiane Terrier, author interview, 2016.

36. Jo Onus, author interview, 2016.

References

Aarons, Victoria, and Alan L. Berger. 2017. *Third-Generation Holocaust Representation: Trauma, History, and Memory.* Evanston, IL: Northwestern University Press.

ACARA. 2012. *Curriculum Design Paper,* Version 3. Sydney: Acara.

Agence France Presse. 2012. "L'UMP dénonce une 'provocation' de Victorin Lurel sur la 'Kanaky.'" *Libération,* August 1.

Ageron, Charles-Robert. 1973. *L'anticolonialisme en France de 1871 à 1914.* Vendôme: Presses Universitaires de France.

Ahmed, Sara. 2014. *The Cultural Politics of Emotion.* Edinburgh: Edinburgh University Press.

Aiken, Kirsten. 2000. "Highest-ranking Indigenous police officer retires." *ABC Local Radio,* June 22. https://www.abc.net.au/pm/stories /s142894.htm.

Aldrich, Robert. 1988. "New Caledonia in French Historiography." In *New Caledonia: Essays in Nationalism and Dependency,* edited by Michael Spencer, Alan Ward, and John Connell, 22–37. St. Lucia: University of Queensland Press.

———. 1989. "Le lobby colonial de l'Océanie française." In *La France et le Pacifique. Revue française d'histoire d'outre-mer,* edited by Paul de Deckker and Pierre Yves Toullelan, 143–156. Paris: Société française d Outre-mer.

Alfred, Taiaiake. 1999. *Peace, Power, Righteousness: An Indigenous Manifesto,* 2nd ed. New York: Oxford University Press.

———. 2004. "Warrior Scholarship. Seeing the University as a Ground of Contention." In *Indigenizing the Academy: Transforming Scholarship and Empowering Communities,* edited by Devon A. Mihesuah and Angela C. Wilson, 88–99. Lincoln: University of Nebraska Press.

———. 2009. "Restitution Is the Real Pathway to Justice for Indigenous Peoples." In *Response, Responsibility and Renewal: Canada's Truth and Reconciliation Journey,* edited by Gregory Younging, Jonathan Dewar, and Mike DeGagné, 179–190. Ottawa: Aboriginal Healing Foundation.

———. 2005. *Wasáse: Indigenous Pathways of Action and Freedom.* Toronto: University of Toronto Press.

———. 2011. "The Psychic Landscape of Contemporary Colonialism." Presentation at the Forum for Aboriginal Studies and Research, University of Ottawa, November 9.

———. 2013. "Being and Becoming Indigenous: Resurgence against Contemporary Colonialism." Presentation at the Narrm Oration, University of Melbourne, November 28.

Anderson, Maureen, and Anne Low. 2007. *History 2.* Milton, NSW: John Wiley & Sons.

Angleviel, Frédéric. 2004. *Les fondements de l'histoire de la Nouvelle-Calédonie.* Nouméa: Centre territorial de recherche et de documentation Nouvelle-Calédonie.

Angleviel, Frédéric, Christiane Douyère, and Bernard Capecchi, ed. 1992. *La Nouvelle-Calédonie: histoire, CM.* Nouméa: Centre territorial de recherche et de documentation pédagogique / Hachette.

Angulo, Alex J. 2016. *Miseducation: A History of Ignorance-Making in America and Abroad.* Baltimore, MD: Johns Hopkins University Press.

Apple, Michael W. 1982. *Education and Power.* London: Routledge.

Atkinson, Wayne. 2001. "'Not One Iota' of Land Justice: Reflections on the Yorta Yorta Native Title Claim 1994–2001." *Indigenous Law Bulletin* 5(6): 19–23.

Attwood, Bain. 2000. "The Burden of the Past in the Present." In *Essays on Australian Reconciliation,* edited by Michelle Grattan, 254–259. Melbourne: Bookman Press.

———. 2005. *Telling the Truth about Aboriginal History.* Crows Nest, NSW: Allen & Unwin.

Australian Bureau of Statistics. 2001. "Education Then and Now." *Year Book Australia 2001,* January 25. http://www.abs.gov.au/ausstats/abs@.nsf /Previousproducts/1301.0Feature Article222001.

Australian Society of Authors (ASA). 2008. *Educational Publishing in Australia. What's in It for Authors?* Sydney: Australian Society of Authors. https:// www.asauthors.org/files/lib/pdf/zReports/ASA_Educational _Publishing_Report2008.pdf.

Aveling, Nado. 2012a. "Indigenous Studies: A Matter of Social Justice, a Matter of Urgency." *Diaspora Indigenous and Minority Education* 6(2): 99–114.

———. 2012b. "'Honest History' Call." *Koori Mail,* 534, September 5, 54–56.

Bancel, Nicolas, Pascal Blanchard, and Françoise Vergès. 2007. *La colonisation française.* Toulouse: Editions Milan.

Barbançon, Louis-José. 2006. "Mémoires oubliées, devoir de mémoire, devoir d'histoire." *Présence Africaine* 173:207–212.

Bedford, Daniel. 2010. "Agnotology as a Teaching Tool: Learning Climate Science by Studying Misinformation." *Journal of Geography* 109(4): 159–165.

Behrendt, Larissa. 2016. "Indigenous Kids Are Still Being Removed from Their Families, More Than Ever Before." *The Guardian,* February 13.

Bell, Duncan. 2016. *Reordering the World: Essays on Liberalism and Empire.* Princeton, NJ: Princeton University Press.

Bensa, Alban. 1997. Preface to *Nouvelle-Calédonie, pays Kanak: Un récit, deux histoires,* by Jacqueline Dahlem. Paris: Montréal: L'Harmattan.

Biondi, Jean-Pierre, and Gilles Morin. 1992. *Les anticolonialistes, 1881–1962.* Paris: Laffont.

Bishop, Julie. 2006. "Forgetting Our Past, Failing Our Future: The Teaching of Australian History." Address to the Australian History Summit Dinner, August 16. Canberra, ACT: Department of Education, Science and Training. https://parlinfo.aph.gov.au/parlInfo/download/media/pressrel/PBLK6/upload_binary/pblk63.pdf.

Blackburn, Kevin, and ZongLun Wu. 2019. *Decolonizing the History Curriculum in Malaysia and Singapore.* New York: Routledge.

Blackmore, W. H., R. E. Cotter, and M. J. Elliott. 1977. *Landmarks: A History of Australia to the Present Day,* 2nd ed. Melbourne: Macmillan.

Blainey, Geoffrey. 1993. "Drawing up a Balance Sheet of Our History." *Quadrant* 37(7–8): 11–15.

Blaxell, Gregory, and Don Drummond. 2006. "Educational and Reference Publishing." In *Paper Empires: A History of the Book in Australia, 1946–2005,* edited by Craig Munro and Robyn Sheahan-Bright, 314–322. St Lucia: University of Queensland Press.

Boler, Megan. 1999. *Feeling Power: Emotions and Education.* New York: Routledge.

Bombay, Amy, Kim Matheson, and Hymie Anisman. 2009. "Intergenerational Trauma: Convergence of Multiple Processes among First Nations Peoples in Canada." *Journal of Aboriginal Health* 5(3): 6–47.

Boyer, Gilles, Pascal Clerc, and Michelle Zancarini-Fournel. 2013. *L'école aux colonies, les colonies à l'école.* Lyon: ENS éditions.

Bradford, Clare. 2001. *Reading Race, Aboriginality in Australian Children's Literature.* Carlton: Melbourne University Press.

Brod, Harry. 1989. "Work Clothes and Leisure Suits: The Class Basis and Bias of the Men's Movement." In *Men's Lives,* edited by Michael S. Kimmel and Michael Messner, 276–287. New York: Macmillan.

Bruy-Hebert, Sylvie. 2010. "Ecole et société en Nouvelle-Calédonie depuis 1850." *HG/NC,* July 14. http://histoire-geo.ac-noumea.nc/spip.php ?article227.

Burke, Gerald, and Andrew Spauli. 2001. "Australian Schools: Participation and Funding 1901 to 2000." *Year Book Australia 2001* 83:433–446. http://www.abs.gov.au/ausstats/abs@.nsf/Lookup/A75909A2108CECAACA 2569DE002539FB.

Burridge, Nina, and Andrew Chodkiewicz. 2012. "An Historical Overview of Aboriginal Education Policies in the Australian Context." In *Indigenous Education: A Learning Journey for Teachers, Schools and Communities,* edited by Nina Burridge, Frances Whalan, and Karen Vaughan, 11–22. Rotterdam: Sense.

Butlin, Noel G. 1983. *Our Original Aggression: Aboriginal Populations of Southeastern Australia 1788–1850.* Sydney: Allen & Unwin.

Calderón, Dolores. 2014. "Speaking Back to Manifest Destinies: A Land Education-Based Approach to Critical Curriculum Inquiry." *Environmental Education Research* 20(1): 24–36.

Camus, Albert. 1947. "La Contagion." *Combat,* May 10.

Cavanagh, Edward, and Lorenzo Veracini, eds. 2016. *The Routledge Handbook of the History of Settler Colonialism.* London: Routledge.

Chappell, David. 2003. "The Kanak Awakening of 1969–1976: Radicalizing Anti-Colonialism in New Caledonia." *Le Journal de la Société des Océanistes* 117:187–202.

————. 2013. *The Kanak Awakening: The Rise of Nationalism in New Caledonia.* Honolulu: University of Hawai'i Press.

Chenntouf, Tayeb. 2006. "La colonisation dans une perspective d'histoire mondiale." *CODESRIA Bulletin* 3–4:12–17.

Clark, Anna. 2006. *Teaching the Nation: Politics and Pedagogy in Australian History.* Melbourne: Melbourne University Press.

Clark, Laurel. 2000. "F. F. Baillière: Book Seller to the University of Melbourne." *University of Melbourne Library Journal* 6, no. 2 (December): 13–26. https://museumsandcollections.unimelb.edu.au/__data /assets/pdf_file/0011/1625519/clark.pdf,

Clarke, Marcus A. H. 1877. *History of the Continent of Australia and the Island of Tasmania (1787 to 1870): Compiled for the Use of Schools.* Melbourne: F. F. Baillière.

Colombel, Claire, and Véronique Fillol. 2009. "La construction identitaire des jeunes océaniens francophones." Presentation at the conference "La Construction identitaire à l'école, approches pluridisciplinaires," Montpellier, July.

Condie, Michael D. 2012. "It's Mabo, It's the Constitution, It's the Vibe. Debates over the 'Active Citizen' and Aboriginal history in the NSW

History Syllabus in the 1980s and 1990s." Honours diss., University of Sydney.

Connell, John. 1987. "New Caledonia: The Transformation of Kanaky Nationalism." *Australian Outlook* 41(1): 37–44.

Cope, Bill. 1987. "Racism, Popular Culture and Australian Identity in Transition." *Centre for Multicultural Studies Occasional Papers* 14:1–20. Wollongong, NSW: University of Wollongong. http://ro.uow.edu.au /cmsocpapers/11.

Corntassel, Jeff. 2011. "Indigenizing the Academy: Insurgent Education and the Roles of Indigenous Intellectuals." *Federation for the Humanities and Social Science* (blog), January 12. http://www.ideas-idees.ca/blog /indigenizing-academy-insurgent-education-and-roles-indigenous -intellectuals.

Coulon, Marc. 1985. *L'irruption kanak: de Calédonie à Kanaky.* Paris: Messidor/ Editions sociales.

Coulthard, Glen. 2013. "For Our Nations to Live, Capitalism Must Die." *Nations Rising* (blog), November 5. https://unsettlingamerica.word press.com/2013/11/05/for-our-nations-to-live-capitalism-must-die.

———. 2014. *Red Skin, White Masks: Rejecting the Colonial Politics of Recognition.* Minneapolis: University of Minnesota Press.

Cour des Comptes. 2016. "Le système scolaire en Polynésie Française et en Nouvelle-Calédonie: un effort de l'état important, une efficience à améliorer." *Rapport Public Annuel,* February.

Cranston, Neil, Megan Kimber, Bill Mulford, Alan Reid, and Jack Keating. 2010. "Politics and School Education in Australia: A Case of Shifting Purposes." *Journal of Educational Administration* 48(2): 182–195.

Curthoys, Ann. 2008. "WEH Stanner and the Historians." In *An Appreciation of Difference: WEH Stanner and Aboriginal Australia,* edited by Melinda Hinkson, and Jeremy Beckett, 233–250. Canberra: Aboriginal Studies Press.

Dahlem, Jacqueline. 1997. *Nouvelle-Calédonie, pays Kanak: Un récit, deux histoires.* Montréal: Editions L'Harmattan.

———. 2002. "L'écriture de l'histoire en Nouvelle-Calédonie entre les accords de Matignon et de Nouméa (1988–1998): de la voix collective d'un manuel scolaire aux positionnements identitaires de ses auteurs." PhD diss., Université Paris 12.

D'Arcy, Paul. 2011. "The Teaching of Pacific History Introduction. Diverse Approaches for Diverse Audiences." *Journal of Pacific History* 46(2): 197–206.

Darlington, Robert, Graham Smithies, and Ashley Wood. 2012. *History Alive 9 for the Australian Curriculum.* Milton, NSW: John Wiley & Sons Australia.

Darlington, Robert, Luke Jackson, and Tom Hawkins. 2012. *History Alive 10 for the Australian Curriculum*. Milton, NSW: John Wiley & Sons Australia.

Davis, Lynne, Chris Hiller, Cherylanne James, Kristen Lloyd, Tessa Nasca, and Sara Taylor. 2016. "Complicated Pathways: Settler Canadians Learning to Re/Frame Themselves and their Relationships with Indigenous Peoples." *Settler Colonial Studies* 7(4): 396–414.

Davis, Sharon. 2016. "As an Aboriginal Woman, I've Learned Education Is Essential to Our Freedom." *The Guardian,* January 31. https://www.theguardian.com/commentisfree/2016/feb/01/as-an-aboriginal-woman-ive-learned-education-is-essential-to-our-freedom.

Dawkins, John. 1988. *Strengthening Australia's Schools: A Consideration of the Focus and Content of Schooling*. Canberra: Australian Government Publishing Service.

Debien Vanmai, Cynthia, and Michel Lextreyt, eds. 2010. *Histoire et géographie. La Nouvelle Calédonie et l'Océanie. Première et Terminale*. Nouméa: Centre de documentation pédagogique de Nouvelle-Calédonie.

de Costa, Ravi, and Tom Clark. 2016. "On the Responsibility to Engage: Non-Indigenous Peoples in Settler States." *Settler Colonial Studies* 6(3): 191–208.

de Suremain, Marie-Albane. 2009. "Entre clichés et histoire des représentations: Manuels scolaires et enseignement du fait colonial." In *La fabrique scolaire de l'histoire*, edited by Laurence De Cock, and Emmanuelle Picard, 76–88. Marseille: Agone.

Deloria, Vine, Jr. 2004. "Marginal and Submarginal." In *Indigenizing the Academy: Transforming Scholarship and Empowering Communities,* edited by Devon A. Mihesuah, and Angela C. Wilson, 16–30. Lincoln: University of Nebraska Press.

Derrida, Jacques. 1996. *Archive Fever: A Freudian Impression*. Chicago: University of Chicago Press.

Dilley, Rob, and Thomas G. Kirsch, eds. 2015. *Regimes of Ignorance: Anthropological Perspectives on the Production and Re-Production of Non-Knowledge*. New York: Berghahn Books.

Dodson, Michael. 1996. "Human Rights and the Extinguishment of Native Title." *Australian Aboriginal Studies* 2(1): 12–23.

Donnelly, Kevin. 2007. *Dumbing Down: Outcomes-Based and Politically Correct: The Impact of the Culture Wars on Our Schools*. Prahran, VIC: Hardie Grant Books.

Donnelly, Kevin, and Kenneth Wiltshire. 2014. *Review of the Australian Curriculum, Final Report*. Canberra: Australian Government Department of Education. https://docs.education.gov.au/system/files/doc/other/review_of_the_national_curriculum_final_report.pdf.

Ellinghaus, Katherine. 2003. "Absorbing the 'Aboriginal Problem': Controlling Interracial Marriage in Australia in the Late 19th and Early 20th Centuries." *Aboriginal History* 27:183–207.

Elmersjö, Henrik A., Anna Clark, and Monika Vinterek. 2017. *International Perspectives on Teaching Rival Histories: Pedagogical Responses to Contested Narratives and the History Wars.* London: Palgrave Macmillan.

Engelbrecht, Alta. 2006. "Textbooks in South Africa from Apartheid to Post-Apartheid: Ideological Change Revealed by Racial Stereotyping." In *Promoting Social Cohesion through Education: Case Studies and Tools for Using Textbooks and Curricula,* edited by Eluned Roberts-Schweitzer, Vincent Greaney and Kreszentia Duer, 71–80. Washington, DC: The World Bank.

Epstein, Andrew B. 2015. "The Colonialism of the Present." *Jacobin Magazine,* January 13. https://www.jacobinmag.com/2015/01/indigenous-left-glen-coulthard-interview.

Etemad, Bouda. 2012. *L'héritage ambigu de la colonisation. Economies, populations, sociétés.* Paris: Armand Colin.

Falaize, Benoît. 2014. "L'enseignement des sujets controversés dans l'école française: Les nouveaux fondements de l'histoire scolaire en France?" *Tempo & Argumento* 6(11): 193–223.

Fanelli, Carlo. 2015. "Critical Education and Insurgent Pedagogies: An Interview with E. Wayne Ross." *Alternate Routes: A Journal of Critical Social Research* 26:405–422.

Feather, John. 1991. *A History of British Publishing.* London: Routledge.

Ferrier, Carole. 1999. "White Blindfolds and Black Armbands: The Uses of Whiteness Theory for Reading Australian Cultural Production." *Queensland Review* 6(1): 42–49.

Fien, John. 1985. "Structural Silence: Aborigines in Australian Geography Textbooks." *Internationale Schulbuchforschung* 7(2/3): 167–172.

Filder. 2009. "Col Dillon reflects on his experience as Australia's first Indigenous police officer." *ABC News: Conversations with Richard Fidler.* March 17. https://www.abc.net.au/local/stories/2009/03/17/2518524.htm.

Fillol, Véronique. 2009. "Pour une didactique du plurilinguisme à l'école calédonienne." *Le français aujourd'hui* 164(1): 53–60.

Firth, Stewart. 1970. "Social Values in the New South Wales Primary School 1880–1914: An Analysis of School Texts." *Melbourne Studies in Education* 12(1): 123–159.

———. 2011. "Culture and Context in the Teaching of Pacific History and Politics." *Journal of Pacific History* 46(2): 207–213.

Fiske, Susan. 1993. "Controlling Other People: The Impact of Power on Stereotyping." *American Psychologist* 48(6): 621–628.

Folds, Ralph. 1987. "The Social Relationships of Tribal Aboriginal Schooling in Australia." *British Journal of Sociology of Education* 8(4): 447–460.

Foley, Gary. 1997. "Native Title Is Not Land Rights." *Koori History*, September. http://www.koorihistory.com/native-title-is-not-land-rights.

Foley, Gary, Andrew Schaap, and Edwina Howell, eds. 2014. *The Aboriginal Tent Embassy: Sovereignty, Black Power, Land Rights and the State*. London: Routledge.

Foley, Gary, and Elizabeth Muldoon. 2014. "Pyning for Indigenous Rights in the Australian Curriculum." *The Conversation*, August 15. https://theconversation.com/pyning-for-indigenous-rights-in-the-australian-curriculum-30422.

Foucault, Michel, and Colin Gordon. 1980. *Power/Knowledge: Selected Interviews and Other Writings, 1972–1977*. New York: Pantheon Books.

Freire, Paulo. 1984. *The Politics of Education: Culture, Power and Liberation*. South Hadley, MA: Bergin and Garvey.

Fricker, Miranda. 2007. *Epistemic Injustice: Power and the Ethics of Knowing*. Oxford: Oxford University Press.

Gaventa, John, and Andrea Cornwall. 2008. "Power and Knowledge." In *The SAGE Handbook of Action Research: Participative Inquiry and Practice*, edited by Peter Reason and Hilary Bradbury, 172–189. London: SAGE Publications.

Gaztambide-Fernández, Rubén. 2014. "Decolonial Options and Artistic/Aesthesic Entanglements: An Interview with Walter Mignolo." *Decolonization: Indigeneity, Education & Society* 3(1): 196–212.

Geiger, William A. 2017. "From the Logic of Elimination to the Logic of the Gift: Towards a Decolonial Theory of Tlingit Language Revitalization." *Open Linguistics* 3(1): 219–235.

Goodall, Heather. 1990. "Land in Our Own Country: The Aboriginal Land Rights Movement in South-Eastern Australia, 1860 to 1914." *Aboriginal History* 14(1/2): 1–24.

Grangier, M. 1950. *Statistiques des effectifs publiques et privés, primaires et secondaires, professionnels, de 1920 à 1951*. Paris: Service de l'instruction publique.

Grosfoguel, Ramón. 2007. "The Epistemic Decolonial Turn." *Cultural Studies* 21(2–3): 211–223.

Gunstone, Andrew. 2004. "Reconciliation, Nationalism and the History Wars." Presentation at the Australasian Political Studies Association Conference, University of Adelaide, September 29–October 1.

Hall, Lisa. 2012. "The 'Come and Go' Syndrome of Teachers in Remote Indigenous Schools: Listening to the Perspective of Indigenous Teachers About What Helps Teachers to Stay and What Makes

Them Go." *Australian Journal of Indigenous Education* 41(2): 187–195.

Handford, John. 2001. "Macmillan Biographies, 1843–1965." In *Macmillan: A Publishing Tradition, 1843–1970,* edited by Elizabeth James, xxi–xxiv. Basingstoke: Palgrave Macmillan.

Hannoum, Abdelmajid. 2010. *Violent Modernity. France in Algeria.* Cambridge, MA: Harvard Center for Middle Eastern Studies.

Hardouin, Magali. 2008. "Programmes scolaires, enseignement et Nouvelle-Calédonie : un enjeu politique majeur pour un territoire en marche vers l'indépendance?" *Spirale* 42:83–93.

Harris, Richard. 2011. "Citizenship and History: Uncomfortable Bedfellows." In *Debates in History Teaching,* edited by Ian Davies, 186–196. Milton Park: Routledge.

Hickling-Hudson, Anne R., and Roberta Ahlquist. 2004. "Teachers as 'Two-Year Tourists' in an Australian State School for Aboriginal Children: Dilemmas of Curriculum, Agency and Teacher Preparation." *Journal of Postcolonial Education* 3(1): 67–88.

Hickman, John. 2016. *Space Is Power: The Seven Rules of Territory.* Lanham, MD: Lexington Books.

Hickman, Heather, and Bradley J. Porfilio. 2012. *The New Politics of the Textbook: Critical Analysis in the Core Content Areas.* Rotterdam: Sense.

High Court of Australia. 1992. *Mabo and Others v. State of Queensland* (No. 2). HCA 23, 175 CLR 1. Canberra: Australian Law Reports.

Hobsbawm, Eric J. 1997. *On History.* London: Weidenfeld and Nicolson.

Howard, John. 2006. "Unity Vital in Battle Against Terrorism." *Sydney Morning Herald,* January 26, 11.

Hutchings, Jessica, and Jenny Lee-Morgan. 2016. *Decolonisation in Aotearoa: Education, Research and Practice.* Wellington: New Zealand Council for Educational Research.

Hutchins, Rachel D. 2016. *Nationalism and History Education: Curricula and Textbooks in the United States and France.* New York: Routledge.

Inglis, Kenneth S. 1974. *The Australian Colonists. An Exploration of Social History 1788–1870.* Melbourne: Melbourne University Press.

Iyengar, Malathi M. 2014. "Not Mere Abstractions: Language Policies and Language Ideologies in U.S. Settler Colonialism." *Decolonization: Indigeneity, Education & Society* 3(2): 33–59.

Jacquier, Yves, Isabelle Amiot, and Christiane Terrier, eds. 2007. *Histoire: cycle 3 Nouvelle-Calédonie.* Nouméa: Centre de documentation péda-gogique de Nouvelle-Calédonie.

James, Matt. 2012. "A Carnival of Truth? Knowledge, Ignorance and the Canadian Truth and Reconciliation Commission." *International Journal of Transitional Justice* 6(2): 182–204.

Johansson-Fua, Seu'ula. 2016. "The Oceanic Researcher and the Search for a Space in Comparative and International Education." *International Education Journal: Comparative Perspectives* 15(3): 30–41.

Jones, Jennifer. 2000. "The Black Communist: The Contested Memory of Margaret Tucker." *Hecate* 26(2): 135–145.

Journal Officiel de la République Française. 1998. *Loi n° 88–1028 du 9 novembre 1988 portant dispositions statutaires et préparatoires à l'autodétermination de la Nouvelle-Calédonie en 1998, art. 85.* Paris: République Française.

Justice, Daniel Heath. 2004. "Seeing (and Reading) Red: Indian Outlaws in the Ivory Tower." In *Indigenizing the Academy: Transforming Scholarship and Empowering Communities,* edited by Devon A. Mihesuah and Angela C. Wilson, 100–123. Lincoln: University of Nebraska Press.

Kartono, Yves. 2017. "Enseignement de la culture et des langues Kanak." *Journal 19 h 30, Nouvelle-Calédonie 1ère,* February 19.

Keen, Suzanne. 2006. "A Theory of Narrative Empathy." *Narrative* 14(3): 207–236.

———. 2007. *Empathy and the Novel.* New York: Oxford University Press.

Kundera, Milan. 1996. "Lost Letters." In *The Book of Laughter and Forgetting.* London: Faber and Faber.

Laidlaw, Ronald. 1986. *The Land They Found: Australian History for Secondary Schools,* 2nd ed. Melbourne: Macmillan Education.

La Nauze, John. A. 1959. "The Study of Australian History, 1929–1959." *Historical Studies: Australia and New Zealand* 9(33): 1–11.

Lantheaume, Françoise. 2007. "Manuels d'histoire et colonisation. Les forces et faiblesses de la polyphonie de l'auteur-réseau, ses effets sur la formation de l'esprit critique." *Lidil* 35:159–175.

Lassauce, Bernard. 2016. "Promouvoir les métiers de l'enseignement auprès des jeunes kanak." *NC1ère,* August 8. http://la1ere.francetvinfo.fr.

Laurens, Cécile, and Jean Vareille. 1984. "New Caledonia and the Society Islands." In *Schooling in the Pacific Islands: Colonies in Transition,* edited by R. Murray Thomas and T. Neville Postlethwaite, 109–142. New York: Pergamon Press.

Lavisse, Ernest. 1913. *Histoire de France: Cours Elementaire.* Paris: Armand Colin.

———. 1942. *Histoire de France. Manuel de Certificat d'études.* Paris: Armand Colin.

Leach, Colin W., Russell Spears, Nyla Branscombe, and Bertjan Doosje. 2003. "Malicious Pleasure: Schadenfreude at the Suffering of Another Group." *Journal of Personality and Social Psychology* 84(5): 932–943.

Léon, Antoine. 1991. *Colonisation, enseignement et éducation: Étude historique et comparative.* Paris: L'Harmattan.

Lévinas, Emmanuel. 1996. *Emmanuel Levinas: Basic Philosophical Writings,* edited by Adriaan T. Peperzak, Robert Bernasconi, and Simon Critchley. Bloomington: Indiana University Press.

Lextreyt, Michel. 2010. "La lettre de rentrée 2010." August 24. http://histoire-geo.ac-noumea.nc.

Lomawaima, K. Tsianina. 2014. "History Without Silos, Ignorance Versus Knowledge, Education beyond Schools." *History of Education Quarterly* 54(3): 349–355.

Losoya, Sandra H., and Nancy Eisenberg. 2001. "Affective Empathy." In *Interpersonal Sensitivity: The LEA Series in Personality and Clinical Psychology,* edited by Judith A. Hall and Frank J. Bernieri. Mahwah, NJ: Lawrence Erlbaum.

Lothian, Kathy. 2005. "Seizing the Time: Australian Aborigines and the Influence of the Black Panther Party, 1969–1972." *Journal of Black Studies* 35(4): 179–200.

Lowe, Kevin, and Tyson Yunkaporta. 2013. "The Inclusion of Aboriginal and Torres Strait Islander Content in the Australian National Curriculum: A Cultural, Cognitive and Socio-Political Evaluation." *Curriculum Perspectives* 33(1): 1–14.

Macintyre, Stuart, and Anna Clark. 2004. *The History Wars.* Carlton, NSW: Melbourne University Press.

Mack, Andrew. 1975. "Why Big Nations Lose Small Wars: The Politics of Asymmetric Conflicts." *World Politics* 27(2): 175–200.

Maddison, Sarah, and Angelique Stastny. 2016. "Silence or Deafness? Education and the Non-Indigenous Responsibility to Engage." In *The Limits of Settler Colonial Reconciliation: Non-indigenous People and the Responsibility to Engage,* edited by Sarah Maddison, Tom Clark, and Ravi de Costa, 231–247. Singapore: Springer.

Malewski, Eric, and Nathalia Jaramillo, eds. 2011. *Epistemologies of Ignorance in Education.* Charlotte, NC: Information Age Publishing.

Marseille, Jacques. 1986. *L'âge d'or de la France coloniale.* Paris: Albin Michel.

Massau, Serge. 2017. "Colonisation, un crime contre l'humanité?" *Polynésie 1ère,* February 23. http://la1ere.francetvinfo.fr.

MATSITI (More Aboriginal and Torres Strait Islander Teachers Initiative). 2014. "Aboriginal and Torres Strait Islander Teacher Workforce Analysis." Canberra: Australian Government. http://matsiti.edu.au.

Maynard, John. 2005. "'In the Interests of Our People': The Influence of Garveyism on the Rise of Australian Aboriginal Political Activism." *Aboriginal History* 29:1–22.

McConaghy, Cathryn. 2003. "On Pedagogy, Trauma and Difficult Memory: Remembering Namatjira, Our Beloved." *Australian Journal of Indigenous Education* 32:11–20.

McGoey, Linsey. 2007. "On the Will to Ignorance in Bureaucracy." *Economy & Society* 36(2): 212–235.

McGonegal, Julie. 2009. "The Great Canadian (and Australian) Secret: The Limits of Non-Indigenous Knowledge and Representation." *English Studies in Canada* 35(1): 67–83.

McGrath, Ann. 2015. *Illicit Love: Interracial Sex and Marriage in the United States and Australia.* Lincoln: University of Nebraska Press.

McGregor, Russell. 1993. "Protest and Progress: Aboriginal Activism in the 1930s." *Australian Historical Studies* 25(101): 555–568.

———. 2009. "Another Nation: Aboriginal Activism in the Late 1960s and Early 1970s." *Australian Historical Studies* 40(3): 343–360.

McGuinness, Bruce, and Denis Walker. 1985. "The Politics of Aboriginal Literature." In *Aboriginal Writing Today: Papers from the First National Conference of Aboriginal Writers Held in Perth, Western Australia in 1983,* edited by Jack Davis and Bob Hodge. Canberra: Australian Institute of Aboriginal Studies.

McKenna, Mark. 2002. *Looking for Blackfellas' Point: An Australian History of Place.* Sydney: University of New South Wales Press.

McKenzie, Phillip, Julie Kos, Maurice Walker, and Jennifer Hong. 2008. *Staff in Australia's Schools.* Department of Education, Employment and Workplace Relations. Canberra: Commonwealth of Australia.

McNeil, Kent. 2004. "The Vulnerability of Indigenous Land Rights in Australia and Canada." *Osgoode Hall Law Journal* 42(2): 271–301.

Meston, Archibald L. 1950. *A Junior History of Australia,* 2nd ed. Melbourne: Oxford University Press.

Mignolo, Walter D. 2002. "The Geopolitics of Knowledge and the Colonial Difference." *South Atlantic Quarterly* 101(1): 57–95.

———. 2005. "Prophets Facing Sidewise: The Geopolitics of Knowledge and the Colonial Difference." *Social Epistemology* 19(1): 111–127.

———. 2013. "On Comparison: Who Is Comparing What and Why?" In *Comparison. Theories, Approaches, Uses,* edited by Rita Felski and Susan S. Friedman, 99–119. Baltimore, MD: Johns Hopkins University Press.

Mignolo, Walter D., and Arturo Escobar. 2013. *Globalization and the Decolonial Option.* Hoboken, NJ: Taylor and Francis.

Milburn, Caroline. 2010. "Wanted: Teachers to Go the Distance." *Sydney Morning Herald,* August 23.

Mills, Charles. 1997. *The Racial Contract.* Ithaca, NY: Cornell University Press.

Mohamed-Gaillard, Sarah. 2009. "Historiographie des territoires français du Pacifique." In *La construction du discours colonial. L'Empire français, XIXe–XXe siècles,* edited by Laurick Zerbini, and Oissila Saaïdia, 149–168. Paris: Karthala.

Mokaddem, Hamid. 1999. *L'échec scolaire calédonien: Essai sur la répétition du même dans l'autre: la reproduction sociale de l'échec scolaire est-elle une fatalité.* Paris: Harmattan.

———. 2007. "Le destin commun à l'épreuve du corps à corps électoral en Nouvelle-Calédonie." In *Pouvoir(s) et politique(s) en Océanie,* edited by Mounira Chatti, Nicolas Clinchamps, and Stéphanie Vigier, 91–132. Paris: L'Harmattan.

———. 2009. *Pratique et théorie kanak de la souveraineté: 30 Janvier 1936, Jean-Marie Tjibaou, 4 Mai 1989.* New Caledonia: Province Nord.

———. 2017. "Anthropologies des mondes en devenir: l'imaginaire non partagé entre Kanaky et Nouvelle-Calédonie." Presentation at the conference "Nouvelle-Calédonie et l'imagination intellectuelle," Latrobe University, October 12.

Mokak, Georgia. 2017. "Do Our Teachers Care Enough about Indigenous Australia to Bring It into the Classroom?" *NITV News,* May 9. http://www.sbs.com.au/nitv.

Moore, Robyn. 2020. "Whiteness=Politeness: Interest-Convergence in Australian History Textbooks, 1950–2010." *Critical Discourse Studies* 17(1): 111–129.

Morrison, Ian. 2013. "The History of the Book in Australia." In *The Book: A Global History,* edited by Michael F. Suarez and Henry R. Woudhuysen, 635–648. Oxford: Oxford University Press.

Moseley, Christopher, ed. 2010. *Atlas des langues en danger dans le monde.* Paris: Editions UNESCO.

Muckle, Adria, Antoinette Burton, Helen Gardner, Keith L. Camacho, and Tracey Banivanua Mar. 2016. "Decolonisation and the Pacific." *Journal of Pacific History* 51(4): 451–462.

Muir, Marcie. 2006. "Case-Study: Postwar Pioneers." In *Paper Empires: A History of the Book in Australia, 1946–2005,* edited by Craig Munro and Robyn Sheahan-Bright, 293–295. St Lucia: University of Queensland Press.

Muldoon, Elizabeth, and Gary Foley. 2014. "VCE's Australian History Study Design Snubs Indigenous Perspectives." *The Age,* November 12.

Murdoch, Walter. 1917. *The Making of Australia. An Introductory History.* Melbourne: Whitcombe & Tombs.

Nakata, Martin. 2002. "Indigenous Knowledge and the Cultural Interface: Underlying Issues at the Intersection of Knowledge and Information Systems." *IFLA Journal* 28(5–6): 281–291.

———. 2011. "Pathways for Indigenous Education in the Australian Curriculum Framework." *Australian Journal of Indigenous Education* 40:1–8.

Ndlovu, Sifiso M. 2006. "The Soweto Uprising." In *The Road to Democracy in South Africa: 1970–1980,* vol. 2, edited by South African Democracy Education Trust, 317–350. Pretoria: University of South Africa Press.

Nicholls, Christine. 2005. "Death by a Thousand Cuts: Indigenous Language Bilingual Education Programmes in the Northern Territory of Australia, 1972–1998." *International Journal of Bilingual Education & Bilingualism* 8(2–3): 160–177.

Nicholson, Mandy. 2016. "How Tanderrum Is Reigniting Culture." *Koori Mail*, November 16, 22.

NITV. 2017. "I Can't Control the Whole School, But I Can Control the Culture of My Classroom." *NITV News*, April 19. http://www.sbs.com.au/nitv.

Noonan, Chris, dir. 1989. *Police State*. Television movie. Australian Broadcasting Corporation.

Openshaw, Roger. 2005. "' . . . Nothing Objectionable or Controversial': The Image of Maori Ethnicity and 'Difference' in New Zealand Social Studies." In *Struggles over Difference Curriculum, Texts, and Pedagogy in the Asia-Pacific,* edited by Yoshiko Nozaki, Roger Openshaw, and Allan Luke, 25–40. Albany: State University of New York Press.

Organ, Michael. 2014. "Secret Service: Governor Macquarie's Aboriginal War of 1816." *Proceedings of the National Conference of the Royal Australian Historical Society,* Mittagong, October 25–26.

Ounei, Susanne. 1985. *For Kanak Independence: The Fight Against French Rule in New Caledonia.* Auckland: Labour Publishing Co-operative Society, in conjunction with Corso (the New Zealand Association for International Relief, Rehabilitation and Development).

Page, Michael. 2006. "Case-Study: Ribgy Limited." In *Paper Empires: A History of the Book in Australia, 1946–2005,* edited by Craig Munro and Robyn Sheahan-Bright, 41–42. St Lucia: University of Queensland Press.

Parkes, Robert J. 2007. "Reading History Curriculum as Postcolonial Text: Towards a Curricular Response to the History Wars in Australia and Beyond." *Curriculum Inquiry* 37(4): 383–400.

———. 2009. "Teaching History as Historiography: Engaging Narrative Diversity in the Curriculum." *International Journal of Historical Learning, Teaching and Research* 8(2): 118–132.

Pearson, Luke. 2015. "The Changes to the National Curriculum Have Nothing to Do with Education." *Indigenous X* (blog), September 24. http://indigenousx.com.au/the-changes-to-the-national-curriculum-have-nothing-to-do-with-education.

———. 2016a. "Luke Pearson: I Was a 'Young Indigenous Leader'—Now I'm Just Some Guy." *NITV,* April 15. http://www.sbs.com.au/nitv/article/2016/04/15/luke-pearson-i-was-young-indigenous-leader-now-im-just-some-guy.

———. 2016b. "Treaty Vs Recognition—The Importance of Self-Determination." *IndigenousX* (blog), April 28. http://indigenousx.com.au/treaty-vs-recognition-the-importance-of-self-determination.

Perkins, Rachel, and Marcia Langton. 2010. *First Australians Unillustrated.* Carlton, NSW: Miegunyah Press.

Perrin, Mandy. 2015. "Editor's Comment: Recognition of the Dignity of Ancestors." *Daily Telegraph,* February 2.

Perron, A. 2016. "Une campagne pour que les enseignants reflètent le pays." *Les Nouvelles Caledoniennes,* August 8. http://www.lnc.nc.

Poigoune, Marguerite. 2017. "Travaux pratiques à Tchamba pour les élèves enseignants." *NC1ère,* March 30. http://la1ere.francetvinfo.fr.

Popkewitz, Thomas S. 1997a. "The Production of Reason and Power: Curriculum History and Intellectual Traditions." *Journal of Curriculum Studies* 29(2): 131–164.

———. 1997b. "A Changing Terrain of Knowledge and Power: A Social Epistemology of Educational Research." *Educational Researcher* 26(9): 18–29.

Powel, Walter W. 1985. *Getting into Print: The Decision-Making Process in Scholarly Publishing.* Chicago: University of Chicago Press.

Probyn-Rapsey, Fiona. 2013. *Made to Matter: White Fathers. Stolen Generations.* Sydney: Sydney University Press.

Proctor, Robert, and Londa L. Schiebinger. 2008. *Agnotology: The Making and Unmaking of Ignorance.* Stanford, CA: Stanford University Press.

Province Nord. 2013. "Quelles recherches scientifiques en province Nord?" *Livre blanc de synthèses et recommandations issues du séminaire organisé à Poindimié* (19–21 juin 2013). Poindimié: Province Nord.

Quijano, Aníbal. 2000. "Coloniality of Power, Eurocentrism, and Latin America." *Nepantla: Views from South* 1(3): 533–580.

———. 2007. "Coloniality and Modernity/Rationality." *Cultural Studies* 21(2–3): 168–178.

Rancière, Jacques. 1991. *The Ignorant Schoolmaster: Five Lessons in Intellectual Emancipation.* Stanford, CA: Stanford University Press.

Reddy, William M. 2001. *The Navigation of Feeling: A Framework for the History of Emotions.* Cambridge: Cambridge University Press.

Regan, Paulette. 2010. *Unsettling the Settler Within: Indian Residential Schools, Truth Telling, and Reconciliation in Canada.* Toronto: UBC Press.

Renan, Ernest. 1882. "Qu'est-ce qu'une nation?" Presentation at the Sorbonne, Paris, March 11.

Reynolds, Henry. 1984. "The Breaking of the Great Australian Silence: Aborigines in Australian Historiography 1955–1983." Presentation at the Trevor Reese Memorial Lecture, Kings College, January 30.

———. 1999. *Why Weren't We Told? A Personal Search for the Truth about Our History.* Ringwood, VIC: Viking.

Rifkin, Mark. 2014. "The Frontier as (Movable) Space of Exception." *Settler Colonial Studies Journal* 4(2): 176–180.

Riggs, Damien W. 2004. "Understanding History as a Rhetorical Strategy: Constructions of Truth and Objectivity in Debates over Windschuttle's Fabrication." *Journal of Australian Studies* 28(82): 37–48.

Roberts, Stephen H. 1929. *History of French Colonial Policy, 1870–192.* London: P. S. King & Son.

Rolls, Mitchell. 2010. "Why Didn't You Listen: White Noise and Black History." *Aboriginal History* 34:11–33.

Rose, Deborah B. 2004. *Reports from a Wild Country: Ethics for Decolonisation.* Sydney: University of New South Wales Press.

Rosenwein, Barbara H. 2010. "Problems and Methods in the History of Emotions. Passions in Context." *International Journal for the History and Theory of Emotions* 1(1): 1–32.

Routledge, Paul. 2012. "Sensuous Solidarities: Emotion, Politics and Performance in the Clandestine Insurgent Rebel Clown Army." *Antipode* 44(2): 428–452.

Ruska, Pekeri. 2016. "On This Invasion Day, I Am Angry. Australia Has a Long Way to Go." *The Guardian,* January 25. https://www.theguardian.com/commentisfree/2016/jan/26/on-this-day-of-mourning-i-am-angry-australia-has-a-long-way-to-go.

Ryan, Lyndall. 2013. "The Black Line in Van Diemen's Land (Tasmania), 1830." *Journal of Australian Studies* 37(1-2): 3–18.

Salaün, Marie. 2005. *L'école indigène: Nouvelle-Calédonie, 1885–1945.* Rennes: Presses universitaires de Rennes.

———. 2013. *Décoloniser l'école? Hawai'i, Nouvelle-Calédonie, expériences contemporaines.* Rennes: Presses universitaires de Rennes.

Sarraut Albert. 1931. *Grandeur et servitude colonial.* Paris: Éditions du Sagittaire.

Saussol, Alain. 1988. "The Colonial Chimera: From Annexation to the Re-Emergence of Kanak Identity." In *New Caledonia: Essays in Nationalism and Dependency,* edited by Michael Spencer, Alan Ward, and John Connell. St Lucia: University of Queensland Press.

Sauvage, Alexandra. 2010. "Teaching the Frontier: Shifting Narratives and Cultural Boundaries in 1990s School Textbooks." In *Frontier Skirmishes: Literary and Cultural Debates in Australia after 1992,* edited by Russell West-Pavlov and Jennifer Wawrzinek, 277–294. Heidelberg: Universitätsverlag Winter GmbH Heidelberg.

Schulz, Samantha. 2017. "Desire for the Desert: Racialising White Teachers' Motives for Working in Remote Schools in the Australian Desert." *Race Ethnicity and Education* 20(2): 209–224.

Schwartzkoff, Louise. 2010. "Family Tree that Survived Governor Macquarie's Mixed Legacy." *Sydney Morning Herald,* November 29.

Scott, Ernest. 1925. *A Short History of Australia.* Melbourne: Oxford University Press.

Semidei, Manuela. 1966. "De l'empire à la décolonisation dans les manuels scolaires français." *Revue française de science politique* 16(1): 56–86.

Shadowwalker, Depree M. 2012. "Where Have All the Indians Gone? American Indian Representation in Secondary History Textbooks." PhD diss., University of Arizona.

Shafer, Mina. 1996. *Visions of Australia: Exploring Our History.* Melbourne: Oxford University Press.

Shafer, Mina, and Denise Brown. 1996. *Visions of Australia: Exploring Our History.* Melbourne: Oxford University Press.

Sharp, Heather L. 2010. "Constructing History: Selective Representations of Indigenous Australians and British Heritages in Queensland History Curriculum." PhD diss., University of Southern Queensland.

———. 2012. "Australia's 1988 Bicentennial: National History and Multiculturalism in the Primary School Curriculum." *History of Education* 41(3): 405–421.

———. 2013. "What We Teach Our Children: A Comparative Analysis of Indigenous Australians in Social Studies Curriculum, from the 1960s to the 1980s." *Social and Education History* 2(2): 176–204.

Simpson, Leanne B., ed. 2008. *Lighting the Eighth Fire: The Liberation, Resurgence, and Protection of Indigenous Nations.* Winnipeg, MB: Arbeiter Ring Press.

———. 2011. *Dancing on Our Turtle's Back: Stories of Nishnaabeg Re-Creation, Resurgence, and a New Emergence.* Winnipeg, MB: Arbeiter Ring Press.

———. 2016. "Indigenous Resurgence and Co-Resistance." *Critical Ethnic Studies* 2(2): 19–34.

Simpson, Audra. 2014. *Mohawk Interruptus: Political Life Across the Borders of Settler States.* Durham, NC: Duke University Press.

Singhal, Pallavi. 2017. "Teachers Burning Out as They Take on Classes Outside Expertise: ACER Report." *Sydney Morning Herald,* April 23.

Smith, Andrea. 2008. "American Studies without America: Native Feminisms and the Nation-State." *American Quarterly* 60(2): 309–315.

———. 2012. "Indigeneity, Settler Colonialism, White Supremacy." In *Racial Formation in the Twenty-First Century,* edited by Daniel HoSang, Oneka LaBennett, and Laura Pulido, 66–90. Berkeley: University of California Press.

Smith, Bryan, Nicholas Ng-A-Fook, Sara Berry, and Kevin Spence. 2011. "Deconstructing A Curriculum of Dominance: Teacher Education, Colonial Frontier Logics, and Residential Schooling." *Transnational Curriculum Inquiry* 8(2): 53–70.

Smith, Linda T. 1999. *Decolonizing Methodologies: Research and Indigenous Peoples.* London: Zed Books.

Snelgrove, Corey, Rita K. Dhamoon, and Jeff Corntassel. 2014. "Unsettling Settler Colonialism: The Discourse and Politics of Settlers, and

Solidarity with Indigenous Nations." *Decolonization: Indigeneity, Education & Society* 3(2): 1–32.

Soula, Virginie. 2014. *Histoire littéraire de la Nouvelle-Calédonie (1853–2005)*. Paris: Karthala.

Spillman, Lyn. 1994. "Imagining Community and Hoping for Recognition: Bicentennial Celebrations in 1976 and 1988." *Qualitative Sociology* 17(1): 3–28.

Spivak, Gayatri. 1988. "Can the Subaltern Speak?" In *Marxism and the Interpretation of Culture,* edited by Cary Nelson and Lawrence Grossberg, 271–313. Urbana: University of Illinois Press.

Stanner, William E. H. 1969. *The Boyer Lectures 1968—After the Dreaming.* Sydney: Australian Broadcasting Commission.

———. 1974. *After the Dreaming.* Sydney: Australian Broadcasting Commission.

———. 1979. *White Man Got No Dreaming: Essays, 1938–1973.* Canberra: Australian National University Press.

———. 1991. *After the Dreaming.* Crows Nest, NSW: ABC Enterprises.

Stastny, Angelique, Sasha Henriss-Anderssen, and Tom Clark. 2016. "The Poetics of Non-Indigenous Reflexive Self-Awareness: Strategies of Embodiment and Delegation in Focus Group Discussions in Australia." In *The Limits of Settler Colonial Reconciliation,* edited by Sarah Maddison, Tom Clark, and Ravi de Costa, 159–176. Singapore: Springer.

Stevenson, Winona L-A. 2000. "Decolonizing Tribal Histories." PhD diss., University of California.

Steyn, Melissa. 2012. "The Ignorance Contract: Recollections of Apartheid Childhoods and the Construction of Epistemologies of Ignorance." *Identities* 19(1): 8–25.

Stoler, Ann L. 2002. "Colonial Archives and the Arts of Governance." *Archival Science* 2(1–2): 87–109.

———. 2011. "Colonial Aphasia: Race and Disabled Histories in France." *Public Culture* 23(1): 121–156.

Strakosch, Elizabeth. 2016. "Beyond Colonial Completion: Arendt, Settler Colonialism and the End of Politics." In *The Limits of Settler Colonial Reconciliation,* edited by Sarah Maddison, Tom Clark, and Ravi de Costa, 15–33. Singapore: Springer.

Sullivan, Shannon, and Nancy Tuana, eds. 2007. *Race and Epistemologies of Ignorance.* Albany: State University of New York Press.

Surun, Isabelle, ed. 2012. *Les sociétés coloniales à l'âge des Empires (1850–1960).* Neuilly: Atlande.

Sutherland, Alexander, and George Sutherland. 1880. *The History of Australia from 1606 to 1876,* 4th ed. Melbourne: George Robertson.

Taumoefolau, Melenaite. 2011. "Decolonising Pacific Studies: Privileging Pacific Languages and Indigenous Knowledges." In *Talanoa Rhythms:*

Voices from Oceania, edited by Nāsili Vaka'uta, 59–68. Auckland: Masilamea Press.

Taylor, Tony, and Robert Guyver. 2012. *History Wars and the Classroom: Global Perspectives.* Charlotte, NC: Information Age Pub.

Teaiwa, Teresa. 2011. "Preparation for Deep Learning: A Reflection on 'Teaching' Pacific Studies in the Pacific." *Journal of Pacific History* 46(2): 214–220.

——. 2017. "Charting Pacific (Studies) Waters: Evidence of Teaching and Learning." *The Contemporary Pacific* 29(2): 265–282.

Tebbel, John. 1987. *Between Covers: The Rise and Transformation of American Book Publishing.* New York: Oxford University Press.

Téin, Gilbert K. 2011. "'Kaloonbat' est son identité véritable." Interview by Edmond Morrel. *Espaces Livres,* October.

Thaman, Konai H. 2003. "Decolonizing Pacific Studies: Indigenous Perspectives, Knowledge, and Wisdom in Higher Education." *The Contemporary Pacific* 15(1): 1–17.

Thomas, R. Murray, and T. Neville Postlethwaite. 1984. "Colonization and Schooling in Oceania." In *Schooling in the Pacific Islands Colonies in Transition,* edited by R. Murray Thomas and T. Neville Postlethwaite, 1–27. Oxford: Pergamon Press.

Thornton, George. 1895. *School History of Australia and Tasmania.* Sydney: Turner & Henderson.

——. 1900. *School History of Australia: Being a Brief Account of the Progress of the Colonies from the Earliest Discoveries to the Year 1900.* Melbourne: A. N. Smith.

Thornton, Patricia H., and William Ocasio. 1999. "Institutional Logics and the Historical Contingency of Power in Organizations: Executive Succession in the Higher Education Publishing Industry, 1958–1990." *American Journal of Sociology* 105(3) (November): 801–843.

Tickner, Robert. 1991. *Aboriginal Reconciliation: A Discussion Paper.* Canberra: Parliament House.

Toro Blanco, Pablo Andrés. 2015. "Towards a New Chile Through the Heart: Aspects on the Construction of a Nationalist Emotionology in School Textbooks During the Pinochet Years (c. 1974–c. 1984)." *History of Education & Children's Literature* 10(1): 583–600.

Tritter, Thorin. 2013. "Canada, Australia and New Zealand." In *History of Oxford University Press.* Vol. III, *1896 to 1970,* edited by William R. Lewis, 619–647. Oxford: Oxford University Press.

Tuck, Eve, and K. Wayne Yang. 2012. "Decolonization Is Not a Metaphor." *Decolonization: Indigeneity, Education & Society* 1(1): 1–40.

Tuck, Eve, Marcia McKenzie, and Kate McCoy. 2014. "Land Education: Indigenous, Post-Colonial, and Decolonizing Perspectives on Place and Environmental Education Research." *Environmental Education Research* 20(1): 1–23.

Tull, Denis M., and Andreas Mehler. 2005. "The Hidden Costs of Power-Sharing: Reproducing Insurgent Violence in Africa." *African Affairs* 104(416): 375–398.

Turner, Bryan S. 1993. "Outline of a Theory of Human Rights." *Sociology* 27(3): 489–512.

Vázquez, Rolando. 2012. "Towards a Decolonial Critique of Modernity. Buen Vivir, Relationality and the Task of Listening." *Capital, Poverty, Development, Denktraditionen im Dialog: Studien zur Befreiung und Interkulturalität* 33:241–252.

Veracini, Lorenzo. 2007. "Settler Colonialism and Decolonisation." *Borderlands e-journal* 6(2). https://ro.uow.edu.au/lhapapers/1337.

———. 2011a. "Introducing 'Settler Colonial Studies.'" *Settler Colonial Studies Journal* 1(1): 1–12.

———. 2011b. "Telling the End of the Settler Colonial Story." In *Studies in Settler Colonialism: Politics, Identity, and Culture,* edited by Lionel Pilkington and Fiona Bateman, 204–218. London: Palgrave Macmillan.

Vernaudon, Jacques. 2013. "L'enseignement des langues kanak en Nouvelle-Calédonie." *Hermès, La Revue* 65(1): 112–118.

Vimalassery, Manu, Juliana H. Pegues, and Alyosha Goldstein. 2016. Introduction to *Special Issue: On Colonial Unknowing. Theory & Event* 19(4).

Vorauer, Jacquie, and Matthew Quesnel. 2016a. "Empathy by Dominant Versus Minority Group Members in Intergroup Interaction: Do Dominant Group Members Always Come Out on Top?" *Group Processes & Intergroup Relations* 21 (4): 549–567.

———. 2016b. "Don't Bring Me Down: Divergent Effects of Being the Target of Empathy Versus Perspective-Taking on Minority Group Members' Perceptions of Their Group's Social Standing." *Group Processes & Intergroup Relations* 19(1): 94–109.

Walsh, Catherine. 2007. "Shifting the Geopolitics of Critical Knowledge." *Cultural Studies* 21(2–3): 224–239.

Watson-Gegeo, Karen A., and David Gegeo. 1992. "Schooling, Knowledge, and Power: Social Transformation in the Solomon Islands." *Anthropology & Education Quarterly* 23(1): 10–29.

Weintraub, Shelly. 2000. "What's This New Crap? What's Wrong with the Old Crap. Changing History Teaching in Oakland, California." In *Knowing, Teaching and Learning History: National and International Perspectives,* edited by Peter Seixas, Sam Wineburg, and Peter Stearns, 178–193. New York: New York University Press.

Welch, Cheryl. 2003. "Colonial Violence and the Rhetoric of Evasion: Tocqueville on Algeria." *Political Theory* 31(2): 235–264.

Weldon, Paul R. 2016. "Out-of-Field Teaching in Australian Secondary Schools." *Policy Insights* 6 (June).

Wénéhoua, Macate, ed. 1996. *Notre pays demain*. Nouméa: Les éditions du Niaouli.

White, Leanne. 2004. "The Bicentenary of Australia. Celebration of a Nation." In *National Days/National Ways. Historical, Political and Religious Celebrations Around the World*, edited by Linda K. Fuller, 25–39. Westport, CT: Praeger Publishers.

Williams, Alan N. 2013. "A New Population Curve for Prehistoric Australia." *Proceedings of the Royal Society* 280 (1761).

Wilson, Angela C. 2004. "Reclaiming Our Humanity: Decolonization and the Recovery of Indigenous Knowledge." In *Indigenizing the Academy: Transforming Scholarship and Empowering Communities*, edited by Devon A. Mihesuah and Angela C. Wilson, 69–87. Lincoln: University of Nebraska Press.

Windschuttle, Keith. 2002. *The Fabrication of Aboriginal History*. Sydney: Macleay Press.

Wolfe, Patrick. 1994. "Nation and MiscegeNation: Discursive Continuity in the Post-Mabo Era." *Social Analysis: The International Journal of Social and Cultural Practice* 36:93–152.

———. 1999. *Settler Colonialism and The Transformation of Anthropology: The Politics and Poetics of An Ethnographic Event*. London: Cassel.

———. 2006. "Settler Colonialism and the Elimination of The Native." *Journal Of Genocide Research* 8(4): 387–409.

Yates, Lyn, and Cherry Collins. 2010. "The Absence of Knowledge in Australian Curriculum Reforms." *European Journal of Education* 45(1): 89–102.

Zembylas, Michalinos, Zvi Bekerman, Claire McGlynn, and Ana Ferreira. 2009. "Teachers' Understanding of Reconciliation and Inclusion in Mixed Schools of Four Troubled Societies." *Research in Comparative and International Education* 4(4): 406–422.

Index

About the Author

Angélique Stastny is an independent researcher with a PhD in political science from the University of Melbourne. She has taught politics and indigenous studies at the University of Melbourne and RMIT University, as well as history at Aix-Marseille University in France. She previously worked as a research assistant for the Indigenous-Settler Research Collaboration (ISRC) at the University of Melbourne and as a postdoctoral fellow at the University of Graz, Austria. Her research focuses on (anti)colonialism and decolonization in the Pacific, Indigenous politics, racism, and critical whiteness. She is the 2021 National Library of Australia Fellow.